atefulness   social cohesion   homophobia
irness   bigotry   gra   ess
nophobia   equity   ion
ercy   sexism   respect   transphobia   freedom
eciesism   inclusion   fascism   forgiveness
timi   wetiko   compassion   celebration
ee   w   classism   ub   nazism
e   ageism   bliss   microaggressions   joy
longing   patriarchy   sizeism   healing
preciation   empathy   racism   entitlement
orance   empowerment   prejudice   happiness
e   colonialism   courage   tenderness
aration   awe   supremacism   peace
ety   enchantment   ableism   trust   selfishness
erty   contentment   extremism   connection
iosity   egotism   passion   fanaticism
ersity   insensitivity   apathy   wellness
lusion   well-being   rejection   understanding
erosity   detachment   tranquility   equanimity
isemitism   serenity   liberty   islamophobia
peration   hinduphobia   interbeing   justice
ogyny   collective identity   oneness   casteism
ality   colorism   sympathy   thankfulness

Praise for *BREAKING BIAS*

"I commend the author and hope this book will help people to come closer to one another through breaking biases on the basis of secondary differences like race, religion, rich or poor that divide us."

— from the Foreword by **His Holiness the Dalai Lama**

"Your biases can hurt other people, but they can also hurt you. They can damage your relationships and degrade your decision-making. But the good news is: they're not your fault, and they can be addressed. Anu is the perfect guide to transform all biases in the modern world."

— **Dan Harris**, *New York Times* best-selling author of *10% Happier* and host of the *Ten Percent Happier* podcast

"Evolving beyond the biases that separate us is the core task of humanity if we are to meet the existential challenges that face us. Anu Gupta is a brilliant scholar and a wonderful guide on this deep-time journey to uncover the root causes of bias in our world and, even more importantly, within ourselves. . . . This timely book is a beacon of hope in our precious, hurting world."

— **Tara Brach, Ph.D.**, best-selling author of *Radical Acceptance* and *True Refuge*

"Learning to see and understand bias is deeply important for our world, especially now. Breaking Bias *is a valuable and illuminating curriculum that will help not only with understanding bias but also ending it."*

— **Jack Kornfield**, author of *A Path with Heart* and *After the Ecstasy, the Laundry*

"Masterful, practical, and wise, Breaking Bias *is essential reading. Weaving together insights from science, history, and awe-inspiring personal reflections, Anu Gupta gives us a powerful handbook for how to break bias from the inside out. Learn how to dismantle systems of oppression, embrace the worth of all beings, and build a world of belonging, right where you are."*

— **Valarie Kaur**, best-selling author of *See No Stranger* and founder of the Revolutionary Love Project

"A tour de force! Part history lesson, part personal science experiment, part tool kit, this book brings together deep wisdom with practical skills to help us all learn how to move out of our conditioned biases and into a new, more connected way of relating to each other. A must-read!"

— **Judson Brewer, M.D., Ph.D.**, *New York Times* best-selling author of *Unwinding Anxiety* and *The Craving Mind*

"Compassionate, vulnerable, and mind-expanding, Breaking Bias *is a powerful guidebook to deepen our understanding of bias and how to break the cycle. Merging modern Western sciences, ancient Buddhist wisdom, and shame-free inquiries, Anu sparks individual awakening for collective change. This book is an invitation to join the movement toward a world celebrating our diversity and honoring our inherent belonging."*

— **Sharon Salzberg**, *New York Times* best-selling author of *Lovingkindness* and *Real Life*

"As a theologian and scholar of psychology and religion whose research is centered in disrupting racism, I've scoured the literature on the subject of bias. Breaking Bias *uniquely captured me and would not let me go. It is beautifully constructed to invite mindfulness, empathy, and transformation. Anu's kindness accompanies the reader on a journey informed by the depth and breadth of his experience, research, wisdom, compassion, and hope for a healed world. A must-read for all who yearn for a more just society."*

— **Rev. Dr. Jacqui Lewis**, senior minister for public theology and transformation at Middle Collegiate Church and author of *Fierce Love*

"Anu Gupta gives us a clear view of how bias takes root in society, ranging from the beginnings of written history to the realities of the modern world. He invites us on an inner journey to take our own beliefs and hold them up to the light. Breaking Bias *will radically shift your perspective on the power structures around you while drawing you a new map of the world. This book inspires change and creates a new vision where isolation and exclusion can be replaced by connection and belonging."*

— **Deepa Purushothaman**, best-selling author of *The First, the Few, the Only*, executive fellow at Harvard Business School, and retired managing partner at Deloitte

"In Breaking Bias, *Anu Gupta's clarity and openheartedness invite us to reflect on the great suffering caused by racial, gender, and all forms of stereotypes, to understand more fully their religious, social, and economic underpinnings, and to explore ways of freeing ourselves from these deeply conditioned patterns. . . . It's rare to find a work that is so unflinching in its analysis and so compassionate and understanding in illuminating the way forward. Highly recommended!"*

— **Joseph Goldstein**, author of *Mindfulness: A Practical Guide to Awakening*

"Breaking Bias *is a triumph! Anu Gupta has developed an invaluable resource for anyone who wants to understand how contemporary social, ethnic, cultural, gendered, religious, and anthropocentric biases came into being, how they spread, and how to break through them! In this book, Gupta offers a comprehensive historical overview of bias with clear articulations of how bias shapes inequity in social, organizational, national, and international policies. This book is a must-read!"*

— **Dr. Kamilah Majied**, author of *Joyfully Just: Black Wisdom and Buddhist Insights for Liberated Living*

"Anu Gupta explores crises of human interrelationality at the level of the soul: questions that prompt deep reflection and offer avenues for even deeper relationships. Doing so as a friend, a teacher, and a scientist, his approach is one that envisions flourishing for all. This helpful and necessary book is a balm."

— **Pádraig Ó Tuama**, author of *Poetry Unbound* and host of the *Poetry Unbound* podcast

"In Breaking Bias, *Anu Gupta offers us a powerful and accessible overview of both the roots of our species' prejudices and the actions we must take to free ourselves from them once and for all. He skillfully weaves historical analysis of various human systems of domination with reflective prompts, guiding the reader through their own thoughtful and gradual process. Anu's relatable stories of his own journey make this sometimes challenging material a joy to read."*

— **Sebene Selassie**, author of *You Belong*

"Anu Gupta is a professional bias breaker. He's brought his wisdom to more than 80,000 people around the world from all walks of life. Yes, he's a master teacher. Yes, he will expertly guide readers through a breadth of impressive knowledge and actionable steps rooted in neuroscience to unlearn and break bias. But most importantly, Anu is an unfailingly kind friend who genuinely wants the best for all of us. How lucky are we to have Breaking Bias *in our hands?"*

— **Barbara Becker**, author of *Heartwood: The Art of Living with the End in Mind*

"Breaking Bias *is a landmark achievement—a beautifully constructed and elegantly written journey into what it means to be a complex, sensitive human being who embraces the fullness of life by confronting individual and societal misperceptions that keep us apart and helping us move beyond them. Building on his incredibly diverse lived experience, Anu Gupta has given us a wonderful book—full of passion, hope, and, yes, love—backed by meticulous research and searing analyses. A timely book, but also one for the ages."*

— **Janet Dewart Bell, Ph.D.**, author of *Lighting the Fires of Freedom* and *Blackbirds Singing: Inspiring Black Women's Speeches from the Civil War to the Twenty-First Century*

"With brilliant prose and infinite grace, Anu Gupta's Breaking Bias *invites every single one of us to look in the mirror and marvel at what we see, then go out into the world and challenge the notions that stand in the way of our ability to look at one another and do the very same. With sacred practices, thoughtful data, and a deep reverence for life,* Breaking Bias *helps us bring greater understanding to the learned and often painful attitudes, beliefs, and behaviors that separate us from ourselves and each other. We can do better. And this timely and crucial book shows us the way."*

— **Rha Goddess**, founder and CEO of Move the Crowd and author of *The Calling*

"What a gift! Breaking Bias *is a call to all of us to grow up to our potential and down to our depths. This is more than a book. It is a beautiful witness to our inherent possibilities and a guide to the transformation that can save us from ourselves."*

— **Dr. Larry Ward**, senior teacher in Thích Nhất Hạnh's Plum Village tradition, author of *America's Racial Karma*, and co-author of *Love's Garden: A Guide to Mindful Relationships*

"In today's interconnected world, the need for equity and healing has never been more pressing. Breaking Bias *equips readers with the tools and knowledge to challenge the status quo, transform bias right away, and catalyze meaningful change. . . . Whether you're a seasoned social entrepreneur or an aspiring changemaker, this book offers invaluable wisdom and inspiration to navigate the complexities of bias and social impact work."*

— **Cheryl Dorsey**, president of Echoing Green

"This is the best articulation that I have read of what bias is, how it comes to be, and how it can be ended. . . . Through powerful and tender stories, spiritual wisdom, and the latest science, Anu lovingly guides us to look honestly and compassionately at our conditioning so we can bring about lasting freedom and well-being for ourselves and our world. This is required reading for all of us!"

— **Kaira Jewel Lingo**, author of *We Were Made for These Times* and co-author of *Healing Our Way Home: Black Buddhist Teachings on Ancestors, Joy and Liberation*

"Breaking Bias *might be the most important book you read in the 21st century. As sweeping as any Yuval Harari book and as challenging as Paul Hawken's, Anu Gupta's powerful and impeccably researched book is a master class in understanding our species: why we are the way we are and how to create a better world where belonging replaces bias. Everyone in a position of power, authority, or influence needs this book."*

— **Susan Davis**, founding president and CEO of BRAC USA and co-author of *Social Entrepreneurship*

"A rigorous and expansive investigation of a human tangle and illness—assumption and bias. I am grateful for Anu's innovative antidote of PRISM, a pragmatic and heartening medicine to confront and transform the root causes of bias. Let's take the medicine together."

— **Koshin Paley Ellison**, Zen teacher and author of *Untangled: Walking the Eightfold Path to Clarity, Courage and Compassion*

"Breaking Bias *is a powerful invitation to examine our subconscious attitudes, beliefs, and conditioning, and to finally rewrite the stories we have told about ourselves and others, to embrace a more inclusive and loving world that comes about when we become the change we seek."*

— **Ananta Ripa Ajmera**, best-selling author of *The Way of the Goddess* and *The Ayurveda Way* and founder of The Ancient Way

"Anu shares a profound journey to breaking bias that we deeply need in order to free ourselves and our society from the ancient neural reflexes of our tribal past. This inner and outer journey is one that could not be more timely and more important for creating the world we carry in our hearts."

— **Douglas Abrams**, co-author of international bestseller *The Book of Joy* and executive producer of *MISSION: Joy*

"Anu Gupta has written a wonderfully accessible book that marries his personal journey with Buddhism and bias-busting. It's moving, practical, and filled with useful strategies. Highly recommended!"

— **Shakil Choudhury**, author of *Deep Diversity*

"Anu has dedicated a lifetime to investigating, deconstructing, and rebuilding how we perceive ourselves and others. In a time where the world feels more divided than ever before, Breaking Bias *is an urgent antidote to the confusion and suffering of modern life, offering wisdom rooted in science and contemplative practice. I genuinely believe this book can transform those who come into contact with its message."*

— **Manoj Dias**, author of *Still Together* and co-founder of Open

"You are holding in your hands a crucial guide for all who are committed to the vital work of dismantling both personal and systemic biases. . . . Gupta's emotional, groundbreaking frameworks and exercises leave a lasting impact, [inviting] deep reflection on our relationship with societal norms and the biases we all hold. . . . Breaking Bias *marks an achievement in the work of antiracism and a world without bias, and I see it as a vital text for anyone wanting to interrogate bias and lead with greater compassion, love, and courage."*

— **Jorge Fontanez**, CEO of B Lab U.S. & Canada

"Anu Gupta's Breaking Bias *is a major contribution in its focus on locating the roots of identity-based biases and the inequities that flow from them. From page one, the reader is centered in such a way that inclusion is inescapable. Gupta connects with readers by channeling his experiences and asking readers to immediately consider their own experiences with the subject matter of bias, exclusion, and inequity. Gupta's approach sets a tone that will encourage lively reflection and conversation. Through this book, readers will be engaged in a process of co-creation of a more inclusive, more just, and more fair society through organic, positive paradigm shifts in culture and community."*

— **Danielle Conway**, dean and Donald J. Farage professor of law at Penn State Dickinson Law

BREAKING
BIAS®

BREAKING
BIAS®

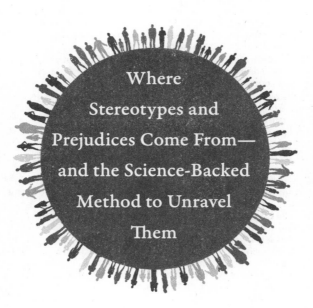

Where Stereotypes and Prejudices Come From— and the Science-Backed Method to Unravel Them

ANU GUPTA, MPHIL, JD

HAY HOUSE LLC
Carlsbad, California • New York City
London • Sydney • New Delhi

Copyright © 2024 by Anurag Gupta

Published in the United States by: Hay House LLC: www.hayhouse.com*
Published in Australia by: Australia Publishing Pty Ltd: www.hayhouse.com.au
Published in the United Kingdom by: Hay House UK Ltd: www.hayhouse.co.uk
Published in India by: Hay House Publishers (India) Pvt Ltd: www.hayhouse.co.in

Interior illustrations: © 2024 by Anurag Gupta and BE MORE, Inc.
Interior illustrations and tables designed by: Joshua Babcock, Ph.D.
Interior layout: Bryn Starr Best
Indexer: Beverlee Day

The endpages are an exercise in breaking bias using the Peters Projection Map of our Earth. This projection accurately represents the sizes of countries and continents relative to one another, regardless of their latitudinal location, unlike traditional Mercator projections (e.g., Google Maps as of 2024) that exaggerate size of landmasses closer to the poles and diminish those near the equator, perpetuating Eurocentric biases.

"Consecrated" by St. Catherine of Siena, from the Penguin publication *Love Poems from God: Twelve Sacred Voices from the East and West* by Daniel Ladinsky, © 2002 used with permission. www.danielladinsky.com

Thích Nhât Hânh, excerpt from "Please Call Me By My True Names" from *Call Me By My True Names: The Collected Poems of Thích Nhât Hânh.* Copyright © 1999 by Unified Buddhist Church. Reprinted with the permission of The Permissions Company, LLC on behalf of Parallax Press, Berkeley, California, www.parallax.org.

Breaking Bias* is a registered trademark of BE MORE, Inc., a certified B Corp that operates globally.

The author of this book does not dispense medical advice or prescribe the use of any technique as a form of treatment for physical, emotional, or medical problems without the advice of a physician, either directly or indirectly. The intent of the author is only to offer information of a general nature to help you in your quest for emotional, physical, and spiritual well-being. In the event you use any of the information in this book for yourself, the author and the publisher assume no responsibility for your actions.

Cataloging-in-Publication Data is on file at the Library of Congress

Hardcover ISBN: 978-1-4019-7731-3
E-book ISBN: 978-1-4019-7732-0
Audiobook ISBN: 978-1-4019-7733-7

10 9 8 7 6 5 4 3 2 1

1st edition, September 2024

Printed in the United States of America

This product uses responsibly sourced papers and/or recycled materials. For more information, see www.hayhouse.com.

*Dedicated to Paramahansa Yogananda
and all the great ones who've guided my path.
And for my mother, grandmother, elders, siblings,
friends, mentors, teachers, students, colleagues, ancestors,
and anyone who shines their divine light to build a world
where every being belongs in the fullness of their diversity.*

CONTENTS

LIST OF FIGURES AND TABLES

FOREWORD

We human beings are social animals and our survival depends on our community. Given this common-sense situation, taking care of others is the best way of fulfilling one's own aspirations. Thus, being considerate of others and cultivating compassion are wise ways to benefit oneself as well.

In our education systems, there needs to be equal emphasis, if not more, on inner mental development, such as warmheartedness, just as is being done with external material development. We need to incorporate education on the common ground that we all want to be happy and that warmheartedness and compassion are the best ways of achieving this. If compassion is part of the education curriculum, a sense of equality will come about automatically. Likewise, if there is compassion in our life, caring for others will come naturally.

In his book *Breaking Bias*, Anu Gupta speaks about why stereotypes and prejudices have no real basis and urges people to be kind to one another. I identify myself with this thinking and I am sure many would benefit from such an approach. As we all belong to our big human family, and since interdependence is part of our reality, a sense of oneness of humanity is crucial for all of us. I commend the author and hope this book will help people to come closer to one another through breaking biases on the basis of secondary differences like race, religion, rich or poor that divide us.

His Holiness the Dalai Lama
15 April 2024

INTRODUCTION

*Our goal is to create a beloved community, and this will
require a qualitative change in our souls as well as
a quantitative change in our lives.*

— DR. MARTIN LUTHER KING, JR.

Beloved Reader, welcome to your breaking bias journey! I am so
happy that you've chosen to read this book. As we embark on this
journey, I'd love for you to grab a journal and pen or a tablet where
you can capture your thoughts, ideas, and emotions.

Let's begin with a short mindfulness practice. Take three deep
breaths, perhaps even close your eyes, and reflect on a word or a
phrase that describes how **you feel** about bias in our society today.
With your pen, write it below or in your journal.

Now take three more in- and out-breaths. Close your eyes if
that's comfortable, and imagine a world without bias. A world where
all human and nonhuman beings can truly belong just as they are
and unleash their full potential. Using a word or a phrase, describe
how **you feel** in such a world and write it below or in your journal.

Notice that I asked you to write how you *feel* in both inquiries,
not what you think or what you believe. This is purposeful because
the world of bias is a world of feelings. Bias is based in emotions.
If bias could be transformed using words or reason alone, you
wouldn't be reading this book. Bias results from habits of the mind.
Unless we become curious about the emotions, thoughts, and

underlying consciousness that trigger these habits, despite having libraries of research and scholarship demonstrating its existence, we'll continue to bear witness to the needless pain, suffering, and inequities it causes across cultures and societies.

The good news is that by noticing, acknowledging, and writing down your feelings, you've just begun your breaking bias journey! You've practiced mindfulness and perspective-taking, two of the five tools that are our gateway to breaking bias. You'll become familiar with the full toolkit, which I call PRISM, as you continue reading this book.

WHY BREAK BIAS?

I believe that breaking bias is one of the most important, if not *the* most important, work we each do in this 21st century. This is because breaking bias goes to the core of who we are as humans: how we live, how we work, how we commune and interact with others, and, most important, how we relate to ourselves, other humans, animals, nature, and life itself.

As you'll learn in this book, dedicated efforts of researchers have identified the causes for why identity-based biases and inequities persist in our world. What we need now is to use our moral imagination and will to push us into applying what we know and to build a world where belonging replaces bias. When your inner skeptic says "how implausible," I invite you to replace that message with "if people can imagine colonizing Mars, why not imagine living on Earth without bias?" We are living in an era when we've transitioned from the information age to the imagination age. It is now up to people like you and me to change our course from conflict and cruelty to understanding and compassion.

The Building Block of Most Challenges

Bias is the building block of most challenges we face individually, locally, and globally. It shows up in our interactions with co-workers, family members, and strangers. It impairs the services we provide in our professional lives, such as health care, education, or policing. It compromises the products we design, such as apps, clothing, and the code for artificial intelligence. It limits the cultural narratives we construct in film, theater, and the arts. It hinders the success of policy solutions we recommend for issues like climate change, disinformation, mass incarceration, and public health crises. Most strikingly, it shows up in how we treat ourselves and one another.

Take a few minutes to reflect below or in your journal on where bias shows up in your personal and professional life. Reflect on why you picked up this book. Why do you want to break bias?

Perhaps you want to live, act, behave, and make decisions in your professional and personal life that are untainted by prejudice. Perhaps you want to understand and heal the harms of bias you have experienced or are experiencing in your day-to-day life, workplace, family, and community. Perhaps you want to stop causing inadvertent harm to yourself and others. Or maybe you want to go deeper and understand the nature of bias itself and what you can do about it—in your family, workplace, community, and country.

I have been in the trenches with this work for all my life. Through my journey, which you'll learn about throughout this book, I have come to *know* in my body, heart, mind, and soul that our motivation for transforming bias has to be rooted in compassion. Compassion actively transmutes the mental hindrance of doubt, suspends disbelief, and opens us to taking action that will alleviate suffering.

This is why in the pages to follow, I invite you to engage in practices that help us access and strengthen our innate capacity for compassion.

What I offer in this book isn't an argument or a prescriptive solution, but a modest offering to meet the polycrisis of our times. This will be our individual and collective journey of unlearning, relearning, unbecoming, and becoming. On this journey, my

sincere prayer and hope is to support you in enhancing your connection with yourself and all your relations; empowering you to use
your expertise and passion to skillfully respond to the existential
crises we face collectively; and enacting possibilities that reimagine
ways you can *be with* yourself, others, and the living Earth.

Before we proceed, let's address the unicorn in the room. I know
the adage is the elephant in the room, but I find unicorns more fun!

The Unicorn in the Room

If you live in the global north, you've likely experienced the
topic of bias as something that is generally about women and
black people. Somewhere in your mind you may wonder, *Why is
this Indian man writing about breaking bias? What's his deal?* So let
me share my very unplanned adventure into becoming a professional bias breaker!

I spent the first 10 years of my life in Chandni Chowk, one
of the most iconic and historic parts of India's capital, Delhi. The
associations you likely have about India—from its colorful architecture, smells, and overcrowded streets, to its religious, linguistic,
and ethnic diversity, to its more-than-humans* like monkeys, ele-
phants, and cows living alongside humans—formed my magical
childhood. In this incredibly overstimulating environment, my
exposure to differences in human appearance and cultures led me
to believe that such differences were normal, and that all humans
were treated equally and with dignity.

Yet, on my rickshaw ride to school every day, I passed by hundreds of men, women, and children begging to make ends meet.
I didn't know who these people were, why they begged, and how
they'd gotten there, but from an early age, I received coded messages

---

* I will use the phrase "more-than-human" interchangeably with "nonhuman"
throughout the book to refer to animals, birds, fish, plants, insects, and the living
Earth. The phrase is used by scholars, indigenous, and animist communities to
describe the interdependence between humans and nonhuman beings. It recognizes
the agency, intelligence, and interconnectedness of the natural world, dissolves the
traditional human-centric view of the world, and invites us to cultivate a deeper sense
of compassion, reverence, and responsibility toward all beings.

such as "Don't touch them. They're dirty." This signaled to my young mind their diminished status in society. Though I was born into a dominant-caste and middle-class animist* Hindu family, I was kept completely oblivious of the social hierarchies that permeated my society. I didn't even know my family's caste (*jati*) or class until I became interested in studying bias in college! But let me not get ahead of myself.

When my family immigrated to America in the mid-1990s, the tables turned, and I slowly became an untouchable. My teachers couldn't pronounce my name. My classmates claimed I ate poop and worshipped cows. And on top of all of that, everyone taunted me for being gay. To me, they were wrong. Indian food is quite nutritious, and as animists, Hindus worship the many manifestations of the single Divine in many forms. Alas, my attempts to correct my bullies were futile. I mean, have you ever met a bully who fact-checked their abuse?

This gay thing, however, got to be a bit too much. One day, I went up to one of my bullies, looked him straight in the eye, and asked him, "What the heck is wrong with being gay? Just like you, I like to smile and laugh. I am a happy person. Why are you picking on me for being happy?"

The poor fellow must have empathized with my suffering. He took me aside and asked me to look up the word *gay* in the dictionary. And I did.

To my utmost delight, I learned that the word *gay* also meant same-sex-loving people. Until that moment, I hadn't had a mental concept or a word to describe how I had felt inside ever since I was a young child. It was as if a huge boulder on my chest was suddenly lifted. I felt liberated because for the first time, I learned that how I felt inside is not an anomaly. That feeling of liberation, however, was short-lived. I quickly realized that being gay was not safe; other students "sensing" that I was gay was the reason why I

---

* I use the word *animism* to describe the diverse cosmologies and ontologies of ancient and current societies that imagine, perceive, and attribute all aspects of being—animals, plants, rocks, rivers, weather systems, humans, art, symbols, words, and others—with consciousness, a sense of aliveness, and reverence.

was being taunted, excluded, and even beaten in school. My survival instincts kicked in. My 12-year-old mind denied, hid, and pushed this part of me deep within my psyche, and moving forward, it did everything it could to assimilate and be as close as possible to what it understood my new home to value: cisgendered, straight whiteness.

I changed everything I could about myself. I altered the way I looked. I watched how I walked, how I carried my body, the pitch of my voice, how I moved my hands so they wouldn't be perceived as feminine. I lost my Indian accent. I spoke in a deeper tone without any inflections, and I even went by the name Andy to distance myself from my Indian heritage. My young mind didn't comprehend how destructive this all was because it was in survival mode.

I just wanted to be left alone and to blend into the background, but there was one problem. I couldn't take off my skin. Pretty much every day, someone on the subway, or in the supermarket, or in the elevator, would ask me, "Where are you really from?" My heart would sink because "New York" was never a satisfactory answer. I was reminded daily of my foreignness, my otherness. At that point, just as I had with my gayness, all I could do was shove those remarks deep within and use my might to do what I thought my new home wanted from me: excel academically and professionally.

That I did. I went to college to study biology and chemistry, and while I loved organic chemistry—I was even a teaching assistant—halfway through my degree, I shifted my focus from the natural sciences to the social sciences and humanities. That began my exploration into the vast field of bias. I studied various human cultures, languages, psychology, history, and political economies. I worked, studied, and lived in Israel, India, Mexico, South Korea, England, Myanmar, and the United States. I interfaced with numerous types of biases: inter-ethnic biases in Myanmar; caste and class biases in India; religious and ideological biases in Islamic societies; race and color biases across the Americas; gender bias in all of these societies; and complete separation from nature and more-than-humans in all industrialized societies. I became obsessed with learning about bias, desperately wanting to understand why some humans and living beings are mistreated in societies for no other reason than simply *being*.

In hindsight, I can appreciate how my younger self was trying to escape the daily reminder of otherness I felt in the United States by learning about other societies and spending time abroad. It was a coping mechanism. Yet, wherever I went, I was questioned: Who was I really? How could I be American with my name and color? Could I be American if I was born in India? Could I be Indian if I was raised in America? And why did I have to choose?

After my graduate work at the University of Cambridge, I returned to America to study law for a budding career in human rights and antidiscrimination law. However, returning to an academic environment that rarely acknowledged bias, and despite understanding this intellectually, the repeated experience of otherness lit the match of self-hatred, self-loathing, and depression that I had suppressed since my tween years.

In 2009, a few days before my 24th birthday, I found myself on the ledge of my 18th-story apartment window, about to jump off.

Looking at the Midtown Manhattan traffic below me, I suddenly became aware of many of the stereotypes I had been reduced to: fatty faggot, Arab terrorist, ugly Hin-doo-doo, and big-nosed idiot. For the first time in my life, I saw these stereotypes as just ideas—ideas that have been perpetuated about me and humans with my attributes for centuries, but ultimately, just ideas. Like most marginalized people worldwide, I'd internalized these ideas as true.

Through an inexplicable moment of grace, instead of jumping forward onto the traffic, I fell backward into my apartment. That moment of grace began my very own breaking bias journey—one that has brought me transformative healing from a lifetime of suffering and accumulated traumas. This journey led me to discover and teach the who, what, where, when, how, and why we as humans do this thing called bias to ourselves and one another, and how we can end this cycle once and for all. This is what I will share with you in this book.

WHAT IS BREAKING BIAS?

Coming so close to ending my life compelled me to seek answers. For many years, I gave up on dating, drinking, and media consumption, which for me were diversions from looking at why I was so angry and judgmental toward myself and others. I studied the cross-disciplinary research in fields like global history, anthropology, political economy, law, neuroscience, and behavioral psychology. I practiced numerous healing modalities such as traditional talk therapy, yoga, eye movement desensitization and reprocessing (EMDR), Indigenous Focusing-Oriented Therapy, breathwork, morphic awakening, Body & Brain Yoga, and somatic experiencing.

I also spent more than 10,000 hours meditating in silence on short and long meditation retreats, contemplating the wisdom from the world's major spiritual traditions.* And most important, I lived with, prayed with, worked with, and befriended humans of subordinated and dominant identities (something we'll explore in the chapters ahead) to not only intellectually understand bias, but to feel its impacts on our individual and collective bodies and psyches.

Through this process, I discovered that as humans, our consciousness operates in two realms: the absolute realm and the relative realm. At the absolute level, we are all the same. We are a part of the same species, and we share sentience with the millions of other species with whom we share this planet. But on the relative level, we each experience life differently based on a myriad of factors. These factors are the causes and conditions that shape our lives.

Bias operates solely in the relative realm, and the many biases we experience, witness, and even enact are a consequence of various causes and conditions. My breaking bias journey brought me face-to-face with these causes and conditions (there are five). In this book, you will become intimately familiar with these causes and conditions and learn to transform them for yourself and for all the lives you touch.

---

* They include Buddhism, Hinduism, Christianity, Islam, Taoism, Sikhism, Judaism, and others.

Breaking bias is the process of making "qualitative changes in our souls as well as quantitative changes in our lives," as so nobly envisioned by our ancestor, Dr. King.[1] These changes begin at the level of each one of our own hearts and minds. I am a living and breathing example of what is possible when we break bias.

At this planetary junction, we face systemic challenges: climate refugees, ecosystem destruction, disinformation, senseless wars, religious and political fanaticism, loss of trust in public institutions, and deterioration of our very own physical, mental, emotional, and spiritual health. We humans make up all of these systems. History teaches us that for systems to change, a critical mass of us individuals—like you and me—have to transform ourselves. This is the work of breaking bias.

To support you in this process, I've developed the frameworks I share in this book using my two sources of learning and healing: ancient Buddhist wisdom* and modern Western sciences. I will encourage you to apply these frameworks to your own relative experiences given your unique humanity.

If at any point what I share does not match your experience, I encourage you to stay curious, be honest, but ultimately, trust *your* experience. Nothing I say overpowers the truth that your body, heart, and soul communicate to you. My ultimate hope is that your breaking bias journey helps you befriend the most important person in your life: yourself!

THE PRISM TOOLKIT: OUR PATHWAY TO BREAKING BIAS

Just as we learn how to cook or drive, biases too are learned. We are *not* born with biases. We are not born to think that women are weaker than men. Or that dark-skinned humans are less attractive than light-skinned ones. Or that rich people are hardworking and poor people are lazy. Each one of these stereotypes is learned,

---

* While my personal spirituality spans animist, Buddhist, Hindu, Christian, and Sufi traditions, I use Buddhist frameworks exclusively because they've been validated by modern neuroscience and nonbelievers.

and they manifest as bias. Just as biases are learned, they can be unlearned by using the PRISM Toolkit.

PRISM is a neuroscience-based toolkit I created to support people in unlearning and breaking bias. I think of PRISM as our companion in *neuro-decolonization*, a term I learned from my meditation teacher and indigenous public health expert, Dr. Bonnie Duran. Neuro-decolonization is the process of cleansing our minds, bodies, and nervous systems of concepts, emotions, and habits that are unwholesome and unskillful, and training them to cultivate the wholesome and skillful instead. With ongoing practice, PRISM makes this outcome possible by transforming the virus of bias in our bodies, hearts, and minds. Collectively, these tools spell out the acronym PRISM: Perspective-taking, pRosocial behaviors, Individuation, Stereotype replacement, and Mindfulness. We begin the practice of PRISM with mindfulness and work our way backward to perspective-taking.

Below you'll find a brief explanation of each tool along with some active words and phrases I will use interchangeably to refer to each tool throughout the book.

1. **Mindfulness**: Mindfulness is the bedrock of breaking bias and the PRISM Toolkit. It is the practice of noticing, of becoming aware or conscious of what is happening in your experience—body, heart, mind—in the present moment; *notice, note, become aware of, bring your attention to, observe, watch*

2. **Stereotype replacement**: The practice of becoming mindful of group-based associations or unwholesome habits and actively replacing them with real, positive counterexamples or wholesome habits; *replace, research, find, identify, substitute*

3. **Individuation**: The practice of investigation and decoupling group-based associations from individuals and experiences with curiosity; *be curious, investigate, inquire, reflect, with interest, examine*

4. **pRosocial behavior**: The practice of cultivating positive mental states and emotions that intend to alleviate suffering

or benefit others, e.g., kindness, compassion, gratitude, joy, radical empathy, and forgiveness; *feel, touch, open, sense, love, hold*

5. **Perspective-taking**: The practice of imagining possibilities of being beyond your lived experience, including the vantage points of other beings; *imagine, visualize, picture, think outside the box*

Practicing PRISM tools will help you interrupt the conscious and unconscious habits of bias programmed in our minds. They will also support you in correcting false beliefs and building new habits of thought toward yourself and others with greater awareness, curiosity, and compassion. In addition, these tools will help you accumulate numerous wellness and well-being benefits like social connectedness, social trust, emotional regulation, stress and anxiety reduction, and memory boosting, as listed in Table 1.[2]

While PRISM can be practiced in many ways, I have found meditation to be the most effective medium for creating lasting behavior change. Science has also shown that up to eight weeks of regular meditation practice supports new habit creation, as well as the breaking of old habits such as binge eating, addiction, and bias.[3]

Benefits of the PRISM® Toolkit				
Perspective-Taking	pRosocial Behavior	Individuation	Stereotype Replacement	Mindfulness
✔ Reduces Bias & Stereotyping	✔ Regulates Negative Emotions		✔ Boosts Memory	
✔ Improves Social Connection	✔ Creates Positive Emotions		✔ Reduces Stress	
✔ Strengthens Relationships	✔ Builds Resilience		✔ Reduces Anxiety	
✔ Builds Social Trust	✔ Enhances Creativity		✔ Deepens Curiosity	

Table 1

Supporting thousands of professionals in advancing diversity, equity, inclusion, and belonging (DEIB) and breaking bias has affirmed for me that in order to take action we have to get out of our heads and integrate what we know with our bodies and hearts. We can read recipes for our favorite dishes all day, but we will not get to taste them until we put them into practice and start cooking.

Our ancestors and elders trained their bodies, minds, and nervous systems in rigorous meditative and spiritual practices to perform nonviolent civil resistance and sit-ins for lasting social change, e.g., the American civil rights and Indian freedom movements. In today's world, the challenges associated with bias have entered all aspects of our daily life. PRISM tools offer us the training we need to be aware of why things are the way they are and to take action to transform them. Throughout the book, I'll invite you to pause and practice these tools as we delve deeper into the causes and conditions that have programmed us with bias.

PREPARING FOR YOUR BREAKING BIAS JOURNEY

Now that we've covered the basics, I want to prepare you for your journey ahead. I have found that the reason why we as a species have not made progress on breaking bias and in related areas like mental health, addiction, and DEIB is not because of a lack of brilliance, academic research, commitment, resources, or even time. Rather, it's because we have not been warned of or prepared for the very personal and painful nature of this work.

There is no way around it—bias goes to the core of who we are, and it hurts! So to do this work effectively, we each need to feel safe so we can be vulnerable and observe, acknowledge, and feel our pain, or we will run away—just like my 12-year-old self did after being bullied for being gay and Indian. At this crucial time in our human history, running away is no longer a viable option. Bias is disrupting our mental health; relationships with our family, friends, and colleagues; workplace and community cultures; national and international politics and economics; and the sustainability of the Earth itself.

Given my personal experiences with bias, I take safety very seriously. For that reason, this book is intentionally trauma-informed and shame-free. I truly believe that each one of us is more than the worst thing we have said and done.* I am not here to make you feel bad, guilty, or ashamed about anything you are or anything you have thought, said, or done because I know, as Ocean Vuong reminds us, *you are gorgeous* in every imaginable way.[4] Now your breaking bias journey is for you to sincerely feel and embody that gorgeousness for yourself.

On this journey, you may encounter shame, blame, guilt, anger, disappointment, sadness, grief, and many other afflictive emotions. I call them all messengers that are asking you to listen, discover, investigate, and play with what they have to share. The five PRISM tools will support you in working with, befriending, and, with practice, inshallah,† transforming these emotions. At the end of the book, in the "Communities and Practices for Support" section, I have provided some additional resources that can support you on your breaking bias journey.

SAFETY MEASURES FOR YOUR BREAKING BIAS JOURNEY

So far, I've brought the work of breaking bias to more than 80,000 professionals from all walks of life—from homemakers, activists, rabbis, and coders to lawyers, doctors, teachers, and politicians. My students have been the C-suite at some of the largest financial and tech firms as well as small-business owners, managers at nonprofits, and administrators at all levels of government. Whether you've picked up this book to become a better pastor, therapist, nurse, or professor or just a better-informed global citizen, like many of my students, you won't be surprised to learn that the key to breaking bias is transforming our minds, or shifting our consciousness.

---

* Gratitude to my law professor, Bryan Stevenson, for helping me appreciate this truth.

† *Inshallah* literally means "God willing" in Arabic, Persian, Urdu, and other languages inspired by Sufism and Islam. It can also be understood as "I hope" in secular terms, similar to its descendant word *ojala* in Spanish.

In *A New Earth,* Eckhart Tolle reassures us that from a deep-time perspective of thousands of years, regardless of how human consciousness may appear, it is evolving toward greater peace, understanding, and compassion.[5] The Vedic wisdom of my ancestors calls this evolution in our consciousness a transition from the Kali Yuga, or the Age of Darkness, characterized by greed, violence, and materialism, toward the Dwapara Yuga, or the Age of Morality.[6] It is apparent in the growing concern many of us have for our fellow human and nonhuman families and the living Earth, and in the shifts from subordination of one people over others to intermarriage and collaboration.

However, for many of us, including yours truly, this evolutionary process of thousands of years is not fast enough. Breaking bias offers you the opportunity to expedite that process for yourself and every single human and nonhuman life you touch.

In my work of taking thousands of people on this journey before you, I've found five shared agreements useful in establishing psychological safety, ease, and trust as you navigate through your breaking bias journey. They are:

1. **Use I-statements**, such as *I think, I believe, I feel, in my experience,* rather than using the royal *we, you,* or *they.* This agreement helps ground us in our lived and felt experiences while permitting others to stay grounded in theirs.

2. **Commitment to dialogue**. This is likely why you have made it this far into this book, but it is important to keep this at the forefront of your mind throughout. As I've learned from bridge-builders like Thích Nhât Hânh and Brené Brown, there are two important ingredients to dialogue: understanding and kindness. As you move through the book, give yourself and others the benefit of the doubt. Stop crucifying yourself and others for what has happened. Instead, be curious. Ask questions to learn and grow. And always, remember: *May I be kind.* Dialogues become diatribes and monologues when kindness leaves the room. Mr. Rogers said it best: *There are three ways to ultimate success: The first way is to be kind. The second way is to be kind. The third way is to be kind.*

3. **Be present**. This journey will take you into the past and throw you into the future. In those moments, ground yourself in the present moment. Modern culture has forced us to be present-phobic, and part of our work together is to befriend it with mindfulness. Throughout our journey, I'll invite you to observe, acknowledge, and feel your somatic experiences (body sensations) that accompany your thoughts and emotions and jot them down in the margins of this book or in your journal.

4. **Investigate discomfort**. This goes hand in hand with being present. Given the deeply personal and painful nature of this work, acknowledge when afflictive emotions arise and become an observer of your experience. What are the sensations you feel? Where in the body are they? What do they feel like? Notice pressure, temperature, and other sensations in your body as well as fears, memories, stories, concepts, and ideas in your mind. Document and investigate them. This is your unique somatic or bodily experience of bias.*

5. **Privacy and confidentiality**. This agreement is for the times when you discuss the contents of this book with other humans. This work is deeply personal and painful, and when you do this work with others, you and other humans will share some deeply painful and personal experiences. This agreement will help you build, strengthen, and repair trust with others because it says to others that your stories are safe with me; you are safe with me.

Please note that this book does not replace seeking therapeutic interventions needed to recognize and heal bias-related harms and traumas. If at any point you experience difficulty managing your emotions, I invite you to pause and seek support. This goes to our shared agreement to be kind, starting with yourself. To support you with the agreements, I give you permission (!) to write in the book. In fact, I request you to always read this book with a pen

---

* In the Buddhist cosmology, this is known as the First Foundation of Mindfulness, i.e., the body.

and a journal handy, because the work of breaking bias is meant to be a conversation.

You'll notice the active gerund break*ing* in breaking bias. That is purposeful. We are actively taking action, individually and together. In the margins of this book or in your journal, jot down your feelings, emotions, stories, ideas, and memories as they arise. This is the practice of mindfulness, of making the unconscious conscious. With practice, you will uncover where bias remains in you at any moment in time and what needs to be healed.

The shared agreements will be your companions in facing and transforming afflictive emotions that may arise as you engage in the work of breaking bias and shifting your consciousness. Each conscious act of breaking bias slowly becomes a ripple in our collective consciousness to transform misunderstanding, hatred, and division in our families, workplaces, communities, and social systems.

Before moving forward, please write an aspiration you have for breaking bias. Acknowledge and sign on the line below that you will try your best to abide by these shared agreements as you move toward this aspiration.

My aspiration in breaking bias is:

I promise to try my best to abide by the shared agreements on my breaking bias journey, including seeking support as a gesture of kindness toward myself.

Sign: Date:

Feel free to write any intentions you have for yourself in moments when you forget the agreements that will help you return to them (e.g., *I will forgive myself, be kind to myself and those I may have harmed, recall my commitment to healing, and return to the shared agreements*).

I will:

FINANCIAL BENEFITS OF BREAKING BIAS

I would be remiss to ignore that our species is currently operating in a global capitalist paradigm* where the currency of money (as you'll learn) has come to overshadow all other currencies, e.g., relationality, kinship, joy, love, and gratitude, among others. Within this paradigm, money may be a deep concern for you when it comes to caring for yourself and your loved ones. If this is so, be assured that research has monetized numerous benefits to breaking bias.

It's shown that holding on to biases is bad for our health.[7] They impair our ability to make decisions and increase our stress, anxiety, and general frustration levels.[8] Socially, bias creates workplaces, communities, and societies that are unfair and in which people lack the skills to deal with conflict, disagreements, and misunderstandings, which create numerous costs, such as attrition, litigation, and poor performance.[9]

Systemically, economists estimate that racial bias alone costs the American economy at least $2 trillion annually in terms of wasted costs and thwarted performance.[10] This number does not include the costs of the inequities, pain, and suffering racial bias creates as we have witnessed in our own hearts and minds due to publicized violence against racialized humans, or the less publicized incidents that you may have experienced or witnessed in your own life.

In addition, if $2 trillion is just the annual cost of racial bias in one country, imagine what the accumulated financial costs of all forms of bias—gender, sexuality, disability, age, religion, nationality, and class, among others—would be in America or countries globally. Yep, that's a lot of wasted time, effort, talent, resources, and physical, emotional, mental energy, and, most important, human potential.

Israeli historian Yuval Noah Harari advises that "For every dollar and every minute we invest in improving artificial intelligence,

---

* Scholars and advocates call it late-stage capitalism, characterized by a globalized economy where everything—not just the material world but also immaterial dimensions, such as nature, ecosystems, more-than-humans, spirituality, coaching, mentorship, family, arts and lifestyle activities—has become commodified and consumable through the exchange of money.

it would be wise to invest a dollar and a minute in advancing human consciousness."[11] To me, he's suggesting that we channel capitalism toward breaking bias.

YOUR BREAKING BIAS JOURNEY AHEAD

The study of bias is a vast academic discipline. As an academic and a seeker, I love studying, researching, and investigating. However, that is not the purpose of this book. My goal with this book is to share with you concepts and frameworks in the simplest and most accessible language to inspire, empower, and enable you to act! I have written it to help you understand the history and evolution of bias and ways to release your own biases.

I will share with you the foundational information you need to start breaking bias. With that in mind, please note that this book is not intended to be a primary or sole resource for the emotional, cognitive, or physical impact of bias in your past, present, or future. If you are interested in learning more or are seeking such support, I provide extensive resource lists.* My sincere hope is that at the least you will apply what you learn in your professional and personal lives so we can all benefit from the bounty of breaking bias.

Breaking bias is an ongoing journey. It isn't a one-time task that you complete and it's done. Rather, it's something we each cultivate and practice by returning to it over and over again. I hope you'll use the frameworks and tools offered in the pages ahead to design your own unique recipe that will create the necessary qualitative and quantitative changes in your heart and life that are required for this consciousness shift.

Your journey ahead has three legs that align with the three parts of this book.

In Part I, The Basis of Bias, you'll learn the foundations of what bias is, how it is shaped, and its various forms and manifestations. In Chapter 1, you'll become familiar with the constellations that

---

* *See* Abridged Bibliography and Communities and Practices for Support; and for additional resources, visit anuguptany.com.

make up human diversity and identities as well as the inner work-ings of our human mind. Chapter 2 will take you through deep time to illustrate the emergence of exclusion and inclusion within human societies. And Chapter 3 will provide you with an overview of the neural mechanisms of how biases are enacted and the four forms of bias.

In Part II, The Making of Bias, you will learn the first two causes and conditions of bias. They are story and policies. The first two causes give form to cultures that ultimately train our individual minds in all identity-based biases. In Chapter 4, using class, eth-nicity, profession, and other identities, you will see how to apply the first two root causes to any human identity in any society. In Chapters 5 and 6, I will apply them to two human identities that have a global reach: race and gender, respectively.

In Part III, Our Training in Bias, you will delve deeply into the three vectors of culture that train all humans in various biases. These are the three remaining causes of bias: social contact, edu-cation, and media. We will begin Part III with an overview of cul-ture in Chapter 7, where I will provide some helpful context and definitions of the remaining three causes. In Chapters 8, 9, and 10, you will explore, reflect upon, and unlearn ways social contact, education, and media, respectively, have trained your mind with conscious and unconscious habits of bias.

Throughout the three parts, I invite you to pause, reflect, and practice PRISM tools to actively support you in unlearning and breaking bias. In addition to these check-ins, I encourage you to trust your body and your naturally arising somatic awareness, and take breaks as you need to balance your attention and metabolize the material. I also share personal stories from my own life as well as from my family, teachers, friends, colleagues, and students. Where appropriate, I have changed the names and identities of people to respect their confidentiality while retaining the learning from their stories.

Thank you once again for being on the breaking bias jour-ney with me. I hope your journey is filled with new insights, resolve, and courage.

PART I

THE BASIS OF BIAS

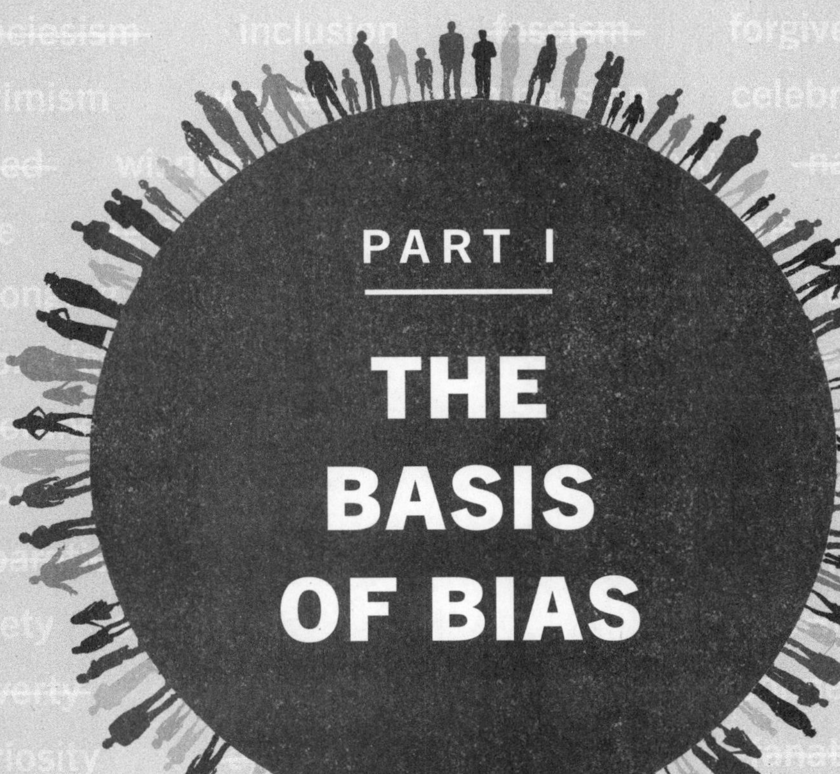

Chapter 1

DIVERSITY, IDENTITY, AND THE MIND

Humankind has not woven the web of life. We are but one thread
within it. Whatever we do to the web, we do to ourselves.
All things are bound together. All things connect.

— CHIEF SEATTLE

In the 21st century, the word *diversity* has gained significant traction. Businesses, nonprofits, governments, and international organizations flaunt it as one of their most prized values. Leaders across industries deliver inspiring speeches and make repeated commitments to upholding diversity.* And diversity has trickled into political rhetoric that unites or polarizes groups of people globally. As a result, understanding diversity is central to our exploration of bias. Before proceeding further, below or in your journal, define *diversity* in your own words.

Diversity is:

---

* For example, the CEO Action for Diversity and Inclusion, the world's largest business-led initiative to advance DEIB in the workplace, with pledges from more than 2,500 CEOs.

I've spent decades exploring, discussing, teaching, and studying diversity, and I've noticed that every person understands it differently, describes it differently, and feels differently about it. This makes sense because no two people, including identical twins, share the same lived experiences. However, to understand bias, we all need a common framework to understand human diversity.

I define *human diversity* as "the authentic representations and expressions of humanity." Diversity is who we are as a species, and it is who each one of us is as an individual member of our species.

As a species, we encompass many nationalities, ethnicities, genders, cultures, religions, professions, and political and economic views. And as an individual, you hold a diversity of identities that span those categories and many more in addition to the roles and functions you serve in your family, workplace, and community. Our human diversity is the landscape that triggers bias in our thoughts, words, and behaviors. In this chapter, I will introduce you to my human diversity framework and familiarize you with important concepts that become the basis for bias.

WHAT HUMANS SHARE ACROSS OUR DIVERSITY

In recent times, there has been an increased awareness of historically marginalized human identities, from LGBTIANBTSQ+* identities to the spectrums of neurodivergent and disabled peoples to religious, ethnic, and indigenous communities such as the First Nations peoples, Yazidis, Baha'i, Sami, and Orang Asli. This increased awareness of human diversity is beautiful because it reveals to each one of us that people and our cultures are not a homogeneous monolith, never have been and never will be. Humans have always and will continue to define, redefine, and create new ways of naming and organizing our humanness.

---

* Lesbian, gay, bisexual, transgender, queer, intersex, asexual, aromantic, nonbinary, two-spirit, questioning. I will use *queer and gender-diverse* or *LGBTQ+ people* to reference humans with these identities.

Practically speaking, however, as humans, we cannot possibly stay mindful of the vast spectrums of human diversity all the time. Scientists say that as humans we can stay aware of three to five discrete ideas in our minds at a time.[1] So how do we reconcile our diversities without feeling victimized by others who may not acknowledge aspects of our beingness that matter to us? And how do we go about in the world relating to other humans in the fullness of their diversity?

My mind used to get caught in these questions as I began my healing process from suicidal ideation, depression, anxiety, and post-traumatic stress disorder (PTSD). On the one hand, I was grateful to be alive. On the other hand, I walked around feeling victimized for being gay, for being a person of color, and for my many marginalized identities. I sought validation for my existence from outside of me—and when those around me made comments that didn't acknowledge my understanding of my history, culture, beliefs, and identity, I felt angry and diminished. My mind was vigilant all the time, in hyper-judgment mode. Just around that time, Lisa, a law school classmate, invited me to go to a yoga class with her.

What went through my mind immediately was something like "Those [*expletive*] colonizers exploiting my culture to make an [*expletive*] business out of my spirituality"—you get the point. But I really respected Lisa. She had inspired me to seek therapy and try various healing interventions. On top of that, her outer appearance was what my mind judged as the "colonizer." As I became mindful of the many judgments in my mind, I discovered my own curiosity and desire to learn yoga and be connected to it. Through that process, I unearthed what had kept me from practicing yoga until that moment: the bullying I experienced as a young person for my Hindu ancestry.

I noticed that I had distanced myself from my own heritage to fit into my American surroundings, while holding resentment toward *all* white European-descent people for practicing what I believed was my culture. I generalized the exclusion I experienced with some white people to all white people. This realization liberated me from my own mental prison for the first time in my life, and off I went to practice yoga with Lisa. My first class felt like returning home to my body. I couldn't remember the last time I'd been in my body, not in my thoughts, ideas, and stories.

Within a few months, I decided to do the 200-hour teacher training. To many, the idea seemed ludicrous. I was in law school to become a lawyer, not a yoga teacher! But I wasn't after the certification, I wanted the training. In my depressed and anxious state, I found that yoga allowed me to stop thinking and for the first time to feel my body. I marveled at my 11 body systems* doing their thing automatically, without any instructions from my conscious mind. I was in awe of my brain, which is less than 2 percent of our body weight but consumes over 20 percent of our energy intake and truly dictates the numerous functions of the body without me knowing it. And I was absolutely amazed by the breath. The breath that I almost lost, how it *just happens* and how focusing on it disclosed the state of my mind and my body.

One day, while standing in a Warrior II pose, my shoulders dropped two inches farther from my ears. I felt so confused that I took a moment to roll my shoulders back up and down. At that moment, I recalled a memory from my time in Korea, when I taught English at a middle school. After school, I used to attend a mixed martial arts class with a prominent teacher, and during our warm-ups, he used to hit my shoulder with a bamboo stick to no avail. I used to be so annoyed by him, but in that yoga class, I finally understood what he had been doing.

For years, I walked around the world with my shoulders tensed up to my ears. And the tension was not just in my shoulders, but also in my jaw, my feet, my hands, and my lower back. The practice of yoga began to create a clearing inside my body.

Alongside a physical clearing, yoga helped me ease mental attachments I had to my marginalized identities. Learning about human anatomy and the inner workings of our incredible, amazing,

---

* The 11 systems in our bodies are the muscular, skeletal, nervous, endocrine, cardiovascular, respiratory, digestive, urinary, immune, integumentary, and reproductive systems. Each of these systems plays an essential role in maintaining the overall health and functioning of the human body.

spectacular, magnificent body systems and brain empowered me to appreciate my humanity differently and understand diversity with a fresh perspective.

For the first time, I appreciated the felt sense experience of my body's physiological and psychological responses and how these systems operated in the same exact manner in the bodies of every human being, regardless of how my mind labeled that body. In the repetition of thousands of asanas, or yoga postures, I experienced that all the ways I separated myself from others on the bases of race, gender, sexuality, size, religion, ideology, disability, etc., are actually my secondary identities.

Our primary identity as a species is as a human being. If you're reading this, what you and I share at the absolute level is our humanity. This insight is the key to understanding human diversity as it has been in the past, as it is now, and as it may evolve in the future. I've since designed the human diversity framework to explain the vastness of human diversity without feeling overwhelmed by the thousands of ways human identities and experiences manifest globally. As humans, we each have just two types of human identities: our primary identity and secondary identities.

OUR PRIMARY IDENTITY

A few months into my yoga practice, I learned about the Woodenfish Humanistic Buddhist Monastic Life Program that gives people under 30 the opportunity to temporarily be ordained as Buddhist monks and practice silent meditation for a summer in Taiwan. I jumped at the opportunity. If I were to live, and live without causing harm to myself or others, I knew I had to get to know my mind. This program gave me the structure and safety I craved.

As I sat silently in my monastic robes, with a shaved head and pursed lips, focusing my attention on my in- and out-breaths, I became aware of the 80 bodies sitting with me. Representing different skin tones, ethnicities, nationalities, genders, and sexualities, they sensitized me to our beingness as humans. This beingness is our primary human identity. Biologists label it by the name of our species: *Homo sapiens*. Geneticists have demonstrated it by decoding the entirety of the human DNA sequence, which is 99.9 percent identical in every human being. Spiritual and humanist figures from ancient to contemporary times have termed it "our common humanity." And political philosophers and theorists recognize it as the inherent dignity within our being.

Having since spent thousands of hours in meditation, I have come to appreciate that our primary identity is composed of five attributes. In Buddhist mind sciences, they are known as the five aggregates of our human existence.[2] They are:

* **Form**: Every human, regardless of their shape, color, anatomy, abilities, and disabilities, has a body form. Despite variations in our body forms, our bodies share six, not five, possible sense organs. These six sense organs allow us six possible sense experiences: eyes for sight, ears for sounds, tongue for taste, skin for touch, nose for smell, and the sixth sense, the mind, for thoughts and emotions. These six sense organs are like the equipment or hard drive of our existence. In addition, people who have one or several sense organ deficits often have supplemental functions that enhance their senses, and even if not, they still have form.

* **Affect** or **vedana** (pronounced VAY-the-naa): Every sense experience we have through our six sense organs (i.e., sight, smell, taste, touch, sound, and thoughts/emotions) has associated with it an affect, valence, or feeling tone that is called *vedana* in Sanskrit. This aspect of our humanity is not the collection of feelings or emotions we experience as humans, but rather the bare affect beneath each sensory experience. This bare affect falls on the spectrum of pleasant, neutral, and unpleasant, what we often label internally as good, okay, or bad feelings. Every human sense experience accompanies one of these three feeling tones. *Vedana* varies for people when it comes to the same experience. For example, the taste of a cheeseburger is quite pleasant for some and unpleasant to others; similarly, listening to classical music, or hiking, or watching TikTok videos carries with it an underlying

vedana. Bringing awareness to affect or *vedana* will be an important part of your breaking bias practice.[3] I will use *vedana* interchangeably with *affect*, *valence*, and *feeling tone* throughout the book.

* **Perception**: The ability of every human to recognize, interpret, and label what they experience through one or more of their six sense organs is known as *perception*. I think of perception as a pair of glasses that helps us make meaning of the external inputs we receive through our sense organs. Perception is dependent on our own subjectivity, conditions, and our six sense organs. We often experience things not as they are, but as we are. For example, in Disney's *The Little Mermaid*, when Ariel first discovers a fork, based on what she has known she perceives it as a comb and not an instrument used to aid eating.

* **Mental formations**: Called *samskara* in Sanskrit, mental formations refer to three primary ways our mind engages thoughts: mental concepts, emotions, and mental habits. Alongside *vedana*, these three elements are an important aspect of bias. I will be using *mental formations* interchangeably with *mental concepts*, *emotions*, and *habits* throughout the book.

    1. **Mental concepts** help you make meaning of your world. With respect to human diversity, mental concepts create the categories and labels that become our secondary identities. For example, we label people without the sense experience of sight as *blind*.

    2. **Emotions** help you feel sensations and experiences in your heart, mind, and body. Emotions are a mental formation because they are labels our minds give, using concepts, to body sensations that we experience in response to an external sensory input: for example, pleasure, pain, happiness, sadness, or anger.

    3. **Mental habits** result from the repeated labeling of people, objects, and experiences with particular concepts and emotions that over time go on autopilot. For example, you assume a person with the name Ashley is female because everyone you've ever met with that name has been female.

✳ ***Consciousness***: Buddhist psychology defines consciousness (known as *vinyana* in Sanskrit) as a continuous stream of awareness with four layers. They are:

1. **Mind consciousness:** the outermost and the most energy-consuming layer, it is the thinking aspect of our awareness that plans, analyzes, worries, judges, etc., during our waking hours; it is turned off while we sleep.

2. **Sense consciousness:** the layer beneath mind consciousness, it enables you and all humans to have and be aware of our six sense experiences during our waking hours, i.e., seeing, hearing, touching, smelling, feeling, and thinking.

3. **Store consciousness:** the largest layer, it is the storehouse of all our perceptions—consisting of concepts, emotions, mental habits, and their accompanying *vedana*— accumulated over our lifetime associated with different forms and experiences; it is operating at all times, even in the absence of our mind consciousness, to modulate and respond to our autonomic needs.

4. **Manas:** the deepest layer within store consciousness that at its core is the belief in a separate self, or the feeling and instinct we each have as "I am," me, and mine.

Regardless of whether you are aware of consciousness from moment to moment, consciousness *is*, and it is what keeps us alive and supports us in functioning in our world. As humans, though we think we are a singular organism, our beings are actually made up of a congress of microbial and bacterial beings. In addition, our bodies consist of at least 30 trillion cells. From moment to moment, we are unaware of all of them, but the instant something comes in contact with our skin or another body part, we become aware of it as touch. This is consciousness in action. For example, imagine you're sitting at a café listening to nice ambient music and staring blankly into space while waiting for a friend. Whether you pay attention to them or not, hearing-consciousness of the music, seeing-consciousness of space, and thinking-consciousness of anticipating your friend's arrival are happening.

Consciousness is a vast topic that is beyond the subject of this book. In elaborating on the four levels of consciousness, I wanted to give you some context for it as an essential part of our primary identity. For our breaking bias purposes, however, moving forward, I will use *consciousness* by itself, without making further distinctions on its various levels.*

The Mind: The Basis of Our Experiences

The mind is the field where, as humans, we experience: (1) *vedana* (pleasant, neutral, or unpleasant feelings), (2) perception of sense experiences, and (3) consciousness, the storehouse of the concepts, emotions, and habits we accumulate over our lives and the ability to be aware of them. Where is the mind? Some say it is the brain, others say it is the brain and the spinal cord, and still others say it includes all nerve endings, and even extends around your body in the form of electromagnetic waves. While there isn't yet a scientific consensus around the physicality of the mind, we know that: we have a mind; our brain is a part of its physical form; and just like our eyes see, our ears hear, and our noses smell, our minds produce thoughts.

These thoughts, whether they arise with or without our will, are what give rise to mental formations, i.e., concepts, emotions, and habits. Some scientists estimate that on average we have 60,000 thoughts a day! And a vast majority of these thoughts, about 90 percent of them, are recurring.[4] This makes sense because many of those thoughts help us get on with our day and build habits like brushing our teeth or feeding the cat, but also habits around how we spend our free time, how we speak to ourselves, and how we respond to a crisis.

As human beings, we are creatures of habit, and every single one of our habits begins with a thought that ultimately becomes

---

* For more information on the four layers of consciousness, *see* Thích Nhât Hânh's *Understanding Our Mind* in the Abridged Bibliography.

our ways of thinking, believing, speaking, and acting. This habit creation mechanism is known as the Hebb's Rule or "neurons that fire together, wire together."[5] In his book *Thinking, Fast and Slow*, behavioral economist Daniel Kahneman labels the outcome of our mental habits—neurons firing and wiring together—as System 1 thinking.[6] System 1 thinking refers to our primary identity's attribute of mental formations; it is fast and automatic, and it draws on past experiences, patterns, and mental shortcuts, i.e., concepts, emotions, and habits, to make rapid judgments without conscious effort. It's the system we rely on for routine tasks, like recognizing different objects, colors, and faces or driving a familiar route.

Bias results from System 1 thinking rooted in our primary identity's five attributes: *mental formations* stored in our *consciousness* about human (and more-than-human) *forms* that become our *perception* toward self and others, and the pleasant or unpleasant *vedana* associated with it. Thankfully, as humans we have the capacity to change habits, what neuroscientists call *neuroplasticity*. Kahneman refers to this ability as System 2 thinking, which is slow and deliberate. System 2 involves mindfulness, investigation, and curiosity through conscious awareness, effort, and practice. On our breaking bias journey, you are actively training your mind to transition from System 1 to System 2 thinking by practicing the PRISM tools.

What We Identify with Becomes Our Reality

If you're like me, you were probably raised to believe that as humans we have five senses. Buddhist mind sciences helped me appreciate what many humans have known for over 2,500 years: what we experience as our mind is a sense organ, and what it produces, thoughts, is a sense experience. The mind scientist who was the historical Buddha characterized the intrinsic nature of the mind as clear and luminous like a precious jewel. Thích Nhât Hânh describes this natural state as "Buddha-nature" or "the Kingdom of God."*

I am not going to lie, I scoffed at these descriptions when I first learned them from my Taiwanese meditation teacher, and for good

---

* See Thích Nhât Hânh's *Living Buddha, Living Christ*. Mystics across traditions quote Luke 17:21, *"the kingdom of God is within you,"* to refer to our mind's intrinsic luminosity.

reason. All my life until that point, I had only experienced my mind as filled with confusion, anger, worry, fear, jealousy, and grief.

However, just a few years later, while on a 10-day silent meditation retreat at Insight Meditation Society, I touched and experienced this luminosity for the first time. The experience itself is indescribable in words, but a few aspects of it included: the release of all worldly concerns, a sense of oneness with all living beings and the living Earth, a feeling of unconditional love and joy, and innumerable sensations of expansion around my heart. This experience is what kept pulling me back to meditation halls, to build a daily meditation practice, and to learn more about the science of meditation.

You're probably wondering, if I experienced such an ecstatic state of oneness, why didn't I just stay there? This is where it gets interesting. While the mind's intrinsic nature is luminous, this luminosity gets covered over by what are known as the three root defilements of the mind: greed, hatred, and ignorance. In Sanskrit, they are known as *kleshas* and they are responsible for the arising of all the unwholesome emotions we experience, such as fear, anger, worry, etc., that disturb the natural tranquility of our minds.* I think of the defilements as seeds in our minds that get stronger or weaker through (1) our cultural conditioning and (2) the thoughts, emotions, and mental habits that we *choose* to cultivate in our minds.

Science shows the existence of these underlying defilements by demonstrating that almost 70 percent of our thoughts gravitate toward negativity, a phenomenon known as "negativity bias."[7] It's as if our minds are Velcro for negative experiences and Teflon for positive experiences. However, science has also demonstrated how the fundamental structure of the brain differs among longtime meditators who've consciously chosen to de-identify with afflictive emotions and practiced cultivating positive emotions such as compassion, generosity, and wisdom—i.e., System 2 thinking.[8]

The key here is identification. *Identification* and *identity* have the same root, which means to "associate with" or "regard as the

---

* *See* the Ekmans' Atlas of Emotions created by neuroscientists in an effort to familiarize secular and non-Buddhist audiences with Buddhist mind sciences: https://atlasofemotions.org.

same as." The repeated process of identifying with concepts and emotions becomes habits that make those experiences who we are. We make them a permanent identity. I'd done that for years by identifying with depression and anxiety as who I am, versus states of mind that my being was experiencing. This is the influence of the defilements, obscuring the natural luminosity of the mind and forgetting our absolute, primary identity as members of the same species.

Such identification gives rise to a false sense of self, commonly known as the ego,* that deludes us into believing that we are separate from the living Earth and all living beings, keeping us stuck in a pendulum of greed and hatred, i.e., believing external things like wealth, fame, and status will bring us lasting happiness and running away from anything that creates pain. In Buddhist mind sciences, succumbing to this mental habit over and over again is the third defilement, i.e, *avidya* in Sanskrit, loosely translated as "ignorance" or "delusion." *Avidya* is a technical word that refers to our human tendency to forget, misunderstand, or misconstrue the big picture. I think of the ego as a conglomeration of the three root defilements.

The good news is that we each have the capacity to retrain and purify our minds. We strengthen this capacity by becoming mindful of the defilements, quitting identifying with them, and weakening them by cultivating their opposite wholesome qualities, such as wisdom, compassion, and generosity. This is the breaking bias journey you're taking through these pages to speed up the evolution of your individual and collective consciousness.

OUR SECONDARY IDENTITIES

If our primary identity is what we share, our secondary identities are what make each human unique. They're also the meat of bias. Our secondary identities describe the labels our society assigns

---

* *Mara* in Buddhism, *Maya* or *Ahamkar* in Hinduism, *Nafs* or *Shaitan* in Sufism and Islam, and *Satan* or *the Devil* in Judeo-Christian cosmology.

to the different manifestations of our human forms and experiences. When we speak about human diversity, we're referring to our secondary identities. See Figure 1.1 for a visual summary of our primary and secondary identities.

Amid the vast diversity of human cultures and identities, we each have only three *forms* of secondary identity: biological, experiential, and social. Let's look at each form more closely.

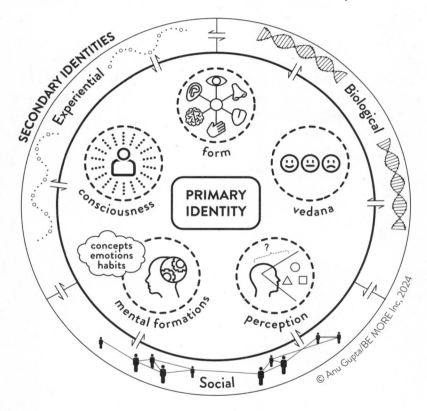

Figure 1.1

Biological Identities

Our biological identities describe the various aspects of our human form based on our biology and genetics. Recall that though every human has a body, the ways that body manifests vary. For example, in some humans one or more of the six sense organs or sense experiences may be impaired in some way.

We have little control over our biological identities. They are how we each are born based on our biological ancestors and other factors that we don't scientifically understand. These identities give our bodies attributes such as our skin and hair color, hair texture, facial features, disabilities, sex, sexuality, gender identity, neurodiversity, genetic conditions, and so on. Some of our biological identities have become the subjects of politics and debate. We will explore why and how in the coming chapters. For now, I'd like you to become aware of and explore some of your biological identities.

PRISM EXERCISE

Pause. Take three breaths and return your awareness to your somatic experience.

In Table 1.1 below, find a select list of biological identity labels, their descriptions, and an empty column. After reading through the label and its description, write your biological identities for that label in the third column. Notice and document your somatic experience as you move through this activity.

▷◁▷◁▷◁ Secondary Identities: Biological ▷◁▷◁▷◁		
Skin Color	The presence or absence of melanin that gives the human skin organ color, e.g., *brown, tan, peach, olive.*	
Facial Features	The color, structure, or size of various facial organs, i.e., the eyes, nose, cheeks, chin, lips, e.g., *dark brown eyes, rounded nose.*	
Disabilities	One or more ways a human's six sense organs or physical bodies may be biologically or genetically impaired, e.g., *blind, deaf, ADHD.*	
Sex	Assigned to humans at birth based on anatomical parts and DNA, e.g., *male, female, intersex.*	
Gender Identity	The way a human perceives their gender. When one's gender identity aligns with their sex, one is *cisgender*; when it isn't, one is *transgender*.	
Sexuality	The gender/s humans feel romantically and sexually attracted to, based on their own gender, e.g., *heterosexual (straight), homosexual (gay or lesbian), bisexual, asexual, another sexual orientation.*	
Body and Hair Type	Attributes of the human body, such as hair color and texture, body size, hip size, height, weight, among others that vary based on ancestry or genetics, e.g., *tall, short, fat, thin, straight or kinky hair.*	

Table 1.1

Experiential Identities

Our experiential identities are identities we acquire over the course of our lives based on three types of experiences: our actions and efforts, the roles and functions we assume, and what happens to us. Depending on our society, we may have some control over these identities. This is an incredibly diverse arena of our secondary identities. Before we move on, I'd like you to whet your understanding of some of your experiential identities.

> **A Note on Trauma:** I define *trauma* as "an experience or experiences that are life threatening and/or emotionally, cognitively, and physically overwhelming." Trauma can be a singular event, chronic, or events that occur repeatedly over time. It includes personal experiences that we may have experienced as children or adults, i.e., physical, emotional, sexual, psychological, environmental, or economic traumas, as well as intergenerational or ancestral, historical, and vicarious traumas. When a human has experienced compounding effects of multiple types of traumas, practitioners call it *complex trauma.*
>
> The many small-t or big-T traumas impact each of us differently based on our nervous system, our various secondary identities, our internal capacity for withstanding trauma (sometimes known as *resilience*), and our will and actions. Humans who've survived traumatic experiences often come together as social groups rooted in that shared experience and that aspect of their experiential identity, e.g., veterans, survivors of childhood sexual abuse, survivors of war. We will be exploring trauma as an experiential identity throughout the book, as well as how PRISM tools can support, mitigate, transform, and even heal the many imprints of trauma in our bodies, hearts, and minds. If you've personally experienced any form of trauma, I encourage you to seek support that feels most aligned with your sensibilities.†

---

* I've found Dr. Bruce Perry and Oprah Winfrey's *What Happened to You?* helpful in understanding the impact of trauma, particularly the trauma of experiencing different forms of bias, on the human body, heart, and mind, *see* Abridged Bibliography.

† *See* Communities and Practices for Support for some ideas.

PRISM EXERCISE

Pause. Take three breaths and return your awareness to your somatic experience.

In Table 1.2 below, find a select list of experiential identity labels, their descriptions, and an empty column. After reading through the label and its description, write your experiential identities for that label in the third column. You'll find a few examples in the second column. Notice and document your body sensations and emotions as you move through this activity, and as a reminder, please take care of yourself and seek support, as needed, when noting any traumatic experiences.

Secondary Identities: Experiential		
Actions		
Education	The experiences and degrees from K–12 and/or tertiary education institutions, e.g., *IIT, NYU, Cambridge, Sorbonne, Michigan State.*	
Professional Training	The experiences of learning the craft of a profession, e.g., *nursing, engineering, teaching, social work, graphic design.*	
Hobbies	The activities and experiences humans engage in for joy and pleasure, e.g., *sports, music, climbing, yoga, meditation.*	
Roles and Functions		
Family	The functions humans have in their family unit, if any, e.g., *spouse, parent, sibling, grandparent.*	
Work	The functions humans have in their workplace, if any, e.g., *manager, coordinator, president, unemployed.*	
Civic	The functions humans have in extracurricular activities, if any, e.g., *nonprofit board member, volunteer, church usher, tutor.*	

Table 1.2

Table 1.2 continued

What Happens to Us		
Age	A human's age and generation, e.g., *baby boomer, millennial, Gen X, Gen Z*.	
Illness or Sickness	A human's experiences with any ailments in the past or present, e.g., *stroke, cancer, long COVID, HIV, diabetes*.	
Disability	Any disabilities humans acquire over the course of their life for any reason, e.g., *loss of a limb, blindness, speech impediment*.	
Trauma	Experiences that are life-threatening or emotionally, cognitively, or physically overwhelming, e.g., *war, mass shootings, rape, sexual abuse, incarceration, car accident, death of a loved one*.	

Social Identities

Our social identities describe the labels and meanings our society assigns to us, often based on our biological and experiential identities. For example, our societies give meaning to biological identities like our sex, skin color, physical appearance, absence of certain body parts or bodily senses, and family ancestry through social identities such as gender,* race, ethnicity, disability, caste, and ethnicity.

Similarly, our societies assign social meaning to experiential identities. We define our level of material wealth as class status; being in a romantic relationship and with whom as being single, married, divorced, gay, straight; or passing professional qualifying exams for law or nursing as having certain professional titles. Our

---

* Gender is a social category that is assigned to human bodies based on body parts and DNA. Our sex does not necessarily reflect our internal sense of gender identity. In the 21st century, humans who don't exclusively feel like a man or a woman have established the social identity of "nonbinary" to label their gender. In the gendered English language that uses *he* or *she* pronouns exclusively, many nonbinary humans go by the singular pronoun *they/them* to escape being misgendered. A similar movement has spread to other languages with binary labels for gender. The evolution of gender in this way is an example of how humans innovate and evolve social identities, and how societies and languages adapt over time. We'll explore gender further in Chapter 6.

social identities are assigned to us by our surroundings, and we generally have little control over them unless we change our surroundings by taking an action such as emigration.

Through socialization, our social identities become a part of our self-concept. Our minds strengthen this self-concept by identification with a social identity as "who I am," and a perceived membership in a group that identity signifies. We will explore various social identities, e.g., race, gender, sexuality, class, and ethnicity, as we move into the root causes of bias in Part II. For now, I'd like you to explore some of your social identities.

PRISM EXERCISE

Pause. Take three breaths and return your awareness to your body.

In Table 1.3, find a select list of social identity labels, their descriptions, and an empty column. After reading through the label and its description, write your social identities for that label in the third column. You'll find a few examples in the second column. Notice and document your body sensations and emotions as you move through this activity.

↑↑↑↑ Secondary Identities: Social ↑↑↑↑		
Gender	Describes the roles and functions people in a society expect from a human based on their sex and gender identity. Pre-modernity, most indigenous societies had three or more genders. In most societies today, gender is a man/woman binary with a growing acceptance of nonbinary people, e.g., *man, woman, nonbinary, other genders.*	
Race	A social hierarchy based on color, ancestry, and appearance in societies that Europeans settled or colonized, e.g., *white, black, brown, indigenous.*	
Ethnicity	Describes a human's connection to a historical place with shared beliefs, history, memories, languages, and traditions, e.g., *Lakota, Mayan, Korean, Khmer, Malay, Bengali, Yoruba, Zulu, German, Tibetan, Irish, Ukrainian.*	

Table 1.3

Table 1.3 continued

Class	Describes a human's attributes such as education, clothing, diction, and/or family name that signify presence or absence of material wealth, e.g., *wealthy, working class, middle class.*	
Marital Status	Describes a human's status of being in a legally recognized relationship with another human, e.g., *single, married, separated, divorced, widowed.*	
Profession	Describes a paid occupation that involved prolonged training and a formal qualification, e.g., *teacher, therapist, engineer, graphic designer, lawyer, yoga instructor, carpenter.*	

INTERSECTIONALITY:
PUTTING OUR IDENTITIES TOGETHER

As you may have already noticed for yourself, we each hold various biological, experiential, and social identities. For me, "the particularity of our humanity based on our secondary identities" is known as *intersectionality*.* For example, some of my secondary identities include being an animist inter-spiritual neurodivergent introverted Indian American polyglot gay immigrant cis man lawyer scientist son brother entrepreneur meditator artist yogi childhood sexual abuse survivor. This is the particularity of my humanity in terms of some of my biological, experiential, and social identities. Each of my identities carries with it a story and a history that ties me to experiences I can share with other humans who share that identity.

You'll notice that some of my secondary identities are visible, while others are hidden. For example, anyone who sees me walk on the street instantly knows that I am physically a nonmobility

---

* The term *intersectionality* was coined by American legal scholar Kimberlé Crenshaw to describe the uniqueness of the experiences of women of color based on the fullness of their secondary identities.

impaired man of color. These are my visible identities. However, they wouldn't necessarily know that I am a gay lawyer or that I grew up monetarily poor or that I suffered from depression unless I volunteered that information to them or they learned about those aspects of my humanity through another source.

In 2008, after a state-wide referendum known as Proposition 8, California banned same-sex marriage after legalizing it a few months earlier. It was a huge disappointment for millions globally. I was a first-year law student, and a gay classmate earnestly asked me, "Why do you hate us [gay people]?" He had bought into the story being publicized that black and brown people were responsible for voting for Prop 8, and that being black or brown was mutually exclusive with being gay. The hidden nature of my sexuality alongside the visible nature of my skin color affected how he perceived me and my intersectionality. In his pain, he couldn't acknowledge that more white people like him had voted for Prop 8 than black and brown people combined, or that I too was gay. This was a loss for me as well as for him, and for the millions of LGBTQ+ people of all colors and their families and relatives.

PRISM EXERCISE

Pause. Take a few deep breaths. Return your awareness to your body and our shared agreements.

In the space below or in your journal, list some of your secondary identities, indicating if these identities are visible or invisible. Remember, there is no right or wrong way for you to *be*. Some of these identities may evolve and change in the future.

SOCIAL POWER: DOMINANT
AND SUBORDINATED GROUPS

Within every secondary identity there exists a hierarchy of being better-than or worse-than based on the mental concepts, emotions, and *vedana* that are socially assigned to different human bodies and ways of being, e.g., gender, skin color, profession, or class. These mental formations and *vedana* attached to different forms of human beingness construct the lens through which we humans perceive ourselves and one another.

In these hierarchies there is generally a dominant group and one or more subordinated groups. Belonging to a dominant group on these hierarchies determines many aspects of a human's lived experiences, including social standing, the ability to do or not do certain things, and access to opportunities and resources.

For example, prior to the 1970s, in most places around the world, women and LGBTQ+ humans (subordinated groups) were not permitted to attend most universities, sit on most juries, or practice law in any great numbers, opportunities that were exclusively restricted to cis straight men (the dominant group). The visible nature of gender prevented a majority of the human population from enjoying such opportunities and privileges. Additionally, such restrictions remain to this day in nations like Saudi Arabia, Iran, and Afghanistan, where humans can be executed for announcing that they are LGBTQ+ or atheists (subordinated groups).

Similarly, until the 1970s, under the White Australia Policy, black and brown humans (subordinated groups), regardless of their wealth or intellect, could not become Australian nationals, a privilege restricted to white Europeans (the dominant group). The visibility of one's skin color prevented a large group of people, including Australia's own indigenous people, who'd lived on the continent for more than 60,000 years, from safely building a life in Australia.

I share these examples to simply illustrate that social identities confer upon humans' advantages or restrictions based purely on their *beingness*, for no fault of their own. In our societies, the unearned advantages humans experience for no other reason than their being or intersectional secondary identities, like gender, race, and class, is what scholars term *privilege*; similarly, the unreasonable restrictions placed on humans based purely on their *beingness*— such as sexuality, religious beliefs, or ancestry—is what scholars term *marginalization*.[9]

PRISM EXERCISE

Pause. Take three breaths. Return your awareness to your body and our shared agreements.

What I've shared thus far is deeply personal and can get confusing, so let's do an exercise to help these concepts come alive for you.

In Figure 1.2, you'll see an image of concentric circles. The center represents secondary identity labels that are most valued in American society; the closer one is to the center, the more social power or ease that particular identity brings to a human; the farther away, the more social marginalization or pain one experiences in society due to that identity. For the secondary identities listed, trace your humanity in relation to the center.

As you complete this exercise, notice which secondary identities bring you ease or pain, and observe your somatic experience, especially the *vedana* of sensations that may arise. Are they pleasant, neutral, or unpleasant? Document any thoughts and emotions that accompany this investigation, especially non-feeling, numbness, or intellectualization. With this exercise, you are strengthening mindfulness and the ability to notice your emotional landscape, an essential aspect of breaking bias.

TIP: You can adapt this diagram for the different societies and communities you inhabit by changing the labels for secondary identities, e.g., the queer community, the Indian diaspora, Christians, Chinese citizens, etc.

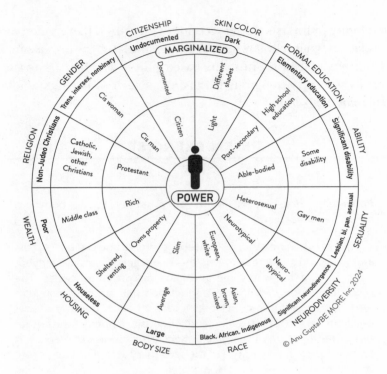

Figure 1.2

CONSEQUENCES OF SOCIAL POWER: EASE AND PAIN

Privilege and *marginalization* have become charged words in some societies. In the space below or in your journal, take a moment to become mindful of your perceptions of these two words by reflecting on (1) the mental concepts attached to each word for you, and (2) the underlying *vedana* associated with them.

For me, the words *privilege* and *marginalization* merely describe how a human's social identity creates ease or pain in their life. For example, in 2022, my two friends who are married to each other bid to purchase the apartment of their dreams in the Upper East Side neighborhood of New York City. This is the wealthiest neighborhood in the city, and, for reasons we'll be exploring in this book, it remains predominantly white to this day.

My friends won the bid, but the seller refused to sell to them, claiming that my friends had somehow misrepresented their finances. They hadn't. However, the seller had learned that my friends are a mixed-race couple and made a comment that the building was not for "people like them." My friends have filed a lawsuit as a result. Beyond the legal aspects of this horrific situation, I reflect on what is happening for the various parties here. Despite having all the social identities associated with wealth, status, and prestige, because my friends are not both white, they don't get the apartment of their dreams and must suffer through the mental anguish and pain of litigation for no other reason than their being. If they had been white, this wouldn't have been an issue, and they would easily have gotten the apartment of their dreams.

This is privilege and marginalization in action, and it mirrors the experiences of any dominant and subordinated group in any social hierarchy globally. For example, white Germans could immigrate; buy land; and get a job in Australia, New Zealand, Argentina, Canada, or the United States in the 1950s, but Koreans could not. Men can drive, pursue any career, and file for divorce in any country around the world, but in many places, women still can't.

Just like that, we each experience privilege and marginalization based on our unique intersectionality. Our privileged identities offer our lives the *feeling of ease* in the form of admiration, social standing, benefit of the doubt, the ability to do or not do certain things, and access to rights, opportunities, and resources; and our marginalized identities create the *feeling of pain* in our lives in the form of harmful assumptions, threats to physical or psychological safety, and exclusion from rights, opportunities, and resources.

The Ease and Pain of Passing

A few years ago, I met with my student Diane, an executive at a large health system. To me, she appeared as a very well-dressed white woman with striking blue eyes and curly hair. I soon learned that she identified as black. Immediately, my mind registered her as mixed-race, i.e., one of her parents is white and the other is of African ancestry, and she, due to the inexplicable magic of genetics, came out looking white. Identity is a very personal topic, and I wasn't even conscious of my mind's automatic story-making around her humanity, but she sensed it.

Within seconds, she informed me that both of her parents are black. She likely has European ancestry given the history of enslavement in the United States, but not by the consent of her ancestors. Over the course of our conversation, she shared with me that her appearance likely helped her professionally. In fact, her mother had prayed every day while pregnant with her for a child with blue eyes so she could have this outcome. I could sense both the ease and the pain in her voice. Ease for her material well-being and professional accomplishments, and pain for how that ease wasn't available to many of her relatives and friends because of their appearance. This is the complexity of our identities.

For many of us, our bodies get labeled in ways where we may be able to "pass" or be closer to the dominant group, which shapes the level of ease we may experience socially but can simultaneously cause tremendous personal pain. As a cis man with a certain set of mannerisms, I too have "passed" as straight in my encounters with people from around the globe. In fact, my way of being allowed me to be invited into many communities that otherwise shun queer people. What Diane shared with me is a layer of cognitive dissonance that many humans who don't neatly fit into social hierarchies experience in their bodies, hearts, and minds.

The Antidote to Pain and Ease

A few months after almost ending my life, I was blessed to be introduced to the life-changing Buddhist practice of loving-kindness. It's a practice of silently and earnestly directing a series of positive affirmations first toward oneself and then slowly directing them outward to other human and more-than-human beings.

Scientists have demonstrated that this powerful prosocial behavior thwarts depression, anxiety, self-loathing, and social distrust and has many other mental, emotional, and social benefits.[10] Beyond the labs, I have experienced the transformational power of this practice in person. At the beginning, my teacher Gina Sharpe instructed me to just do it—no ifs, ands, or buts—for 20 minutes *daily* for two months. Well, those two months turned into two years and now to more than a decade, and it has turned my world inside out.

As a mid-20-something, I couldn't even imagine "coming out" to my parents and my extended Indian family. I had accepted that I would remain in the closet and lead a very unhappy life that publicly denied this part of my being. Yet loving-kindness had something else in store for me. The practice of offering loving and kind affirmations to this painful part of my identity over time led me to not only accept this identity but to be *honored* by it. I remember repeating to myself, "I am honored to be gay. I am honored to be queer. I am honored to be experiencing my humanness in this way." These shifts are subtle, but just as we water and care for the seeds we plant for months or even years before they sprout, loving-kindness slowly works to transform the defilements in our minds that cover up our minds' natural luminosity.

For me, these defilements were the ignorance of my worthiness, hatred of myself, and craving to be someone other than who I am. This is why the practice of loving-kindness when directed toward oneself is a radical antidote for any social identities that cause us pain.

Just as we can strengthen love and kindness for ourselves, we can also train our minds to cultivate it for others. For any dominant and privileged identities that we have, we can cultivate compassion for those who are marginalized or subordinated on that identity's hierarchy. This capacity to feel is what my teacher Sharon Salzberg calls the "quivering of the heart." This capacity of our human body, heart, and mind is what inspires and empowers us to act in the name of what is fair, just, and good.

For me, as a brown Indian man, this practice allowed me to feel the pain of women and girls around the world, of black people, of indigenous people, of trans people, and many others as my own and compelled me to respond by founding my organization and doing what I can to alleviate their suffering. Modern neuroscience is catching up with what ancient wisdom traditions have preached for millennia: mercy, empathy, compassion, and loving-kindness are the keys to healing divides within us and in our families, workplaces, and communities.[11]

Now that you have a grounding in human diversity, identities, and mind—the basis of bias—I want to invite you to practice and experience loving-kindness before continuing your journey.

PRISM PRACTICE: LOVING-KINDNESS

Pause. Find a quiet, comfortable, and safe place where you can be free of distractions for at least 10 minutes.

TIP: Read the instructions before starting so you can complete the exercise without needing to open your eyes during the practice.

To begin, find a position for your body that is upright. Place your hands comfortably on your lap or knees, and bring your eyes to a gentle close while guiding your attention to your breath.

Take 5 to 10 deep and soothing breaths, keeping your attention on the full length of each inhale and exhale.

First, direct loving-kindness toward a subordinated social identity that brings you pain in your society. Imagine this part of your being, and repeat the following four phrases silently toward this identity 5 to 10 times at a comfortable pace. Feel free to adapt the phrases so they feel natural to you.

Well-Wishes for Self:
> May I be happy.
> May I be healthy.
> May I be safe.
> May I live with ease.

Second, direct loving-kindness toward a dominant social identity that brings you ease in your society. Imagine this part of your being, and repeat these phrases silently toward this identity at a comfortable pace, 5 to 10 times. Feel free to adapt the phrases so they feel natural to you.

Well-Wishes for Self:
> May I be happy.
> May I be healthy.
> May I be safe.
> May I live with ease.

Next, direct loving-kindness toward a loved one, e.g., a family member or a friend who does not share your privilege and may experience pain due to that social identity. Visualize this being in your mind, feel their pain, and repeat these phrases to them at a comfortable pace, 5 to 10 times.

Well-Wishes for a Loved One:
> May you be happy.
> May you be healthy.
> May you be safe.
> May you live with ease.

Next, open your circle of loving-kindness toward a neutral being or a stranger, i.e., someone you have no strong feelings toward, like a store clerk, a receptionist, or a driver you saw on the road, who does not share your privilege and may experience pain due to that social identity. Visualize this being in your mind and repeat these phrases to them at a comfortable pace, 5 to 10 times.

Well-Wishes for Another:
> May you be happy.
> May you be healthy.
> May you be safe.
> May you live with ease.

Lastly, extend loving-kindness to all beings everywhere, including yourself. Imagine loving-kindness radiating outward toward all people, living beings, and the living Earth.

Well-Wishes for All Beings:

May we be happy.
May we be healthy.
May we be safe.
May we live with ease.

After completing the above, you can open your eyes and stretch. Take a few minutes after this practice to reflect and journal on your somatic experience. Remember, regular repetition of this practice supports building the habit of loving-kindness. It can be a powerful way to elevate your mood and to feel connected to yourself and others.

Chapter 2

EXCLUSION AND INCLUSION

Of all beings that exist on Earth, human beings are the youngest.
And of all human cultures, Western culture is the youngest.

— TREMEMBÉ ELDERS VIA VANESSA ANDREOTTI

In this chapter, I am going to be your pilot through deep time to show you how human minds evolved to create societies rooted in exclusion consciousness. This mindset programs us in secondary identity-based biases. For me, researching, understanding, and accepting this history from the perspective of human consciousness helped usher in the possibility of breaking bias, as it extricated me from my mind's defilements that kept me stuck in the dualisms of us versus them, good versus bad, and right versus wrong. It was also incredibly healing because it helped me depersonalize my mental wounds, apply the PRISM tools to heal those wounds skillfully, and take action that is onward leading.

As we jump in, in the space below or in your journal, I'd love for you to apply what you've learned so far and define *exclusion* and *inclusion* in your own words.

Exclusion is:

Inclusion is:

I define *exclusion* as "restricting certain humans from access to activities, opportunities, protections, resources, or rights because of their secondary identities," and *inclusion* as "ensuring that those who've been historically excluded have equal, equitable, and fair access to activities, opportunities, protections, resources, or rights" because when they do, all humans will.

BEFORE HUMAN "HISTORY"

Western science* speculates that early species of humans first evolved on our planet some 2.5 million years ago, which is a blip in our planet's 4.6 billion years of existence. The current scientific consensus is that earliest humans lived in eastern Africa and then slowly spread across the globe and developed numerous ways of being concurrently across the continents. Within the span of 2.5 million years, our human species of *Homo sapiens* likely evolved from our various human and more-than-human ancestors at least 315,000 years ago based on the most recent archeological discovery.[1]

Because there is no written evidence to say otherwise, the dominant story among scientists is that for most of the tens of thousands of years since, our ancestors led nomadic and pastoral lives in small bands and tribes as foragers, gatherers, fishers, and hunters. Being genetically identical to how we are today, they too possessed the five attributes of our primary identity that I outlined in Chapter 1. However, in this dominant story, their livelihoods were concerned with staving off hunger and keeping themselves and their loved ones safe and healthy from external dangers, such as inclement weather, wild animals, and other tribes of humans. Through the hardware of our six sense doors, our human ancestors understood, conceptualized, and imagined different realities that became the precursors of human cultures globally.

---

* As opposed to scientific traditions rooted in Vedic/Hindu, Buddhist, Mayan, and other indigenous cosmologies that reference cycles of settled and centralized human existence based on their complex, deep-time calculations.

We have scarce recorded evidence on how humans lived and communed with one another during this vast period of human existence from 2.5 million years to 5,000 years ago. The first known human writing system, cuneiform, is estimated to have been established around 3000 B.C.E. Thus, Western science, and those operating in that paradigm, call the very long period of human existence, exploration, and expansion before cuneiform *prehistory*. In prehistory, humans spread across the world, and our species of humans became first the dominant and then the only remaining form of humans on our planet.

PRISM EXERCISE

Pause. Take three breaths. Return your awareness to your body sensations, recalling our shared agreements.

In the space below or in your journal, take a few minutes to define *civilization*. Then, notice and describe the *vedana* and mental formations associated with this word in your mind.

Define *civilization*:

Vedana:

Mental formations (concepts, emotions, habits):

For you, the word *civilization* may carry positive associations and a pleasant *vedana* that create a perception of being better and more desirable than other types of societies. Based on many dictionaries, including Oxford and Webster, the top definition for *civilization* on Google is "the stage of human social and cultural development and organization that is *considered advanced*."

Considered advanced by whom, though? How is *advanced* defined? What are the consequences of not being "considered advanced"? I was first asked to interrogate this word by my college professor Shiva Balaghi in a postcolonial gender seminar. I quickly sensed the unconscious baggage associated with this word, which played a central role in how a specific form of exclusion paradigm became globalized in the age of modernity.

In this chapter, we will explore how this happened and its relationship to bias. Moving forward, I will use the neutral phrase *centralized societies* to refer to cultures that our minds have been conditioned to define as *civilizations*.

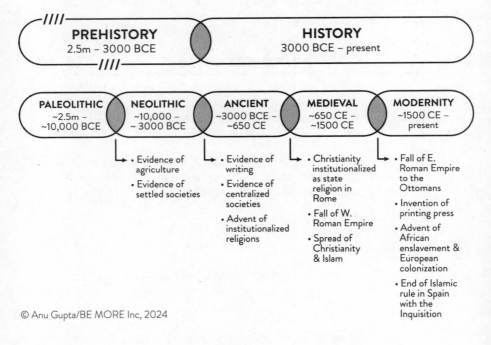

© Anu Gupta/BE MORE Inc, 2024

Figure 2.1

BEGINNING OF HISTORY

Scientists speculate that starting around 10,000 B.C.E., based on archaeological evidence, some human tribes in different parts of our Earth left their nomadic hunting and gathering ways to create human settlements by domesticating animals and cultivating plants. This last period of prehistory—beginning about 12,000 years ago—is known as the Neolithic age. See Figure 2.1 for an outline of the time we'll be traveling through in this chapter.

Over thousands of years, *some* of these human settlements developed writing forms and transitioned into centralized societies, ushering our species into the period scientists have labeled *history*. Four major features of centralized societies separate prehistory, which constituted the vast majority of known human existence as a species, from what we understand as *history*:

* Demarcated *ownership* or claim over certain land or territories of the Earth

* Physically altering the natural environment within those territories with complex architecture and systems for various human purposes, including storing food, obtaining clean drinking water, and disposing of waste

* Administering, organizing, and exerting control over large groups of humans within those territories through shared concepts and emotions and their associated *vedana*, e.g., religious belief systems, a centralized political or government apparatus, and written or oral language

* Division of labor of human populations into social hierarchies of dominating and subordinated groups based on secondary identities

Archaeological evidence indicates that the first centralized societies spontaneously came into being and developed in six modern-day regions: Iraq, Egypt, India, China, Peru, and Mexico. What's important to note is that beyond the borders of these centralized societies, and sometimes even within their territories, there existed hundreds of what anthropologist David Graeber and archaeologist David Wengrow call "social experiments" of human settlements, cultures, and ways of being.[2] These experiments included the ways of being of our Neolithic ancestors, decentralized societies, and nomadic cultures. I want to highlight this point because the mental concept of *civilization* traps us into disregarding and diminishing these diverse ways of being with one another of our human ancestry. Let's explore why.

COMPARING MIND

Have you ever found yourself stuck in comparing mind, thinking or feeling that you are better than or worse than another human for *any* reason? Perhaps for your intellect, achievements, looks, beliefs, culture, athletic or artistic abilities, or even the fact that you are committed to improving yourself by reading this book?

Circle one: Yes   No

I have posed these questions to thousands of people, and I have yet to receive a single no. I won't lie—for most of my life, my mind was doing this on autopilot, comparing and judging my brown skin, my big nose, and the fat around my waist with others. I remember countless hours in front of the mirror imagining if only these parts of my being could change. I'd always thought this was just how we are and how our minds work—until I read about a provocative exchange between Western neuroscientists and longtime Tibetan meditators, including the Dalai Lama, at a gathering organized by the Mind and Life Institute in the early 1990s. A Western scientist expressed that she found it difficult to practice loving-kindness (the prosocial behavior practice you learned at the end of Chapter 1) toward herself. She bravely shared that she felt guilty, selfish, and unworthy of such well-wishes. The self-loathing that she described felt very familiar to me, and to many people in the audience; however, it puzzled the Tibetans. At first, they couldn't grasp the idea of the widespread self-loathing and self-judgment in Western societies because in their minds, each human just *is*, a part of nature.

Learning about this exchange reminded me of the liberating truth that I knew as a young child, that I just am. Not better than or worse than. I am. Can you repeat that out loud for me? I am. It is our minds that attach various concepts, emotions, and *vedana* to who and what we are, which ultimately becomes the lens or the perception through which we view ourselves and others.

PRISM EXERCISE

Pause. Take a few breaths. Bring your attention to your somatic experience, remembering our agreements.

In the space below or in your journal, write one secondary identity that makes you feel better about yourself and identify the story of hierarchy that comes with it. Examples:

- *Earning a lot of money.*
  Money gives me respect from my friends and family.

- *Being a white-collar professional.*
  Having these degrees makes one smarter than others.

- *Having a slim body.*
  I am admired by others at social events.

Notice that attached to this feeling of "being better than others" are three aspects of your primary identity: **mental formations** and their accompanying pleasant *vedana* that become the **perception** of what is good or not good/bad. Perception is what makes us aware of a secondary identity—such as body size, skin color, or gender; it instantaneously triggers in our mind (1) a concept and an emotion stored in our minds with respect to that secondary identity, and (2) an accompanying feeling tone, or *vedana*.

Perception rooted in comparing mind when attached to a secondary identity births the seed of exclusion consciousness responsible for social hierarchies. Powered by the defilement of ignorance, these hierarchies first begin in our minds, and our individual and collective belief in those hierarchies then get reflected in our communities, institutions, systems, and cultures.

INCLUSION AND EXCLUSION CONSCIOUSNESS: *INTERBEING* AND *WETIKO*

In his book *When Awareness Becomes Natural*, Burmese meditation master Sayadaw U Tejaniya writes that we humans are not only a part of nature, we are nature. Modern science confirms this ancient wisdom by demonstrating that 60 percent of our body weight is made up of water and the remainder of natural elements: organic compounds, gases, and minerals like calcium, phosphorous, sulfur, and potassium, among others. Not only that, geneticists have shown that we share some degree of our DNA and genes with all of nature, e.g., 50 percent with bananas, 80 percent with cows, and 98 percent with chimpanzees! We are nature.

What science has proven at a molecular level, our *interbeing*,* our Paleolithic, Neolithic, and many other ancient ancestors knew and practiced for millennia, and many existing cultures today still do. The concept of interbeing holds all aspects of nature as "sacred," that is, worthy of respect and reverence. We hear the echoes of this cosmology in most indigenous, animist, and spiritual communities that imagine humans and more-than-humans as "relatives." This ontology or *mindset of being* transcends dualistic thinking and hierarchies. It is what I interchangeably call *inclusion consciousness* or *ubuntu,* a Zulu concept that also describes the interconnectedness and interdependence of all things in the universe.

Inclusion consciousness actively works to deactivate the defilements in the mind. It builds mental formations that gravitate toward interdependence, cooperation, reciprocity, generosity, compassion,

---

* *Interbeing* is a concept that was coined by the Vietnamese Zen master and peace activist Thích Nhất Hânh. It describes the interconnectedness and interdependence of all things in the universe. It acknowledges that we are not isolated individuals, but rather are deeply connected to each other and to the natural world. It invites us to recognize that our actions have an impact on others and on our planet, and that we are all responsible for creating a more compassionate and sustainable world.

and forgiveness. This mindset isn't a relic of a bygone era. It is here now and a part of the cosmology of hundreds of human cultures today. The culture I grew up with in India had some aspects of inclusion consciousness.

According to animist traditions, including my own, most of our planetary and human history was dominated by inclusion consciousness.* However, a separation or exclusion consciousness arose within *some* human settlements in the Neolithic period. Indigenous wisdom refers to this system of thought and being as *wetiko* (pronounced way-ti-koh). *Wetiko* is an Algonquin word for a cannibalistic spirit and mindset that is driven by greed, excess, and self-consumption. Operating under the defilements of greed, hatred, and ignorance, in the words of Alnoor Ladha and Martin Kirk, *wetiko* "deludes its host into believing that cannibalizing the life-force of other beings (others in the broad sense, including animals and other forms of Gaian life) is a logical and morally upright way to live."[3]

Exclusion consciousness is a mindset marked by separateness, domination, competition, exploitation, accumulation, selfishness, cruelty, and retribution. As some Neolithic cultures transitioned into centralized societies, this mindset birthed various human hierarchies rooted in secondary identities, such as gender, descent, class, religion, and occupation, that excluded certain humans from activities, resources, rights, and opportunities for no reason other than their being.

I view our human history as a contest between these competing mindsets, which gave rise to different forms of exclusion and inclusion paradigms. The age of modernity globalized a certain type of exclusion paradigm that remains our dominant reality. In the last century, however, there has been a rise of inclusion consciousness, which gives you—and each one of us—the unprecedented opportunity to transition our species into a new inclusion paradigm. Let's walk through this history together.

---

* The Hindu tradition calls it the Age of Truth, or Satya Yuga. *See* Sri Yukteswar's *The Holy Science* in the Abridged Bibliography.

EXCLUSION PARADIGMS IN THE ANCIENT AGE

I grew up bearing witness to various exclusion paradigms in India and the United States. My early caretakers, like millions of migrant workers across India, were hired help generally from rural Indian villages who consciously or unconsciously believed a false narrative about their inferiority. They were not too different from the indigenous-descent Mexican migrant workers I've worked with in the United States. Similarly, in the classrooms of prestigious global universities, I've interacted with wealthier, generally but not exclusively white classmates who believed that they were somehow superior and wanted to "save" people in the global south by helping those people to become more developed like them. This is exclusion consciousness in action.

Exclusion consciousness thrives on separateness and comparing mind, and when institutionalized, it becomes an exclusion paradigm. During the ancient age, exclusion paradigms varied regionally in centralized societies. For example, the identity-based hierarchies practiced by the ancient Greeks, Romans, and Egyptians differed from those of the Chinese, Indians, Nahuatls, and Persians.

From about 3000 B.C.E. to 600 C.E., centralized societies came to dominate a portion of our planet's landmass. One of the central features of all centralized societies was division of labor and occupational class hierarchies based on social identities. As these centralized societies captured greater landmass, they instituted their hierarchies over larger human populations, assimilating and infecting many animist cultures.

Under these exclusion paradigms, a human's intersectionality (e.g., descent, ethnicity, language, beliefs, religion, gender, or disability) dictated all aspects of their lives. For example, in most centralized societies, a human's gender determined whether they could work outside the home, run for office, or enter certain professions, and whom they could marry. The perception accompanying each human's intersectionality generally located them on two hierarchies: a human hierarchy of better or worse than other humans based on secondary identities, and a meta-hierarchy of humans, nonhuman beings, and the Earth in an individual's and collective's consciousness.

For individual humans, the repeated exposure to and awareness of these hierarchies reinforced their self-concept and concept of the other (i.e., in-group and out-group). As more and more people are trained in those mental formations, the exclusion consciousness becomes a part of a collective's consciousness, giving rise to each society's unique exclusion paradigm.

Under each exclusion paradigm, humans within centralized societies suffered tremendously or exerted tremendous power over others based on where they found themselves within these hierarchies. While these centralized societies fought innumerable wars with one another to conquer more land and spread their mindset of domination and separateness to other territories, there existed numerous cultures and societies outside and even within their boundaries that did not subscribe to their exclusionary mindset. These cultures, mostly animist, lived in harmony with one another and the natural world.

This does not mean they didn't engage in violence or destruction of the Earth or other species—as humans, they were just as subject to the mind's defilements.* However, in such circumstances, many animist cultures utilized mental concepts that curbed their behavior toward one another, including their response to violence and destruction in the forms of restorative justice, reconciliation, and healing justice. For example, indigenous societies prior to European contact did not have prisons. Their cosmologies could not countenance using effort, time, and resources to discard their fellow humans—no matter what deeds they had done—in such a way.

In addition, in ancient centralized societies, there were illuminated humans like Krishna, Zarathustra, Moses, Lao-tzu, Mahavira, Buddha, Epictetus, Jesus, and Muhammad, who, akin to animist cultures, challenged their society's exclusion consciousness through their deeper realization of *ubuntu,* i.e., human oneness and interdependence with more-than-humans.† They espoused compassion,

---

* For example, the animist Romans, Mongols, Egyptians, Incas, Cholas, and other centralized societies operated from a mindset of domination that was powered by *wetiko* and the defilements of greed, hatred, and ignorance.

† There were likely many non-male humans as well, but due to the social ranking of gender that designed history, their names and legacies are lesser known.

understanding, forgiveness, and love and taught others how to cultivate interbeing through these means. They embodied a state of consciousness that any human can reach through introspection, knowing one's mind, and speaking and behaving in a manner rooted in that consciousness, i.e., ethics, virtues, and morality. They inspired social, cultural, and religious revolutions that continue to offer us peace and comfort, ecstasy and joy. For me, it's not important whether these beings were divinely inspired or divine themselves; what's important is their message.

TRANSITION TO THE MEDIEVAL AGE

From the mid-600s to the mid-1400s C.E.—the medieval era—centralized societies came to dominate more of our planet's landmass. Several important human events mark the transition from the ancient to the medieval age, including Constantine's conversion to Christianity and the establishment of the Roman Catholic Church, the fall of the Western Roman Empire,* and the establishment of the first Islamic caliphate in the Arabian Peninsula. In the medieval age, the messages of the illuminated beings Jesus Christ and the Prophet Muhammad were written down to pass on a spiritual legacy and guidance, but they were subsequently institutionalized by certain groups of humans for the purposes of domination and empire. As a result, two competing exclusion paradigms came to politically dominate most centralized societies in Europe, North and East Africa, the Middle East, and Central and South Asia.

These two paradigms fought innumerable wars with one another, including the Crusades for more than 200 years (1096–1300 C.E.). While there were further splits within each exclusion paradigm—disagreements over succession, creating Sunni and

---

* Many successor kingdoms emerged that are the predecessors of many modern-day European nations, including: Visigoths (now Spain, Portugal, parts of France and Italy), Ostrogoths (Italy and parts of the Balkans), Vandals (North Africa), Franks (France and Germany), Burgundians (Switzerland and parts of France), and Anglo-Saxons (England). These successor states were generally organized around ethnic or tribal identities, and they often adopted elements of Roman culture and administration in their own systems of government.

Shia traditions, and the Great Schism creating the Eastern Orthodox and Roman Catholic traditions—a meta-narrative prevailed in each centralized society of superiority over all other humans and nonhumans stemming from identification with a certain interpretation of Christianity or Islam. It's important to note that the humans who subscribed to these supranational religious identities retained their tribal or ethnic identities, such as the Franks, Greeks, or Kurds, or created new ethnoreligious identities, like the Turks, Russians, or Armenians.

Both paradigms adopted strict policies around heresy, blasphemy, and apostasy to eliminate any dissent or objections. They also established the concepts of *infidel, savage, heathen*, and *pagan* to refer to humans who did not share the dominant religious identity and attempted to eliminate animist human cultures that retained a connection with Earth. In doing so, they severed their connection with their own biological ancestors and ancestral beliefs, including many animist and Earth-based traditions.

As Christian or Islamic rule spread across our Earth's landmass, many human cultures voluntarily or forcibly succumbed to political Christian or Muslim rule. As a result, their exclusion paradigms became the infrastructure for bias, exclusion, and marginalization in those societies. These paradigms are known as the Great Chain of Being (GCB) in European Christendom and as the *Dhimmi* system in the Islamic world. They both provide the basis for many forms of institutionalized biases that are still in force around the world. Let's dig deeper into each.

Europe's Exclusion Paradigm in the Medieval Age

Have you ever heard of the Great Chain of Being? In the space below or in your journal, guess what it might be based on what you know so far.

Great Chain of Being is:

If you don't know what it is, don't worry! I went through most of my education without knowing what GCB was or even that it existed. Yet an implicit belief in it is the hidden undercurrent of social hierarchies that remain to this day. I see it as the master conceptual puppeteer of social engineering. I first discovered it in Nell Irvin Painter's *The History of White People*, and understanding it has helped me make sense of how the human animal could cause so much death and destruction to other humans, more-than-humans, and our planet Earth.[4]

The GCB mental concept has roots in ancient Greek philosophy, particularly in the work of the influential philosophers Plato and Aristotle. They believed that the universe was governed by a set of eternal and unchanging laws and everything had a "natural" place in a cosmic hierarchy. This exclusion consciousness shaped the way humans thought about the nature of reality and their role in the universe. Their cosmology assigned each human a set of duties and responsibilities based on their position in a preordained social hierarchy. It was the basis for the Roman Empire's organized social hierarchy with the emperor on top, followed by members of the aristocracy, the middle classes, peasants, and enslaved people.

After the fall of the Western Roman Empire, as Christianity spread across Europe, the Roman Catholic Church revised this cosmology to establish its divine authority across the continent and used that divine authority to allow various tribal warriors to proclaim themselves "divine" monarchs, who in turn used this cosmology to legitimize their rule and enforce its feudal social class systems.

In the GCB worldview, an anthropomorphic masculine God, the "Heavenly Father," is the ultimate source of all existence and the creator of a hierarchically ordered universe. All beings exist in a fixed and predetermined order as follows: the Church, the monarchy, the nobility or rich humans, working humans, and the "beasts" (i.e., animals, birds, insects), with plants and the Earth at the bottom. Women are placed below men on each rung, and non-Christians—including Jews, Muslims,* and animists—are

---

* Medieval Europeans called Muslims *Saracens*, likely derived from the Arabic *sarakin*, meaning "desert people."

considered infidels, savages, and beasts, hence, eliminated from society altogether or existing on its margins.

Under the GCB, the idea of private ownership of land didn't exist, so marauding kings and queens claimed total ownership over their territories and fought numerous wars with one another to expand these territories and infect them with their *wetiko*. There was widespread exploitation of the working people; *biophobia** (hatred and fear of nature and more-than-humans) and repulsion toward all human elements labeled as pagan, animist, or feminine were implicit in this exclusion paradigm.

Across European Christendom, animals and nature were objectified as things to be subordinated, dominated, and used exclusively for human welfare, and thousands of women and gender-diverse humans were persecuted for witchcraft and paganism for their affinity for and knowledge of nature, plants, and animals. This cosmology also labeled human nature as inherently sinful, bad, and evil. It is no wonder why this period is popularly known as the Dark Ages.

Under the GCB exclusion paradigm, subjugated people were reared in self-loathing environments that produced some very unhappy humans. They were trained to hate their own existence and to feel separate from themselves and their natural environment, while seeking forgiveness and repentance from external Church authorities for no other reason than their *beingness*. These are the roots of the self-loathing that remains in cultures influenced by this consciousness. I continue to witness it among many of my students reared in religious ideologies that stem from separation and domination.

Within the territories of these centralized societies, however, despite being violently suppressed, the light of inclusion consciousness remained alive among humans like Catherine of Siena, who wrote the following:

---

* A term I learned from Lakota elder Tiokasin Ghosthorse.

All has been consecrated.
The creatures in the forest know this,
The earth does, the seas do, the clouds know
as does the heart full of
love.
Strange a priest would rob us of this
knowledge
and then empower himself
with the ability
to make holy what
already was.

— *St. Catherine of Siena (1347–1380)*

The Islamic World's Exclusion Paradigm in the Medieval Age

In the medieval age, as Islam spread across West Asia, North Africa, and Spain, these societies experienced what is termed a "golden age," with the sciences, philosophy, and the arts flourishing through the exchange of ideas credited to these societies' tolerance of difference. Before we jump into the Islamic world's exclusion paradigm, in the space below or in your journal, I'd like you to take a moment to define *tolerance*. How do the word and its associations land in your body? Document any concepts and emotions, and the *vedana* accompanying them.

Define *tolerance*:

Vedana:

Mental formations (concepts, emotions, habits):

We begin here because many scholars hail the *Dhimmi* paradigm in comparison to medieval Europe's absolutely intolerant GCB paradigm. But what about *Dhimmi* compared to other centralized, nomadic, and decentralized societies across the Americas, Africa, Australia, and parts of Asia? As a college student, when I asked this question in my Islamic studies classes, I'd receive uncomfortable stares and pauses that over time revealed to me the ignorance of some of my instructors about ways of being beyond the two dominant exclusion paradigms.

Unlike the GCB, which was deeply hierarchal around wealth, occupation, and descent, the *Dhimmi* system was rooted in two innovations. First, a purported absolute equality between male humans who adopted Islam, regardless of other secondary identities, such as ancestry, class, or ethnicity. This appealed to many subordinated humans in centralized societies who were previously excluded or marginalized because of their occupation, class, ethnicity, or another identity; it also enabled the swift spread of Islam across centralized cultures.

However, it didn't deliver on its promise, as most humans remained in their pre-Islamic social and economic conditions, while those in control used their other secondary identities such as their descent (e.g., a claim to be a descendant of the Prophet Muhammad), ethnicity (e.g., Arab, Mongol, Tatar, Turk, or Persian), occupation, or wealth to create new hierarchies. While the specifics of these hierarchies varied with the diversity of regional cultures, this system guaranteed humans who joined the dominant group one thing: the *feeling* of superiority to non-Muslims (note: comparing mind).

This feeling relates directly to the system's second innovation: tolerance and protection of humans termed as *ahl al-dhimma* or "people of the Book." To fully appreciate the basis of this idea, I find it helpful to understand the regional context in which the Prophet Muhammad's revelations spread across the Arabian Peninsula before his transition in 632 C.E. At the time, the region was under the control of many competing and corrupt desert-based animist cultures, both centralized and nomadic. The Prophet's

teachings and leadership enabled these diverse groups to experience intergroup peace, harmony, and stability through a new way:
Islam, which means complete surrender to the one Divine, akin to
the beliefs of monotheist Christians and Jews and in contrast to the
outward-facing idolatry of some pre-Islamic Arab tribes.

In this context, the group identity that became Islam perceived
itself as good, other monotheists as okay, and all others, including
their own ancestors, as idol worshippers, *kafir* (nonbelievers), *jahil*
(ignorant), and bad. Islam was brought to new territories westward
and eastward through the lens of this perception. I'd like you to
notice the interplay of mental concepts, emotions, and *vedana* that
gave rise to such a perception.

As Islam was brought to new territories, despite its offer of
equality, many human groups did not want to adopt it and thus the
Dhimmi system came into being. Under this system, people of the
Book, or Christians and Jews, could practice their religion as long as
they paid a *jizya*—a tax—to the authorities for their protection. This
worked perfectly as Islam spread northward and westward through
the Christian Byzantine empire and various Christian kingdoms
and Jewish settlements and tribes.

However, as Islam traveled eastward, it encountered new religious and spiritual groups that were largely absent in the Arabian
Peninsula, like the Yazidis, Zoroastrians, Jains, Hindus, and Buddhists, among many other animist traditions. From what they
knew of pre-Islamic Arab tribes, Muslims perceived these groups
as idol worshippers and hence perpetrated inordinate violence,
suppression, and destruction on them as they had on the pagan
and animist traditions of pre-Islamic Arabia. As a result, numerous diverse ways of being, particularly those rooted in animism,
were either eliminated, absorbed into regional Islamic practices,
or pushed to the margins of societies, most notably the Yazidis
in West Asia. Over time, as some tolerant Muslim rulers learned
about the actual belief systems of these traditions, they folded
groups like the Zoroastrians, Hindus, Buddhists, and others into
the *Dhimmi* system.

This is the *Dhimmi* system in a nutshell. In the transition from the medieval age to the age of modernity, as Constantinople* fell to the Ottomans in 1453, the *Dhimmi* system spread farther across modern-day Turkiye and parts of eastern and southern Europe. In addition, it spread westward across the Indian subcontinent to centralized and decentralized societies of Southeast Asia.

Like the GCB, the *Dhimmi* paradigm creates a human hierarchy based on religious beliefs. However, unlike the GCB, it sometimes tolerates subordinated groups. What's important to recognize about subordinated group tolerance is that it is permitted because the dominant group needs it—for example, for taxes or skills, or to give certain groups of people a feeling of superiority despite their subordination on the grounds of another secondary identity.

I have experienced this feeling of superiority firsthand while living and working in impoverished, excluded, and marginalized Muslim communities in India, Myanmar, and Malaysia. I have no doubt that some of the people I lived and worked with deeply respected and even loved me, and they invited me to adopt Islam many times.

Through our conversations, I learned that they didn't care to know about Buddhist or Hindu cosmologies. Heck, in some cases, they didn't even fully appreciate Islam, but they were identified with the identity of Muslim, which made them *feel* that they were better than other humans. This is the trap of exclusion consciousness. In trying to be better-than, we are made to forget that we *are*. Not better. Not worse. Not even equal, we just are. For this reason, to me, tolerance is insufficient because just as it is granted, it can be taken away. This was the case historically, and it remains the case for non-Muslims in much of the Islamic world, as well as for subordinated ethnic and religious minorities, including Muslims, beyond it.

With respect to the Islamic world's exclusion paradigm, the historical trauma of domination, exclusion, and marginalization remains alive in numerous non-Muslim communities. Whether I am with my Hindu and Sikh relatives or with colleagues who are Bangladeshi Buddhist, Malaysian Taoist, Arab Christian, Persian

---

* The former seat of the Eastern Roman or Byzantine Empire.

Zoroastrian, Turkish Chaldean, or Iraqi Yazidi, I have noticed an identical stream of Islamophobia that is generally not about Islamic spirituality, but about what some humans did to their ancestors and cultures in the name of Islam. I have found that their unrecognized, unhealed, and unreconciled intergenerational trauma often fuels their hatred of or indifference to the marginalization and exclusion experienced by humans who happen to be Muslim today. This too is *wetiko*.

With that said, despite being violently suppressed, many humans across the Islamic world reminded their contemporaries of *ubuntu* as captured by the following words:

> Every war and every conflict between human beings
> has happened because of some disagreement about names.
> It is such an unnecessary foolishness,
> because just beyond the arguing
> there is a long table of companionship
> set and waiting for us to sit down.
> What is praised is one, so the praise is one too,
> many jugs being poured into a huge basin.
> All religions, all this singing, one song.
> The differences are just illusion and vanity.
> Sunlight looks a little different on this wall
> than it does on that wall
> and a lot different on this other one,
> but it is still one light.
> We have borrowed these clothes,
> these time-and-space personalities,
> from a light, and when we praise,
> we are pouring them back in.

> — *Jalal al-Din Muhammad Rumi (1207–1273)*

MODERNITY'S EXCLUSION PARADIGM: CAPITALISM

European colonization standardized the GCB globally, including in Islamic societies colonized by European nations. This period, which we are still in today, is the beginning of what scholars

Vanessa Machado de Oliveira and Báyò Akómoláfé call the age of capitalist modernity/coloniality or white modernity,* an era that ushers white Europeans into a period of economic prosperity and political change at the expense of all the centralized and animist societies they colonized and decimated.[5]

In short, a bunch of guys from Western Europe got on ships with the purpose of expanding their nations' territories. They landed on new continents and perceived the human and more-than-humans of these places through their GCB lens: savages, beasts, and objects to dominate and subjugate. Tolle's description that "thoughts [mental concepts] can spread like a virus and if they proliferate in the collective psyche, they distort our perceptions and cause us to act as if they were true and then they manifest as our reality" fittingly describes the way Europe's *wetiko* came to dominate the world in the age of modernity.[6]

Following global expansion and exploration, some dominant-class Christian European cis male thinkers shared their perceptions of the world outside their borders through their GCB lens. As demonstrated by Western scholars like David Graeber and David Wengrow in *The Dawn of Everything,* indigenous scholars, and scholars from the global south, through exposure to ideas from indigenous, Islamic, and Asian societies, these thinkers ushered Europe into modernity's era of Enlightenment and industrialization. They proffered ideas of political and economic liberalism to reform and replace their exploitative feudal systems.[7]

However, they limited the application of these ideas to humans like themselves. In the 18th and 19th centuries, these ideas titrated through the GCB lens became the inspiration for our modern-day economic and political systems, including federalist or centralist democracies, communism, socialism, and capitalism, as well as fascism, Nazism, and white supremacy.

The history of modernity is incredibly complex, region-specific, and frankly maddening. I know because I spent decades with the books, documentaries, podcasts, and live testimonies of

---

* I will refer to it as *modernity* for short.

the subordinated and dominating peoples globally.* What I want to highlight is that the GCB exclusion paradigm devolved into new mental concepts, including:

* *Race*, a descent-, geography-, and color-based hierarchy that is ubiquitous in societies colonized and settled by Europeans, something we'll delve deeper into in Chapter 5

* *Exclusionary interpretations of Christianity* that supplanted many indigenous and Earth-loving mindsets, homogenizing the subordinate status of women and criminalizing people's gender identities and sexualities globally, something we'll review in Chapter 6

* *Theriocides*, or deliberate slaughter of nonhuman beings, and *ecocide*, destruction of the natural environment

* *A commodified and transactional view* of ourselves, others, nature, and all aspects of the living Earth that has come to dominate our global consciousness today as neoliberalism and late-stage capitalism, something we'll uncover further in Chapter 7

You'll learn about some of the human personalities who enabled the above as you continue reading. For now, all you need to know is that these humans were operating from an anthropo-centric exclusion consciousness that fundamentally saw humans like themselves (wealthy, landowning, literate, white, European, heterosexual, Christian, male) as "civilized" and superior to the rest of humanity, more-than-humans, and nature; and thus, they could do as they pleased with them (which they did and continue to do). They not only used animal-like imagery to justify ruthless subordination and elimination of black, brown, and non-Christian peoples, but perpetrated the same fate on more-than-humans and nature globally.

---

* I've included a list of some of my primary resources for this history in the Abridged Bibliography.

Figure 2.2

For example, until the mid-1800s, it is estimated that up to 60 million buffalo roamed the American plains. These animals were revered by the numerous indigenous societies who relied on them for their way of life. By 1890, their numbers were reduced to fewer than 535 animals.[8] The aim of the American theriocide policy was to remove indigenous people to make way for white settlers across the American continent, a policy rooted in *wetiko*, i.e., feeling separate from indigenous humans, more-than-humans, and the Earth. Figure 2.2 shows an image from 1892 that captures the extent of the buffalo slaughter carried out by white settlers in the American Midwest.[*] To this day, the unaddressed legacies of European colonialism remain the biggest challenge to conservation, environmental sustainability, and a concerted response to climate change.[9]

The mental concepts derived from GCB are not of a bygone era, but remain with us to this day. I was teased and tortured for being a cow-worshipper as a kid, as if respecting life in another sentient being were wrong. This is also why black people, including

---

[*] © Wikimedia Commons. "Men standing with pile of buffalo skulls, Michigan Carbon Works." Detroit Public Library. Retrieved January 9, 2024.

the likes of Serena Williams, Meghan Markle, and Barack Obama, are to this day dehumanized with comparisons to monkeys and chimps. This is *wetiko*, exclusion consciousness that diminishes humans of color. It also prevents us from remembering humanity's evolutionary heritage, our anthropological African heritage, and the sentience of nonhuman beings. As someone who was raised to revere the spirit in monkeys as Hanuman, one of the most celebrated Hindu deities, I recognize that such speciesist and racist language is the continuation of exclusion consciousness to this day.

PRISM EXERCISE

Pause. Take three breaths. Bring your attention to your body and recall our shared agreements. In the space below or in your journal, document what's arising in your body, heart, and mind.

I'd now like you to practice perspective-taking and imagine being the European humans who conceived and practiced domination and colonialism.

Imagine how they felt around different colors of humans and why. How did they feel about women? Gay people? Non-Christians? Animals? The poor? The Earth? Beyond that, how did they feel about themselves? Reflect on what might be rooted beneath their sense of superiority. Imagine being in their bodies and minds. What does it feel like? Document your experiences and the *vedana* that accompanies them.

SPREADING EUROPE'S *WETIKO* VIA CAPITALISM GLOBALLY

One of the traps of the history I've shared with you is to fall into the dualistic thinking of good versus bad and right versus wrong. I spent many years fuming with anger and hatred toward Western colonial powers, building nostalgic stories of how non-Western societies were before the West wreaked such havoc across the world. We know from indigenous scholars that European colonization obliterated and erased many inclusion paradigms they practiced. With that said, in pre-European colonialism there existed many centralized and noncentralized societies with their own exclusion paradigms, such as the Aztecs, Mongols, Hawaiians, Ottomans, Persians, Indians, Chinese, and Japanese.

In the modern era, these societies too saw many illuminated beings who were violently suppressed for attempting to share and spread their inclusion consciousness—Guru Nanak, Kabir, Mira bai, Thích Nhât Hânh, the Dalai Lama, Bahá'u'lláh, Sri Aurobindo, Paramahansa Yogananda, Daisaku Ikeda, and many others. Like their predecessors, their message continues to provide meaning, comfort, and inspiration to many humans, but the collective consciousness of their societies, much like the West's, remains rooted in various exclusion paradigms. European colonization instituted its exclusion paradigm on top of these societies' existing exclusion paradigms, while deliberately planting seeds of divisions via divide-and-conquer policies.

Starting in the 19th century, through Western Christian missionary efforts, many subordinated humans learned European languages and applied Europe's Enlightenment ideas to their own condition. They used European Enlightenment ideas of human equality and inherent human dignity to demand civil and political equality, self-determination, and eventually independence from colonial rule.

They also used these ideas to extricate their societies from precolonial exclusion paradigms. This culminated in global freedom movements from Indonesia and India to Algeria and Angola in what is considered the global south. Within nations settled by Europeans, like the United States, Brazil, Australia, and South Africa, it resulted in the movement for civil rights for black and brown people and women, as well as ongoing movements to recognize the *beingness* of humans irrespective of sex, color, sexuality, disability, and gender identity.

If you're a student of 20th-century history, you know that what followed was unimaginable destruction, death, and human and nonhuman suffering: the Armenian genocide, the Bolshevik Revolution, the Holocaust of European Jews, China's Cultural Revolution, the killing fields in Cambodia, export of Arab-centric Islam* to replace syncretically nuanced traditions of Islam across the Islamic world, and more.

Simultaneously, from the 1950s, capitalism, the dominant Western exclusion paradigm, evolved into neoliberal capitalism, a worldview that commodifies all human and nonhuman aspects of life with a monetary value and determines our worth and purpose in life solely by money. This shift was powered by abstract mental concepts put forth by humans of particular dominant intersectional identities from Western nations with degrees in economics and finance.†

Through international monetary policies and adoption of economic reforms in the footsteps of Western nations, these ideas have crippled the economic welfare of most humans globally, including in the West, created a planetary environment where one nonhuman being goes extinct every five minutes, or up to 100,000 species annually, and our planet faces an existential crisis of climate collapse.[10]

Take a breath with me here, and feel the impact of these words on your body, heart, and soul. For me, as difficult as it is, this has been important to acknowledge and *feel* so I can respond skillfully. The transactional nature of neoliberal ideas and policies are the causes and conditions for the many challenges we experience worldwide, such as inequality, loneliness, unhealthy workplace cultures, mental health crises, and climate change. Sadly, the mind-virus of *wetiko* also seeped into 21st-century social change movements

---

* Such as Wahhabism, Deobandism, and Salafism.

† The term *neoliberalism* has roots in the work of white economists who were part of the Mont Pelerin Society, founded in 1947, which included influential thinkers like Friedrich Hayek and Milton Friedman. Neoliberalism became the dominant force in national and international economic policies, starting in the 1970s. *See* Harvey's *A Brief History of Neoliberalism*.

by replicating Western hierarchies along the lines of race, gender, class, and nationality, among others: think of Occupy Wall Street, Me Too, and the Women's March.

This is the state of our world today, with a dominant exclusion paradigm of neoliberal capitalism and a dozen other exclusion paradigms operating at the national and regional levels.

WHAT DOES THE DOMINANT EXCLUSION PARADIGM WANT?

I will never forget an interview Harry Belafonte gave about his last conversation with Dr. King, in the days leading up to Dr. King's assassination. Dr. King said to Mr. B., "I've come upon something that disturbs me deeply. We have fought hard and long for integration, as I believe we should have, and I know we will win, but I have come to believe that we are integrating into a burning house."[11]

Fifty years later, I believe his words are true not only for America, but also for our global economic and political systems. In the postcolonial era, nations from the global south have been forcibly integrated into an economic system that is literally burning our planet. Despite decades of efforts by indigenous communities and brave activists like Wangari Maathai, Winona LaDuke, Jane Goodall, Vandana Shiva, Kumi Naidoo, and millions of others, our leaders continue to prioritize ceaseless monetary growth. To our leaders, in her 2019 speech at the United Nations General Assembly, Swedish climate activist Greta Thunberg said the following:

> You have stolen my dreams and my childhood with your empty words. And yet I'm one of the lucky ones. People are suffering. People are dying. Entire ecosystems are collapsing. We are in the beginning of a mass extinction,

and all you can talk about is money and fairy tales of eternal economic growth.[12]

This calls out the cannibalistic mindset of *wetiko*, which deludes humans in positions of power into indifference, entitlement, and violence. America's Cree people are said to have described the consequences of *wetiko* as follows: "When the last tree is cut down, the last fish eaten, and the last stream poisoned, you will realize that you cannot eat money."

Let me illustrate this with an example. At my local supermarket, I often see a small plastic cup of pineapple for $1.50. I read on its plastic packaging that the pineapple was grown in Thailand, was packaged in Argentina, and is now being sold in New York. A one-way economy ticket between these three places would cost over $6,000, so how could this product be less than 0.025 percent of that cost? Because of an economic mental concept known as *externalities*, i.e., any social costs like exploitation of humans, environmental costs like ecosystem annihilation, or climate destruction by pollution of the air and water, are not a part of market prices. They are just assumed to be "transaction costs" of doing business.

Economist Milton Friedman provided the intellectual framework that popularized neoliberal ideology in his 1970 article "The Social Responsibility of Business Is to Increase Its Profits" and nothing else.[13] Why? Because he claimed that despite all evidence to the contrary, businesses foster innovation for the progress of human *civilization*. He was awarded the Nobel Prize in Economics a few years later.

I once asked an Amazon executive what the end goal of such progress and civilizing mission was. He immediately responded, "To know and control all aspects of nature." When I pushed back with "What about the sacredness of nature?" he sarcastically responded, "Nothing beyond the human mind is, to use your word, 'sacred.'" This is the narrative—whether conscious or not—of many modern-day leaders in tech, finance, and law.

In 1971, a year after Friedman published his case, the Last Poets presciently released the song "White Man's Got a God Complex."

Today, neoliberal capitalism has spread this complex, *wetiko*, to all corners and cultures of the world, from Asia, Africa, and the Americas to even some indigenous societies globally where human affairs are exclusively concerned with the accumulation of money and "fairy tales of eternal economic growth."

In the words of civil rights elder Ruby Sales, what we face today is a deep spiritual crisis,[14] one fueled by disembodiment and separation: from our bodies, from other human bodies, from more-than-humans, and from the living Earth. In worshipping the mind and building cultures that feed our egos, we have forgotten that we have a body and that we too are nature.

PRISM EXERCISE

Pause. Take three full breaths, return your awareness to your somatic experience, and remember our shared agreements.

The history I've shared with you is hidden from us outside of select graduate courses and academic textbooks. These perspectives may be new to you. They may feel inadequate and superficial, and they are. I've tried to recount in as few words as possible what billions of our ancestors—of all colors, cultures, genders, abilities—have lived through, experienced, and felt in their bodies since the rise of exclusion paradigms.

I want you to take a moment to breathe and feel your body. (Remember you have a body?) Notice your somatic experience and how you *feel* right now. What thoughts and emotions are arising? Notice if there is shame, blame, or anger. Where in the body is it? What is the *vedana* associated with these thoughts and emotions?

Now, stop reading and move your body. Do 50 jumping jacks. Dance. Stretch. Yell. Scream. Do whatever you feel like you need to do to get out of your head and *feel* your body. Go do it and come back after you feel more embodied.

There is nothing to do or fix right now. What I have shared with you happened and it is happening. It is a consequence of trillions of causes and conditions. Notice if your mind tries to search for solutions or for people to blame. That's okay; it only wants to help you find relief from the discomfort you're experiencing.

This is what the political science and legal courses I took attempted to do: gloss over the history and call it *realpolitik* or go overwhelmingly deep and erect good/bad, colonizer/colonized dichotomies. In all scenarios, these mental concepts kept me from *feeling* in my body the pain of what happened and what is happening.

This exclusion paradigm is both our history and our present. Regardless of our secondary identities, we are all entangled in it, and it is in our DNA—of both the oppressor and the oppressed. In the footsteps of many wisdom-keepers from across cultures and traditions, acknowledging and feeling this discomfort in your body with modesty, humility, and compassion is the first step toward healing and, *inshallah*, skillful response that is onward leading.

THE RISE OF INCLUSION CONSCIOUSNESS

Recall that for the vast majority of human prehistory and history, our species existed in alignment with one another and with the natural and more-than-human world. Even as different exclusion paradigms arose in centralized societies and made their mark across human cultures, many animist cultures and wisdom-keepers kept the spirit of interbeing, of inclusion consciousness, alive.

In addition, we know that humans who wrought and continue to wreak unconscionable havoc on one another and on the Earth through scorched-earth policies and ecocides often sought, and continue to seek, comfort in the messages of illuminated teachers like Moses, Jesus, Muhammad, Krishna, Buddha, and others for greater strength and courage. I am struck by how many builders of walls, how many defenders of apartheid and laws that prevent women and LGBTQ+ people from experiencing equality, sought and seek solace in one or more of these illuminated humans.

As Thích Nhât Hânh noted, the seeds of inclusion are in the builders of walls just as they are in the rest of humanity. When we water these seeds, we strengthen concepts, habits, and emotions that channel our thoughts, words, and behavior toward interdependence, cooperation, reciprocity, generosity, compassion, and forgiveness. Cultivating these states also diminishes the power of the ego-making defilements that fuel unwholesome and unskillful ways of being.

I find it comforting that in the last century, in direct opposition to the global exclusion paradigm, at least five interrelated waves have made an indelible mark on planting, nourishing, and spreading the seeds of inclusion consciousness at a global mass scale in the ocean that is our collective consciousness. I will briefly share each below.

1. Intergroup Dialogues

In direct opposition to the exclusion paradigm, numerous contemplatives, poets, seekers, and conservationists in the West began a dialogue with Eastern wisdom traditions in the 19th century that ushered in various contemplative movements such as transcendentalism, theosophy, and others. These movements actively instilled in these seekers curiosity and a desire to learn from the wisdom of the colonized. They welcomed wisdom-keepers like Vivekananda, Paramahansa Yogananda, Thích Nhât Hânh, the Dalai Lama, and D. T. Suzuki, who brought their Earth-based wisdom of interbeing to the West. In addition, many Westerners went to Asia to learn, practice, adopt, and share the benefits of these wisdom traditions.

These dialogues inspired widespread incorporation of inclusion consciousness, even if at a subtle level, through the Beat generation, New Age movements, and the mainstreaming of body, heart, and mind practices like yoga, meditation, tai chi, tapping, and many others, transmitted via studios, YouTube channels, and mobile apps globally. I am personally a beneficiary of these dialogues. Most of my Hindu, Buddhist, Sufi, and Taoist yoga, meditation, and energy-healing teachers were raised in the West.

2. Political Soul Force

In response to the centuries of extraction, exploitation, and ecocide, Mohandas Gandhi inspired hundreds of millions of humans to demand self-autonomy and freedom using the principle of *satyagraha*, or soul force. Gandhi, like most of us, was not a perfect human, as at one point in his life he held despicable views about African people. Over time, he broke his biases and inspired a movement rooted in inclusion consciousness that sought to transform many faces of exclusion consciousness simultaneously, such as colonialism, materialism, patriarchy, casteism, ethnocentric nationalism, racism, and environmental destruction.[15]

Indian nonviolent civil disobedience seeded in the hearts and minds of millions the idea that peace is the way to create peace. It inspired the leaders of the American civil rights and anti–Vietnam War movements of Dr. King and Thích Nhât Hânh. It laid the possibility for the anti-apartheid struggle in South Africa that, under the leadership of Desmond Tutu, Nelson Mandela, and many others, culminated in a peaceful transition of power and social catharsis with the Truth and Reconciliation Commission. And it continues to dominate the strategies of numerous freedom and equality movements globally, including many indigenous movements for sovereignty; the Burmese, Tibetan, and Palestinian freedom movements; and the women's and LGBTQ+ movements in Iran and across the Islamic world. Ultimately, *satyagraha* demonstrated the power of simplicity, compassion, and love as a victorious response to brute force, materialism, and militarism.

3. International Norms

In 1945, after colonizing nations fought two brutal wars with one another and the world witnessed the destruction humans can cause with genocides and nuclear weapons, the United Nations was established to usher our world into an era of peace, tolerance, and understanding. Under its auspices, in 1948, the global humanist and spiritual wisdom traditions were brought together in the adoption of the Human Rights Charter. The Charter was a tremendous achievement because it recognized and respected human diversity for the first time in human history. It standardized a global sensibility for inherent human rights that were external to any religious, political, or cultural belief and did not promote any hierarchies.

In addition, the Charter established norms for nations worldwide to guarantee specific rights to humans regardless of their secondary identities, such as the right to education, health, food, employment, political participation, and others. It intentionally set aspirational norms to evolve humanity beyond identity-based hierarchies, hatred, and wars; it foreshadowed the end of European colonial rule and the freedom movements in Western nations such as the United States, Canada, and Australia; and it ushered in greater consciousness of climate and environmental destruction, e.g., *Silent Spring* by Rachel Carson, which was first published in 1962 and influenced the Western consciousness around protection and preservation of the natural world.

Many of the Charter's norms were enshrined in the constitutions of newly independent nations and within the laws and policies of colonizing nations. The Charter also led to the creation of international human rights law, i.e., the many human rights conventions and treaty bodies that protect specific human identities from discrimination and establish mechanisms to ensure their inclusion.[16] In numerous nations globally, it continues to influence policies and practices that protect humans based on sex, race, ethnicity, and disability, among other secondary identities.

4. Mind Sciences

In the late 20th century, as many Western practitioners gained palpable personal benefits from Eastern and indigenous wisdom traditions such as meditation, yoga, tai chi, Ayurveda, Chinese medicine, plant medicine, and others, they documented these benefits in academic journals through numerous experiments using the language of Western science. With the support of this evidence, traditions that were suppressed and deemed "savage" by colonial powers became mainstream with the sprawling studios and retreat centers globally earning livelihoods for millions of people.

In particular, with advances in the mind sciences and neuro-technology, scientists have demonstrated the efficacy of many ancient Asian, African, and Native technologies, such as meditation, breathwork, somatic practices, and plant medicines, in physically transforming the structure of the brain and supporting durable behavior change in overcoming, for example, addiction, PTSD, anxiety, depression, and many other afflictions that plague our contemporary world. Some of these practices are the basis of PRISM tools that overall support us in transforming our mindsets and behavior.

5. Returning to the Sacred

Above all, more and more people are abandoning the false promises of materialism and exclusion paradigms in search of peace, compassion, and oneness. Against the mainstream movements, these efforts are still burgeoning around the world, and they promise something that no amount of wealth, power, domination, or control can guarantee: inner fulfillment and happiness. As Grace Lee Boggs reminded us, cultivating this inner ground enables us to imagine a life, a family, a community, and ultimately a world that is rooted in inclusion.[17]

We see it not only in the increased interest in animist, Buddhist, Hindu, Sufi, Jewish, and Christian contemplative practices, but also in the revitalization of numerous animist practices from the Philippines to Nigeria and Colombia to Greenland that for millennia supported our fellow humans in integrating our heads with our hearts and bodies. I often say that the longest journey we'll ever take is from our heads to our hearts and bodies. This was my journey. And this is our journey—to remember that we are nature.

Identifying and studying the impacts of these five waves together is how I was able to appreciate the wisdom of my ancestors and Eckhart Tolle's message: human consciousness is organically evolving toward inclusion. However, despite a growing inclusion consciousness, from a deep-time perspective, we will likely remain in the exclusion paradigm for several hundred if not thousands of years to come unless we overcome one single roadblock: bias.

Breaking bias is the gateway to transition us from the exclusion to the inclusion paradigm. The work of breaking bias is rooted in each one of our primary identities because it enables us to become intimate with and transform our perceptions and shift our consciousness. In other words, breaking bias is about making the unconscious conscious by correcting misinformation and strengthening positive states like curiosity, compassion, imagination, joy, and forgiveness.

PRISM PRACTICES

Pause. Take three breaths and bring your attention to your body sensations.

* Notice with curiosity—without needing to fix it—*wetiko* in the field that is your mind. Where is it in the body? Memories? Dreams? What does it feel like? What stories does it repeat to you about who you are as a human, in comparison with other humans? more-than-humans? What aspects of your day-to-day interactions and surroundings feed the root defilements (greed, hatred, and ignorance) of *wetiko*? In other words, where does your hatred pop up? What brings your greed forth?

* Investigate with awareness the state of *ubuntu* in your mind. Where is it in the body? Memories? Dreams? Aspirations? What does it feel like? What stories does it repeat to you about your beingness in relation to other humans? more-than-humans? What aspects of your day-to-day interactions and surroundings strengthen *ubuntu* and the antidotes to *wetiko*, i.e., wisdom, compassion, and generosity?

* Inquire with interest and visualize your ancestries from the ancient age to the very present. What dominant and secondary identities did they likely share with you? Can you be sure about all of their secondary identities? Did they have any secondary identities (spirituality, beliefs, profession, class) that you've been conditioned to perceive as "other"? For the latter, notice any stories (in the form of judgments and thoughts) or afflictive emotions like anger, sadness, or hatred that arise for

you. Practice loving-kindness toward yourself for holding these emotions. Then, if possible, practice it toward those ancestors, starting with the wisest ancestors in the ancient past and slowly moving closer toward the medieval to modernity to the present times.

✳ Imagine and visualize your descendants, from your biological or chosen families, from the very present to 5,000 years ahead. What secondary identities do they share with you? List 5 to 10 wishes, dreams, and aspirations you have for them. Then, list 5 to 10 actions you can take with your head, heart, and hands to fulfill these wishes for them.

✳ Look at the image below, which was taken from the Voyager 1 spacecraft on its outbound flight on February 14, 1990, from about 4 billion miles away. In this image the Earth is a mere point of light, a crescent only 0.12 pixel in size. Our planet was caught in the center of one of the scattered light rays resulting from taking the image so close to the sun. Then read the passage that follows from astronomer Carl Sagan's 1994 book *Pale Blue Dot*. Based on what you learned in this chapter, notice how these words land in your body. Underline any words that stand out to you. Document any emotions or thoughts that arise in your mind, e.g., sorrow, hope, doubt, irritation, empathy.

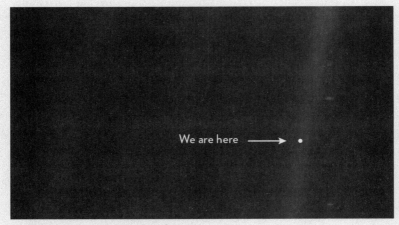

We are here ⟶ •

© Anu Gupta/BE MORE Inc, 2024

Look again at that dot. That's here. That's home. That's us. On it everyone you love, everyone you know, everyone you've ever heard of, every human being who ever was, lived out their lives. The aggregate of our joy and suffering, thousands of confident religions, ideologies, and economic doctrines, every hunter and forager, every hero and coward, every creator and destroyer of civilization, every king and peasant, every young couple in love, every mother and father, hopeful child, inventor and explorer, every teacher of morals, every corrupt politician, every "superstar," every "supreme leader," every saint and sinner in the history of our species lived there—on a mote of dust suspended in a sunbeam.

The Earth is a very small stage in a vast cosmic arena. Think of the rivers of blood spilled by all those generals and emperors so that, in glory and triumph, they could become the momentary masters of a fraction of a dot. Think of the endless cruelties visited by the inhabitants of one corner of this pixel on the scarcely distinguishable inhabitants of some other corner, how frequent their misunderstandings, how eager they are to kill one another, how fervent their hatreds.

Our posturings, our imagined self-importance, the delusion that we have some privileged position in the Universe, are challenged by this point of pale light. Our planet is a lonely speck in the great enveloping cosmic dark. In our obscurity, in all this vastness, there is no hint that help will come from elsewhere to save us from ourselves.

The Earth is the only world known so far to harbor life. There is nowhere else, at least in the near future, to which our species could migrate. Visit, yes. Settle, not yet. Like it or not, for the moment the Earth is where we make our stand. It has been said that astronomy is a humbling and character-building experience. There is perhaps no better demonstration of the folly of human conceits than this distant image of our tiny world. To me, it underscores our responsibility to deal more kindly with one another, and to preserve and cherish the pale blue dot, the only home we've ever known.

As you proceed to the next chapter, reflect on ways you can be more kind in service of preserving our pale blue dot. Reflect on any habits that can support you in embodying this aspiration.

STEREOTYPES AND THE FOUR FORMS OF BIAS

*Until we make the unconscious conscious,
it will direct our life and we will call it fate.*

— CARL JUNG

Read the following paragraph, notice what arises in your mind, and write your reflections below or in your journal.

A father and his son are in a car accident. The father dies at the scene and the son is rushed to the hospital. At the hospital the surgeon looks at the boy and says, "I cannot operate on this boy, he is my son." How can this be?[1]

Trying to solve this riddle likely brought several possibilities to your mind. Before we jump into the solution, let me take you back to 2012, when I first shared the riddle with my mother. She read it and looked very confused. She asked if there was a typo. After about five minutes of back-and-forth, her final answer was: "The dead father was the surgeon, who had really not died, or his ghost was in the operating room."

In response, I asked her what she had done the previous weekend. She said she was on call. I asked her, "What do you generally do when you're on call?" Irritated, she blurted out, "Surgeries."

Suddenly, it clicked. She took her hands to her face to cover the shame and embarrassment she felt. My mother, who is a surgeon, had not imagined the surgeon in the riddle being a woman.

When I first encountered this riddle as a law student, I too came up with various answers: adoptive father, stepfather, the other gay father, and even a Catholic priest—i.e., Father—until I was given the "answer": the surgeon could be the mother. This is the power of associating mental concepts like *surgeon* with gender so that over time these associations become mental habits and create a perception through which we perceive other humans.

Until very recently in human history, i.e., the 1970s, the perceptions we held did reflect our social realities due to the identity-based hierarchies enforced in centralized societies, whether they were rooted in gender, race, religion, or class.

For example, in the 1960s there were very few certified female or indigenous surgeons in Canada because they were categorically excluded from receiving such training. In the postcolonial era, however, that is no longer the case. For example, in 2021, almost 40 percent of all surgery trainees in the United States were female.[2] While that's not parity, it is still a significant number. Yet, for many people, our perceptions about a human's inner and outer capabilities remain tied to social identities, such as gender. These associations are the basis of how bias is birthed in our minds, with widespread implications for all aspects of our personal and social lives. This is what we'll be exploring in this chapter.

LET'S PLAY TAG: THE ASSOCIATION GAME

I want to begin by inviting you to play what I call The Association Game (TAG).[3] I generally play this game out loud with my students, but the worksheet version is just as good. To play the game, you'll need a pen or pencil and a timer.

In Figure 3.1, you'll see a matching game with two sections, 1 and 2. Each section has two categories of words listed in the top row: pleasant and unpleasant words, and insects and flowers. In the rows below, you'll see an image or a word in the center. All you need to do is start the timer and check each circle in the column that matches the word in the categories listed in the top row. The catch is that you have to finish the game *as quickly as possible*, ideally within 30 seconds. Once you complete the exercise, indicate at the bottom the number of errors you made and the amount of time it took you to complete each section. Don't overthink it, just go!

SECTION 1

Insects or pleasant words		Flowers or unpleasant words	Insects or pleasant words		Flowers or unpleasant words
☐		☐	☐		☐
☐	gentle	☐	☐	enjoy	☐
☐		☐	☐		☐
☐	evil	☐	☐	poison	☐
☐		☐	☐		☐
☐	damage	☐	☐	heaven	☐
☐		☐	☐		☐
☐	cheer	☐	☐	gloom	☐
☐		☐	☐		☐
☐	vomit	☐	☐	ugly	☐
☐		☐	☐		☐
☐	hurt	☐	☐	happy	☐
☐		☐	☐		☐
☐	love	☐	☐	friend	☐

Number of seconds ⬭   ⬭ Number of errors

© Anu Gupta/BE MORE Inc, 2024

Figure 3.1

SECTION 2

Flowers or pleasant words		Insects or unpleasant words	Flowers or pleasant words		Insects or unpleasant words
☐	🦋	☐	☐	🦂	☐
☐	gentle	☐	☐	enjoy	☐
☐	🌼	☐	☐	🪰	☐
☐	evil	☐	☐	poison	☐
☐	🌿	☐	☐	🦟	☐
☐	damage	☐	☐	heaven	☐
☐	🌺	☐	☐	🪲	☐
☐	cheer	☐	☐	gloom	☐
☐	🪰	☐	☐	🌸	☐
☐	vomit	☐	☐	ugly	☐
☐	🌹	☐	☐	🐛	☐
☐	hurt	☐	☐	happy	☐
☐	🌼	☐	☐	🌺	☐
☐	love	☐	☐	friend	☐

Number of seconds ⬭   ⬭ Number of errors

Figure 3.1, continued

How did playing the game feel? How many mistakes did you make in each section? I want to acknowledge that you may have experienced resistance. Your mind may have been analyzing what this exercise means for you instead of paying attention to the task at hand. That's okay; bring mindfulness to that resistance. Even though TAG is a straightforward matching game, you may have found that it was easier for you to complete section 2, where insects were paired with the unpleasant words and flowers were paired with pleasant words. This is what scientists call *implicit concept association*, i.e., flower—pleasant, insect—unpleasant.

VEDANA AND STEREOTYPES

Imagine a cockroach crawling up your leg. How do you feel? Now imagine the smell of roses. How do you feel? For the vast majority of us, likely unpleasant *vedana* and pleasant *vedana*, respectively. In reality, at this moment, you're likely not close to a cockroach or a rose, yet your sixth sense organ, the mind, can imagine these concepts and make you feel an underlying *vedana* associated with them, which triggers a reaction of thoughts and emotions.

Vedana gives stereotypes their power. As humans, we generally want more of what has pleasant *vedana* and run away from anything that is unpleasant. Just as we have mental concepts attached to flowers and insects, we have mental concepts attached to human secondary identities, such as skin color, size, height, and gender.

I define *stereotypes* as "false mental formations attached to subordinated identities." Stereotypes exist *only* for subordinated identities, not dominant ones. This is because stereotypes pigeonhole the fullness of a human with a subordinated identity into a few false ideas and generalizes it for anyone with that subordinated identity. False mental formations attached to dominant identities, such as "all cis men are physically strong," are *generalizations* rather than stereotypes, because humans with dominant identities who don't fit the generalization usually receive the benefit of the doubt and the privilege of being a unique individual.

For example, in the United States, the ideas that people with Southern accents are ignorant, Asian people are good at math, and black people are good at sports are commonly known stereotypes. You are likely familiar with these stereotypes and may have succumbed to them yourself, but for now, take a moment to just reflect on how foolish these stereotypes are. Could it be that every single one of the 50 million or so people with Southern accents is ignorant? Or that the more than 4 billion humans our minds designate as "Asian" are good at math? Or that every single one of the approximately 1.2 billion black people is good at sports? Pretty silly, right? Yet we fall into these stereotypes all the time.

Whether positive or negative, stereotypes are harmful because they sever our connection with others. They prevent curiosity and interest. Instead, they let false concepts dictate our perceptions and thereby our verbal, nonverbal, and behavioral reactions to humans with those social identities. As an Asian American, I have experienced this firsthand. At most social events, I am used to strangers assuming that I work in IT or sharing stories about their favorite Indian food or their last trip to India. I have learned a tremendous amount about my birth nation from these strangers, but one day I started wondering why folks couldn't find a way to relate to me outside of my ethnicity.

When that curiosity was triggered, I quickly realized that I wasn't fully innocent either. In the past, whenever I met a person of Korean descent, I went out of my way to share with them that I had lived in Korea and had so much appreciation for Korean culture. As I investigated this behavior, I saw how it prevented me from building meaningful connections with humans of Korean descent. This is when I started practicing the PRISM tool of individuation: dissociating group-based associations from an individual. Practicing individuation helped me become mindful of the stories that arose in my mind. It led me to question my desire to connect with others based on who my mind imagined them to be—in other words, on my experience and ego—versus who they were.

THE SCIENCE OF STEREOTYPING

Fortunately, in the last three decades science has demonstrated the existence of stereotypes in our minds and their influence on our decision-making beyond a reasonable doubt.[4] Before sharing the findings of this research, I want to acknowledge why this research was conducted in the first place.

Growing up as a queer brown man in America, I accepted that bias and inequity were a part of life because I, like many people with subordinated identities, experienced these inequities first-hand. However, as I became a functioning adult, I found myself in educational and professional environments where I interacted with humans who didn't experience these disparities, were misinformed about them, or didn't know about them at all. As a result, they denied their existence outright. Their assumption: the law guarantees equality and therefore there is equality, or the law prohibits discrimination and so there is no discrimination *unless you prove otherwise.*

This is the mark of an exclusion consciousness. It is wedded to separation and worships the rational mind. As a result, since the 1970s, as legal equality has spread among Western nations, advocates and scholars concerned about inequities have needed to design elaborate experiments to prove the impacts of bias on the lived experiences of humans with subordinated identities. As a young researcher, I used to agonize over the wasted resources, talent, and inefficiencies expended in proving what seemed obvious, such as that bias exists or that it impacts hiring decisions or policing. But my concern about wasted resources was relieved once I recognized how pervasive exclusion consciousness really is among humans with dominant identities who exercise authority and influence in our societies.

Perception, *Vedana,* and Stereotypes:
The Stereotype Content Model

From the 1980s to the present day, public polls consistently show that a majority of Americans believe they hold unprejudiced views and treat people equally regardless of race, gender, and other secondary identities. In that same time frame, social science research, however, repeatedly demonstrates that Americans with subordinated identities experience significantly higher rates of inequality, marginalization, exclusion, and prejudice across life areas.[5] For example, black and brown humans confront numerous obstacles in accessing health care, education, and housing than white people; or women and gender-diverse people experience much higher rates of sexual objectification or harassment in the workplace than cis men.

Starting in the 1990s, cognitive scientists designed many experiments to demonstrate a link between people's perceptions and actions, despite their beliefs, and social inequality. In one series of experiments, scientists asked thousands of Americans to rate how they perceived humans with certain social identities on a scale of *warmth* and *competence*. They found that a majority of Americans rated middle-class white people with high warmth and high competence, Asians or feminists with low warmth and high competence, and poor people with low warmth and low competence. They placed the content of stereotypes held by a majority of the respondents on a scale of warmth and competence as shown in Figure 3.2, known as Behaviors from Intergroup Affect and Stereotypes, or BIAS, and called their findings the Stereotype Content Model.[6]

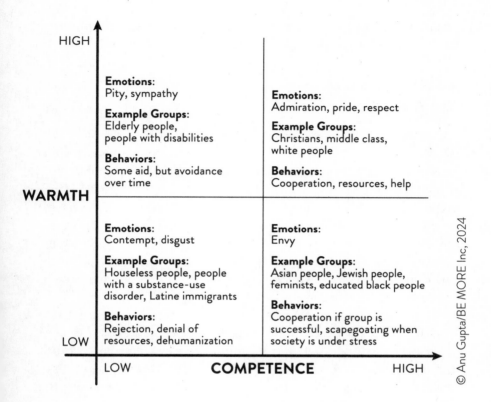

Figure 3.2

I was really excited to learn about this research because it used Western scientific language and methods for ancient Buddhist wisdom. In other words, the constituent parts of the Stereotype Content Model align with our primary identity attributes: *warmth* for pleasant or unpleasant affect or *vedana,* and *competence* for positive or negative mental concepts or stereotypes. This body of scholarship demonstrated that the underlying *vedana* and concepts Americans hold about different groups shapes their perceptions of and behaviors toward humans with different secondary identities.

The Stereotype Content Model can be applied to highlight patterns of stereotyping toward subordinated groups in other societies, e.g., Roma people in Europe, North Africans in France, Tamils in

Malaysia and Singapore, subordinated castes and religious minorities in South Asia, and indigenous people in Latin America.

Measuring the Strength of *Vedana* of Stereotypes: The Science of Implicit Bias

Remember how we played TAG earlier in this chapter? In another series of experiments, in the mid-1990s, researchers invented a digital instrument that could measure our responses to TAG; they called it the Implicit Association Test (IAT). Basically, as with TAG, images or words are flashed on a screen and you have to place them in the correct category by swiping left or right (on a phone) or pressing *E* or *I* (on a keyboard) as quickly as possible. On the back end, the instrument measures the number of errors and the response time at the *microsecond level* (!). The instrument stops if you take too long or make too many errors.

Since the IAT was invented, millions have taken it and scientists have demonstrated that a *majority* of people have an easier time associating pleasant words and positive concepts with dominant identities, such as white, male, straight, thin, and nondisabled, and associating unpleasant words and negative concepts with subordinated identities, such as black and brown, fat, queer and gender-diverse, and disabled. This may include people who consciously advocate for equality as well as a plurality of people from subordinated identities. In fact, a person's results often have nothing to do with their identities or conscious views because the instrument measures our implicit or unconscious associations.

For example, on the race IAT conducted with images of black and white people, the data show that more than 30 percent of black people have an easier time associating positive words and concepts with white people and negative words and concepts with black people; similar facts and figures can be stated for other subordinated groups like women, queer people, fat people, and disabled people.[7] If you find this hard to believe, recall what I shared with you about my mother's response to the surgeon riddle.

This instrument's ease of use birthed a large body of scholarship on the science of implicit bias, allowing researchers to test and demonstrate the connection between unconscious associations among doctors, prosecutors, police officers, teachers, and hiring professionals and identity-based disparities in health care, education, hiring, criminal justice, housing, and beyond. With thousands of peer-reviewed studies, the science of implicit bias has laid to rest any doubts about the connection between stored stereotypes and *vedana* in the human mind and decision-making. In other words, having stereotyped perceptions about different human identities impacts a person's behavior toward those humans.[8]

THE PLAY OF PERCEPTION: CONSCIOUS AND UNCONSCIOUS BIAS

Bias is a reaction to the stereotypes stored in our minds. It manifests in our thoughts, words, or actions. Conscious stereotypes are beliefs we hold, rooted in comparing mind, that are known to us; for example, believing light skin is more beautiful than dark skin or rich people are more hardworking than poor people. Unconscious stereotypes, conversely, are due to habits of thought that we are generally unaware of, e.g., the concept of "male" attached to "surgeon," or the concept of being thin as more attractive.

Just as stereotypes are conscious or unconscious, bias too has two forms: conscious (explicit) bias and unconscious (implicit) bias. I define them as follows:

* Conscious bias is *learned false beliefs* about a secondary identity that are accepted as true and distort how we perceive, reason, remember, and make decisions.

* Unconscious bias is *learned habits of thought* about a secondary identity that distort how we perceive, reason, remember, and make decisions.

PRISM EXERCISE

Pause. Take three full breaths and return your awareness to your somatic experience.

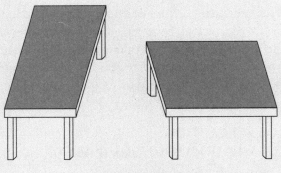

Figure 3.3

Look at the two tables in Figure 3.3. Which one has the longer table surface?[9] The left one, correct? In reality, they are both the same length. If you don't believe me, find a tracing paper to measure them.

This optical illusion was created by cognitive scientist Robert Shepard to demonstrate the power of perception and that seeing is not always believing. You can do all sorts of mental gymnastics, but these two table surface will never look identical, even though you have tested for yourself that they are. Similarly, our perception ensures that two human beings—though we share our primary identity—will never look the same.

Perception instantaneously converts our sense organs' contact with another human's secondary identities into mental formations (concepts, emotions, and habits, including stereotypes, that each have an associated *vedana*). These in turn trigger our reactions (thoughts, words, or actions) or biases.

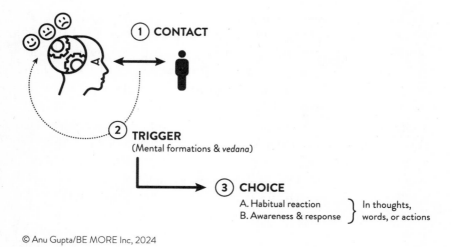

Figure 3.4

Figure 3.4 shows the instantaneous process of how bias gets triggered and decision points after it is triggered. The way bias gets triggered has three nodes: contact, trigger, and reaction or response. First, our sense organs make contact with the awareness of our own or another's secondary identities. Second, that contact triggers in our mind any stored mental formations and *vedana* associated with those identities. These mental formations arise from the unique lifetime of inputs our minds have received from our *cultural conditioning* about different identities.

In response to the trigger, we have a choice: to react (System 1 thinking: habitual reactions) or to become mindful of triggered concepts, emotions, and *vedana* and *choose* our response (System 2 thinking). By practicing PRISM tools, we can actively transition our minds from reactivity and System 1 thinking to skillful response and System 2 thinking.

Identifying this mechanism inspired me to stop practicing law and start my social enterprise, BE MORE with Anu, because it gave me ways to transform and end bias. As someone who experienced bias for my many intersectional identities and who witnessed various forms of biases globally, identifying this mechanism gave me hope.

Just as I practiced various mindfulness-based modalities to heal the depression, anxiety, and self-loathing I experienced, I started applying these tools to the stereotyping and bias that I witnessed in my thoughts and enacted in my words and actions. The results were astounding. Not only did I start feeling better about my humanity, but I also started feeling more connected to all humans and nonhumans. With the support of my sister, Vasudha Gupta, this is how the PRISM tools came to be. Practicing PRISM tools allows us to become aware of stereotypes, interrupt our habitual reactions, and choose to respond differently. Over time, this supports us in building new neural pathways and mental habits that foster behavior change toward ourselves and others.

CULTURAL CONDITIONING

In 2012, as a young lawyer working at the Vera Institute of Justice, I began to present my research to my church community, meditation sanghas, and professional colleagues who worked in frontline marginalized communities globally. After every presentation and conversation, I witnessed a sense of vindication in my audience because science could finally explain their lived experiences. They were so used to being gaslit or denied their repeated experiences of bias, but the mind science explaining why this happened felt validating to them. However, some of my community members began to challenge me to go deeper.

Achebe Betty Powell, one of my church elders and a veteran civil rights activist, took me aside and shared with me that "cultural conditioning" seems like a lazy excuse to not hold people accountable for their actions. She had spent five decades fighting for equality as an advocate for civil rights, women's rights, lesbian and gay rights, and disability justice, and she asked me, could cultural conditioning alone explain Trayvon Martin's murder a few months earlier? Could it alone explain the full display of cruelty of everyone from media commentators and politicians to everyday Americans toward this young boy who happened to be black?

She was on to something. I knew that exclusion consciousness and the three defilements in our minds fuel the thoughts, words, and behaviors that manifest as bias, but if we are all the same human animal, what causes some of these animals to mistreat others so cruelly? While the science of implicit bias laid to rest doubts of the existence and behavioral impacts of stereotypes and bias, beyond "cultural conditioning," it didn't specify the causes and conditions that program human minds with stereotypes and biases.

Causes and Conditions of Bias: How We Learn Bias

After I immigrated to America, learning and information gathering were the primary ways I coped with physical and emotional discomfort I experienced due to bias. After years of practicing PRISM, I recognized that I'd established this habit for two reasons: to rationalize why people around me carried certain biases toward me, and, more importantly, to keep from feeling in my body the impact of the harm I experienced.

Being with information felt safe, but I realize now that it kept me numb to the somatic discomfort of bias. I mention this here to invite you to remember our shared agreements and to be aware of, feel, and investigate your own somatic experience of discomfort.

Accepting Achebe's challenge, I returned to the research and analyzed it to identify *five* root causes and conditions for every form of identity-based bias stored in our minds. Yep, just five so you can remember them on one hand. They are: a story or stories, policies, social contact, education, and media. We will explore the five root causes in depth in Parts II and III.

THE FOUR FORMS OF BIAS

Identifying the five causes and conditions of bias has been liberating for me and my students because it gives us a pathway to address bias by appreciating its learned nature. If your doubting mind jumps in, remind it that for multiple millennia, many animist cultures lived not only without hierarchies within their human tribes but also without such hierarchies in the natural and the more-than-human worlds. To prepare you for your breaking bias journey ahead, I want to summarize the four forms bias takes in our lives.

Biases are harmful reactions or decisions we make toward ourselves or others based on stereotypes. These harmful decisions manifest at four levels: internalized bias, interpersonal bias, institutional bias, and systemic bias (see Figure 3.5). Regardless of their form, all biases begin with concepts and emotions in the form of thoughts with an accompanying *vedana*. As these thoughts get repeated and reinforced over periods of days, years, and a lifetime, they become habits that are unconscious or conscious biases. Let's review the mechanics of each form of bias, as that will be essential to your personal breaking bias journey.

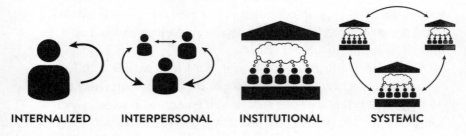

INTERNALIZED   INTERPERSONAL   INSTITUTIONAL   SYSTEMIC

© Anu Gupta/BE MORE Inc, 2024

Figure 3.5

Internalized Bias

Internalized biases are how we perceive ourselves and how we perceive others are perceiving us stemming from the five causes of bias. For example, growing up in the United States, my mind was generally exposed to negative portrayals of people with my intersectionality—i.e., people of color, Indians, queer people—in the media and my school curriculum. In addition, I personally experienced physical, emotional, and psychological harms in my social environments due to my secondary identities. Without any counterexamples of positive images or interpersonal experiences of compassion and acceptance, over time my mind internalized or, consciously and unconsciously, started equating my humanity with those stereotypes.

I define *internalized bias* as a "form of conscious and unconscious bias where harmful mental formations influence our thoughts, words, and actions toward ourselves." Think of it as that nagging voice in your head that mocks you for your appearance, actions, or any number of our secondary identities. For most of my teenage years, this voice would say things like *you're ugly, you're too fat*, or *no one really likes you because you're Indian, an immigrant, gay*, or something else.

Internalized biases follow the same contact–trigger–reaction mechanism outlined in Figure 3.4. As stereotypes that are stored in our minds get triggered by some sense experience, our minds react with a host of stories, ideas, concepts, and emotions in the form of thoughts, words, or actions that are harmful to ourselves. While these reactions are a consequence of the causes and conditions that program our minds with bias, internalized biases are exclusively about us; they are how we perceive, think, and feel about ourselves and how we perceive, think, and feel others perceive us. As they strengthen in power with habitual repetition, they present themselves as internalized inferiority or superiority complexes due to our intersectional identities such as color, race, gender, wealth, alma mater, profession, or abilities.

There are numerous permutations for the mental formations that show up as internalized bias, such as the habit of calling oneself "stupid," or the emotion of feeling unworthy, jealous, or proud in relation to another human. All internalized biases are a function of conscious or unconscious belief in stereotypes and a hierarchy of better-than or worse-than that creates one of two false thought forms: victimhood or entitlement.

At an absolute level, regardless of whether we are rich, poor, thin, fat, male, female, or something else, we *are*, we exist, we are neither better- nor worse-than. However, by believing false stories, our minds place a judgment on how we are—better or worse than a separate, external "other"—which becomes our self-concept and identity. See Figure 3.6 for an overview of this dynamic and some common faces of internalized bias.

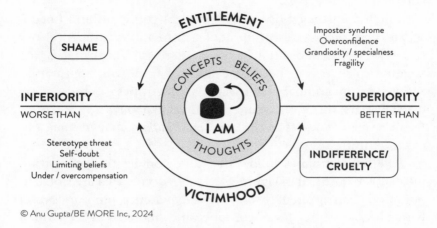

© Anu Gupta/BE MORE Inc, 2024

Figure 3.6

Internalized bias keeps us in an exclusion consciousness of victimhood or entitlement. Victimhood and entitlement are two sides of the same coin, or, in the words of social movement strategist Alnoor Ladha, "two heads of the same Hydra."[10] Eckhart Tolle describes that behind every negative self-concept is the hidden desire to be better than others, and behind the need for superiority is the hidden fear of inferiority.

For me, the dynamic of victimhood has shown up as stereotype threat,[11] limiting beliefs,[12] self-doubt, overcompensation, and undercompensation* for my subordinated identities such as skin color, sexual orientation, and body size, and the dynamic of entitlement has shown up as specialness, grandiosity, overconfidence, fragility,[13] and imposter syndrome[14] for my dominant identities, particularly my sex, gender identity, education, and profession.

---

* Undercompensation is the psychological phenomenon in which we succumb to the stereotypes about our humanity and accept them as true. Bryan Stevenson often shares a heartbreaking example of undercompensation: black, brown, and poor young people who live in under-resourced, heavily policed, and underinvested communities across the United States giving up on their lives because they expect to end up in prison like many adults in their communities.

Internalized Bias and Victimhood

In 2013, I was on a weeklong silent retreat at the Spirit Rock Meditation Center. While practicing mindfulness of thoughts, I came to notice the thought forms of victimhood in my own mind. These thoughts were associated with my most apparent social identities, being a gay man with brown skin and average build.

In the safety of a practice container held by meditation teacher Spring Washam, I began to peel back the layers and investigate the mental formations associated with victimhood. Over the course of a week, I discovered two aspects of my self-concept that popped up as victimhood. I am sharing each of these pieces with their associated *vedana*.

1. **Painful concepts and stories accompanied by unpleasant *vedana*** in the form of beliefs and memories rooted in my past hurts caused by bias, and my identification with what happened to me because of my subordinated identities. These thoughts registered in my mind as "They beat me; they humiliated me; they colonized my people; they enslaved us" or conditional thoughts like "If I were white, straight, [insert dominant identity], then I wouldn't have had these experiences."

2. **Painful emotions accompanied by unpleasant *vedana*** such as animosity, jealousy, resentment, anger, fear, and grief that were rooted in what Brené Brown calls "shame," i.e., *there is something wrong with me*.[15] As I investigated the shame, I experienced it as a conglomerate of thoughts rooted in stereotypes and emotional and psychic pain that wasn't just my pain, but generations of pain of so many different people whose stories and histories I carried in my consciousness. These are the ways historical and intergenerational traumas connected to my secondary identities manifested in my experience.

The *vedana* associated with the somatic experience of painful thoughts and emotions is *very* unpleasant. For most of my life, I avoided these painful thoughts and emotions. Outside of the silent retreat container, when these mental formations were triggered, I'd find comfort in a host of unwholesome habits like overeating, overworking, or seeking comfort in alcohol, relationships, and porn to avoid feeling this pain and to distract my mind-body with momentary pleasant *vedana*. Often these understandable avoidance mechanisms become lifelong addictions and dependencies that continuously fuel more suffering in ourselves, those we love, and the lives we touch through our decisions.

Fortunately for me, and unfortunately for my unwholesome habits, I was required to take the five Buddhist precepts on this retreat.* More importantly, I had given my phone to the retreat teachers, so I had no way of distracting myself with a host of "mental intoxicants" or "false refuges" like work, news, friends, shopping, or porn. This meant, in the safety of our sacred silence, I was left with no choice but to observe, acknowledge, and feel my shame and pain.

Luckily, Spring instructed me to continuously practice pro-social behaviors of loving-kindness and forgiveness toward what was arising in my experience. These tools gave me the healing strength to stay present with and feel the incredibly unpleasant *vedana* of painful thoughts and emotions that kept me identified with victimhood. I felt this pain in my body as vibrations, sensations, and movements of energy, one after another, that over time released my attachments to my victimhood self-concept. I continued to practice this process of awareness with loving-kindness for years to come, but on that retreat, it opened the door to victimhood's favorite hideout, entitlement.

Internalized Bias and Entitlement

Over a period of years, as my identification with victimhood loosened, I started to notice that my mind was getting lost in a host of new types of mental formations that felt good:

---

* They include abstaining from harm to self and other beings, taking what isn't freely given, sexual activity including masturbation, lying, and indulging in any intoxicants that could cloud the mind.

1. **Pleasurable concepts and stories with pleasant**
   vedana in the form of future projections and imaginings
   that attempted to resolve 1 and 2 above. Those scenarios
   exclusively involved some form of revenge, accountability,
   subordination, assimilation, or even elimination of the
   dominant group that perpetrated harm against me or "my
   people," justified by the repeated use of conditionals like
   should, i.e., how I or my people or the world should be, and
   if-then scenarios, e.g., if rich white men are no longer in
   office, my people and I will be safe and happy.

2. **Pleasurable emotions with pleasant *vedana*** such
   as specialness, schadenfreude, pride, overconfidence, and
   grandiosity.

These concepts, stories, and emotions were the work of entitlement. Entitlement is the mask victimhood wears and it is rooted in not feeling, that is, in indifference or numbness. When it is forced to feel, the victimhood consciousness's pain is so great that it shows up as cruelty or other unwholesome mental states. From the lens of loving-kindness, I had compassion for why my mind succumbed to entitlement; I was hurting and entitlement helped me relieve the pain of victimhood. From the perspective of wisdom, however, I saw that this aspect of internalized bias fueled exclusion consciousness, and it was singularly responsible for the many physical, emotional, and psychological harms I caused others.

A flood of memories arose that crystallized the mechanics of entitlement. Entitlement created in me a separate self-concept of being "better than" or more deserving, intelligent, or beautiful than others in response to victimhood. It manifested most prominently as specialness, grandiosity, pride, and indifference.

These mental formations can be conscious or unconscious, and they brought me face-to-face with some very uncomfortable beliefs I held around my gender, ethnicity, intellect, and profession: the beliefs that because I am a man, I am inherently stronger than women, and that I am smarter than people of non-Asian descent. I saw in my own mind many experiences of confusion and memories of resentment and fragility toward others when these false beliefs did not reflect my reality, like the time a female classmate repeatedly beat me at arm wrestling, or when my black classmates outperformed me in math and science.

This wasn't all, however. To sustain this mask of superiority, my mind called such experiences "exceptions to the rule" so it could go on feeling better about itself, *and* I noticed the mind's tendency to stop others who might diminish this self-concept. In reality, this desire for feeling better actually stemmed from my victimhood, from all the hurts and pain I was carrying from the ways I felt diminished, othered, and harmed.

I have since come to appreciate that regardless of the number of dominating identities a human has, victimhood associated with one's subordinated identities is almost always running the show. The mental formations that conglomerate to form entitlement are so difficult to see because they are wholly dependent on victimhood.

I share my experiences not to judge myself. Who am I to judge when I wasn't even aware that I was stuck in this dynamic? With that said, I have come to recognize that my identification with victimhood was masking a tremendous amount of pain I was carrying. Acknowledging, feeling, and healing that pain is our work of breaking bias.

The work of breaking bias begins with internalized bias because it brings down the walls of separation we have unskillfully erected between our authentic selves, other humans, and more-than-humans. Practicing mindfulness helps us loosen our attachment to the thinking mind and strengthen our awareness of the observer behind the thinking.

Until we see and heal the shame and the varying diminishing self-concepts associated with our victimhood, we will operate from a sense of entitlement without even being aware of it. Since discovering this interplay of internalized bias, I have seen it play out in every single instance of interpersonal, institutional, and systemic bias I've observed. I'll describe this interplay in the coming pages, but let's first take a moment to reflect.

PRISM EXERCISE

Pause. Take three full breaths and recall our shared agreements. Bring your attention to the space you're in and feel your feet on the ground below. Notice how you feel and with a few gentle breaths relax any tension that may be present in your body.

In the space below or in your journal, list one internalized bias you have about yourself due to a secondary identity. Reflect on the mental formations (concepts, emotions, habits), *vedana*, and somatic experience that accompany it. Take deep breaths and particularly long exhales as you do this exercise bringing mindfulness to *vedana* of your somatic experience, and feel it.

As you bring awareness to the feelings and sensations, notice if the experience shifts. If completing this exercise feels overwhelming, please return to it later. Instead, get embodied by dancing to your favorite song or going for a run. If physical movement is not accessible to you, engage in an activity that will help you to get out of your head into your body, e.g., tapping, body scan, or breathwork.

Interpersonal Bias

In 2021, I went on a small tour shuttle in Hawaii. Due to COVID restrictions, only 12 people were allowed on the shuttle, and I was the last one to enter the shuttle with my partner. As I walked down the middle aisle, I heard a white man speaking to me. At first, I could not understand him, but I intuitively sensed that he was attempting to speak to me in an Indian language. I was used to strangers saying "Namaste" or "Hare Krishna" to me, but I was unfamiliar with the word he was saying.

After several awkward glances and *excuse me*'s through my mask, I was able to discern that he was trying to greet me in Punjabi with *Sat Sri Akal.* I was surprised, as that is generally a greeting exchanged by Sikhs. Though I have Sikh ancestors, he would have no way of knowing that because I don't wear a turban. So why would he approach me with such a greeting?

He pointed to a silver bracelet I'd purchased at J.Crew, which, to be clear, looked nothing like a Sikh *kada*, a thick metal bangle. What I thought was a fashion statement appeared to him to be religious insignia. Based on the stereotypes stored in his mind, the stimuli of a brown human wearing a silver bracelet when filtered through the lens of those stereotypes impacted how he perceived, reasoned, and made decisions to communicate with me. This is a classic example of interpersonal bias—contact, trigger, and reaction.

For the next five minutes, I watched heat, annoyance, confusion, and grief arise in my body for being stereotyped and interrupted as I went about my day, and most importantly for his lack of curiosity. If he wanted to greet me, a simple "Good morning" would have been sufficient. I share this experience because even though I study, teach, and train people on this subject, my body—just like every human body—still *keeps the score,* as Bessel van der Kolk put it in his book title, and responds accordingly irrespective of what my mind thinks.

I have heard thousands of similar stories: Asian Americans being greeted with *Konnichiwa* or Latine people being perceived as Indian and asked to recommend the best curry in town. Research on weapon bias has shown more lethal consequences of such perceptions for humans with dark skin, such as harmless things like a pen appearing to be a weapon.

Interpersonal bias occurs between humans, in relation to each person's internalized biases. It complements a concept of other against a self-concept. Interpersonal biases are the most widely understood type of bias; they include classism, racism, antisemitism, casteism, sexism, homophobia, ableism, ageism, and other hierarchies of -isms that harm humans.*

I define *interpersonal bias* as "harmful mental formations that influence our thoughts, words, and actions toward others." They

---

* These biases can also be internalized due to the five causes of bias.

can be conscious or unconscious and they range from unkind judgments and ideas about others, to unkind speech, such as microaggressions, gaslighting, and verbal abuse, to unkind actions that threaten and harm the physical safety of other humans.

Interpersonal Bias: Thoughts and Emotions

Interpersonal biases begin at the level of conscious or unconscious concepts and beliefs that produce thoughts and emotions. These mental formations generally play out a concept of self and a concept of other. While the outer layer of the self-concept is entitlement, beneath it there is always victimhood. The concept of other is informed by learned stereotypes that generalize humans with certain secondary identities. While we can never assume what a human is thinking, humans often disclose their beliefs to others, especially in contexts where they feel there is trust and safety.

Here are just a few examples from my own life. My Egyptian classmate at Cambridge passionately informing me that 99.9 percent of Egyptians are Muslim, when in fact Egypt has a sizeable minority of non-Muslims; or in an advising meeting, my law school professor matter-of-factly stating that poor black women need to stop collecting welfare checks by having babies; or a French couple I befriended on a backpacking trip to Croatia sharing that Roma people are a nuisance to the European Union.

I am sure you can recall instances where a family member, friend, colleague, or even a stranger said something about humans' social identity that was tinged with stereotypes. Those words disclose the thought patterns, mental habits, and *vedana* with which humans with certain identities are perceived around the duality of familiar versus other and good versus bad. When unchecked, humans enact these thoughts in words and actions, sometimes with horrific consequences.

Interpersonal Bias: Words and Actions

Enacting interpersonal bias with words and/or actions always has two parties: the responsible and the harmed. For example, my female students who are physicians, regardless of age, ethnicity, or seniority, consistently report that their patients have asked them, "Can I talk to the doctor?" when they in fact are the doctor. Sometimes, there is also a witness who may experience vicarious harm. For example, when I worked in Korea, one fellow teacher often used the word *gay* in a demeaning way. She didn't know I was gay or that some of her Korean colleagues were too. I certainly felt hurt every time this happened, but my colleagues who witnessed the harm also felt shame, guilt, and a whole host of afflictive emotions.

Additional instances of interpersonal-biased behaviors include: Individual teachers and judges discipline or sentence immigrant children and adults more harshly than their white counterparts in American, European, and Canadian classrooms and courtrooms. American real estate agents value the homes of black and brown humans lower than those of their white counterparts.[16] Individual retail professionals decline to service potential customers, as was the case with Oprah Winfrey at a luxury store in Switzerland.[17] And individuals commit mass murder against people with a specific social identity, as in the 2015 Charleston massacre at an African American church, the 2019 mass shooting at two Christchurch mosques, or the 2019 massacre of Latine shoppers in El Paso.

The neural mechanism for the ways interpersonal bias is enacted is identical across societies, whether it's gender and ethnic bias in Germany, Iran, or Malaysia; racial bias in France, Canada, or Australia; or religious bias in Saudi Arabia, India, or Serbia. What differs across cultures and identities is the gravity and the patterns of harm caused by the responsible parties *and* the experience of the harm within the body, heart, and mind of the harmed party.

While the experience of harm varies for the harmed party, the harmful actions and words of the responsible party are always consciously or unconsciously triggered by identification with the mental formations and *vedana* of stereotypes. Beneath the stereotypes is a separate self-concept giving rise to us-versus-them formations and entitlement shrouding victimhood.

Interpersonal bias severs trust, safety, and kinship between humans and causes psychic and emotional pain that, when unacknowledged and unhealed, continues to feed and fuel conflict. At the core of interpersonal and internalized biases are false stories. These stories foment beliefs of separate self-concept and victimhood, exacerbating intergroup conflict while disintegrating trust and social cohesion within families, organizations, communities, and societies.

The mental formations that trigger interpersonal biases are especially dangerous in times of economic or political instability, when charismatic leaders can institutionalize them by manipulating masses of people to do the unconscionable. In *The Heart of Man*, Erich Fromm, a German Jewish scholar who fled the Nazi regime, very clearly lays out this formula.

> A society that lacks the means to provide adequately for the majority of its members . . . [these leaders] provide these members with a narcissistic pride . . . which is the only and a very effective source of satisfaction . . . of the inflated image of itself as the most admirable group in the world. . . Even though I am poor and uncultured I am somebody important because I belong to the most admirable group in the world—"I am white" or "I am an Aryan."[18]

Or I am Japanese, I am Han Chinese, I am a Turk, I am Greek, I am Sunni, I am Shia, I am heterosexual, I am a real woman, I am [fill in the blank].

Identification with a secondary identity, when shrouded in entitlement and multiplied across thousands and millions of people, has been the mechanism for human horrors across history, and especially in the age of capitalist modernity. From enslavement, colonization, and the slaughter of nonhuman beings to the 20th-century genocides of Armenians, European Jews, and Rwandan Tutsis, to the mass violence that accompanied the partitioning of India, Cyprus, and the former Yugoslavia; the January 6, 2021, attack on the U.S.

Capitol; Russia's war in the Ukraine; and the Israeli government's treatment of Palestinians, we see the same imprints of entitlement consciousness: humans possessed by a self-and-other concept doing the unthinkable to other humans, animals, and nature.

To me, these dynamics highlight the need for us to remember our interbeing. This may be hard for you to envision at this moment, so let's do an exercise.

PRISM EXERCISE

Pause. Take three breaths and return your awareness to your body and feel your body sensations.

Now, take a moment to reflect on how many biological ancestors in the last 100 years produced the human you are right now. Go on, take a guess: _____.

What about 250 years? _____.

What about 500 years? _____.

It would be 14, 1,022, and at least 1 million, respectively, and this is a conservative estimate assuming that each one of your ancestors became a parent at around the age of 25 (my parents became parents at 24, and both sets of my grandparents were teenage parents), and it doesn't account for siblings, stepparents, adoptive parents, guardians, and all the other familial configurations common across cultures. Each one of the 8 billion people globally have this many ancestors, and as scientists have shown, we are all literally one another's relatives.[19]

Now, given what you know about yourself—what you look like, your family history, and your cultural background—with curiosity, awareness, and gratitude, reflect on the peoples of different colors, cultures, religions, political ideologies, and class backgrounds whose biological imprint may be in your DNA. In doing this exercise, I hope you'll appreciate interbeing in your lineage.

Institutional and Systemic Bias

The key word in *institutional bias* is *institution*, so let's start by examining that. In the space below or in your journal, take a moment to become mindful of your associations with the word *institution*. What comes to mind?

Generally, sterile, empty buildings or conference rooms, right? That may be the perception; however, institutions are actually groups of humans who work together toward a common goal or purpose. Within institutions, humans are assigned different roles and functions with various levels of decision-making authority, power, or influence. Institutions provide a framework for human interaction and cooperation by regulating and organizing human behavior through a set of rules, policies, customs, norms, and modes of behavior.

I define *institutional bias* as "shared biases of humans who have decision-making authority or influence over an *institution* that impacts many people." For example, a small-business owner deciding how their employees can wear their hair at work; or a five-member government body deciding the K–12 history curriculum in a city, state, or nation; or the nine-person American Supreme Court permitting or prohibiting what humans can do with their bodies, e.g., whom they can marry, their reproductive autonomy, or their medical care access; or producers, directors, and casting directors choosing humans with a "certain look" in their storytelling.

Institutional biases are embedded in the policies, practices, customs, norms, and modes of behavior that privilege and marginalize humans based on their secondary identities. They stem from the decisions of humans in positions of authority and influence. These humans exercise their internalized and interpersonal biases, i.e., their concepts of self and other, through their decisions impacting many humans and more-than-humans they do not know.

Think about it this way: individual humans are the building blocks of all institutions and systems. The daily micro-decisions of these humans on behalf of institutions, such as corporations, nonprofits, churches, or governments, when colored by bias, slowly aggregate into institutional biases, which aggregate into systemic biases, whether it is in health care, technology, banking, law, or philanthropy.

Systemic bias is an outcome of institutional biases, and it demonstrates their society-wide consequences: human suffering as exhibited by inequities in social, economic, cultural, and political life outcomes between humans of different social identities; and wasted human talent, potential, and creativity as well as financial resources.

The Three Buckets of Institutional Bias

To help you manage the afflictive emotions and overwhelm that can be triggered by institutional and systemic bias, I have created a manageable framework that identifies three buckets (yep, just three) where systemic inequities and costs show up across institutions.

They are human relationships (HR), service delivery, and product design. Within institutions, HR is internally facing with respect to how humans interact, behave, and make decisions toward one another. Service delivery and product design are externally facing because they are about the services and/or products humans within institutions are creating and offering to their beneficiaries, customers, or stakeholders.

Human relationships or HR: Ecologist and economist Satish Kumar inspired me to use this phrase instead of *human resources*. To me, it crystallizes the relational aspect of our beingness as social animals instead of being a commodity, an object, or a "resource." HR covers the gamut of human interactions, behaviors, and decisions that affect the recruitment, retention, advancement, and compensation of humans, as well as how humans communicate with one another, how tasks are assigned, how feedback is given, and how conflict is resolved. In the 21st century, with increased mobility of humans across borders and legal protections from discrimination, HR within institutions is shifting.

Service delivery: This bucket refers to the services a human provides or sells to others on behalf of an institution. For example, education, health care, public safety, spirituality, therapy, or any good, such as clothes, food, or real estate. Shared stereotyped perceptions among the service providers in these interactions aggregate into institutional and systemic bias. For example, regardless of class or status, over 20 years of implicit bias science has documented that black humans receive lower-quality care from health care providers, to the point where even celebrities like Serena Williams and Beyoncé had trouble birthing their daughters. This isn't because their providers were explicitly racist, but because some habit of thought and associations prevented them from listening to the pain of their patients. Systemic inequities across systems—whether in philanthropy, venture capital, law enforcement, education, or housing—are functions of the humans who make decisions on behalf of those institutions.

Product design: This bucket refers to goods and products humans design that we use for our day-to-day lives. They include tangible items like clothes, makeup, and pharmaceuticals as well as intangibles like artificial intelligence algorithms, software, music, movies, advertising, digital content, insurance, and financial services. As our daily lives get more enmeshed with artificial intelligence, biotechnology, and the algorithms that power these technologies, we become susceptible to the biases encoded in them based on the stereotypes held by their human developers. This applies to facial recognition technology, credit-worthiness assessment, and surveillance technology, as well as the disinformation campaigns that have affected election results in all parts of the world.

Obstacles to Remedying Institutional Bias

Institutional biases vary across institutions, societies, and cultures. Since the 1970s, despite rising inclusion consciousness, shifting global norms, and the adoption of laws prohibiting discrimination across the globe, there have been at least three obstacles to remedying institutional biases, all rooted in the internalized and interpersonal biases of institutional decision-makers.

Dog whistle politics: This refers to the use of seemingly innocuous but coded language, symbols, and gestures by influencers and decision-makers to appeal to the victimhood experienced by dominating groups while scapegoating subordinated humans. For example, in democratic nations, institutional leaders use the terms *wokeism* and *law and order* to stoke fear and signal to the masses that they will keep them safe, while also implying that subordinated humans are more likely to commit crimes. As in Nazi Germany, such rhetoric is being used to ban books and knowledge in many nations around the world, including the United States, the Philippines, and India. In the American context, Michelle Alexander's *The New Jim Crow* and Ian Haney López's *Dog Whistle Politics* meticulously detail how this phenomenon created mass incarceration and is used to terrorize and criminalize black and brown communities. Dog whistle politics is the work of *wetiko*, and it is about the use of overt coded language to justify disinvestments, policies, and actions that sustain suffering and inequity.

Drained pool politics: Also *wetiko* in action, this type of politics speaks to public and private decisions made by institutional leaders to sustain suffering and inequity by enacting or enforcing policies that harm everyone, but provide members of the dominating groups with an "inflated image of itself." Coined by American scholar Heather McGhee, the phrase refers to the thousands of public policies adopted by American local, state, and federal lawmakers in the post–civil rights era that sustain race-based inequality, suffering, and harm. Her point is that ultimately these policies harm everyone, including humans with dominant identities. For example, after racial segregation was deemed unconstitutional, local governments across the United States chose to close public swimming pools instead of encouraging white Americans to share those pools with non-white Americans. Similarly, lawmakers consciously chose public investments in overpolicing poor communities instead of using those funds to offer these humans services that would alleviate their suffering. The result? No one gets a public pool, people of all colors are affected by mass incarceration, and everyone is worse off.

While *dog whistle* and *drained pool politics* were coined to refer to race-based inequities in the United States, they apply to hierarchies across identities and societies. Some examples are anti-LGBTQ+ rhetoric that translates into "don't say gay" policies, restrictions on reproductive autonomy, and the justifications for repression of social protests and the press in Hungary, Iran, and the Philippines. Ultimately, drained pool and dog whistle politics work because of the third and the strongest of all obstacles: absence of kindness.

Absence of kindness: After COVID-19 struck New York City in March of 2020, for almost a full year, I heard sirens of ambulances outside my building carrying patients to the nearby hospital, and then helicopters monitoring protests after George Floyd's public murder. During this time, many of us saw, heard, and experienced death and destruction up close. The question I continued to ask was: How is it that in the most technologically and scientifically advanced nation in the world, we lost more than a million lives to COVID-19? How is it that despite all of the evidence, scholarship, and research pointing to inequality and injustice, we are unable to stop outlandish cruelty toward our fellow human beings?

At this point in our human history, we have accumulated a lot of head-based knowledge and information needed to explain why things are the way they are. What we lack is the essential training in kindness. Kindness is the capacity of our heart-mind to balance understanding with a genuine friendliness and concern. The principle of non-harming sits at the core of kindness—non-harming toward ourselves and others. In the words of the most famous drag queen in the world, RuPaul, "If you can't love yourself, how the hell are you gonna love somebody else?"

Breaking institutional bias first requires breaking biases, particularly habits of entitlement or victimhood, within ourselves, especially if we are in positions of authority and our decisions impact many people. Cultivating prosocial behaviors like loving-kindness enables us to shift from the autopilot of System 1 thinking toward System 2 thinking.

It was kindness that enabled New Zealand prime minister Jacinda Arden to show up at Christchurch mosques with humility and reverence after New Zealand's Muslim community was targeted by an Islamophobic mass shooter. It was her kindness that inspired the entire nation to never speak the name of the man responsible for the violence, but to focus instead on the dignity and well-being of those who had been harmed and of their families. And in the interest of her own well-being, it was kindness directed toward herself that led Arden to resign in 2023.

UNLEARNING THE PROGRAMMING

The work of breaking bias is not just up to presidents and prime ministers, it is for all of us. Each of us exercises some level of authority, influence, and power over other humans and nonhuman life. The three buckets of institutional bias begin at the individual level, in our own bodies, hearts, and minds, that ultimately become systems. Thus, in order to change systems, we must begin with changing ourselves.

When we break bias within ourselves, we also strengthen our capacity to make decisions that transcend the dualism of self and other, us versus them, feeling more grounded in ourselves, our families, and our organizations, communities, and nations.

Countless humans have transcended this internal dynamic to liberate themselves from the shackles of bias. In modern times, they were the incredibly diverse humans who led independence, civil rights, and anti-apartheid movements globally. They were the Liberian women of various religious beliefs who peacefully ended decades of political gridlock in their nation; and the green belt and Chipko movements in Kenya and India. These humans cultivated prosocial behavior capacities like loving-kindness and radical empathy to transcend the lens of victimhood and entitlement that would perceive the injustices and inequities of their societies as happening *to them*, so they could respond to them as opportunities to create change *through them*.

Our elder Ruby Sales calls this capacity having "clear sight," consisting of hindsight, foresight, and insight. Strengthening this capacity of clear sight will be the next leg of our breaking bias journey in Part II, where we will delve deeper into the first two root causes and conditions of bias: story and policies.

PRISM PRACTICES

Pause. Before you begin, take three full, juicy breaths and feel your somatic experience.

✱ Write one stereotype you notice in your mind about a secondary identity, e.g., race, religion, gender, sexuality, or wealth. Reflect on how you learned this stereotype. If it was a personal experience, write the details. If you heard it from someone, who? And in what context? If you read about it or watched it in the media, say where and describe the portrayal.

You can likely infer that it is impossible for every single human with this social identity to hold such negative attributes. Take some time to identify one real-life counterexample to the stereotype. Next time you notice this stereotype in your mind, replace it with this real-life counterexample. This practice will weaken your identification with the stereotype over time.

Select one of your identities that causes you pain or makes you feel not good enough or victimized. Take 15 to 30 minutes to complete the following meditation. Notice, feel, and document the thoughts and emotions that accompany your experience of victimization. What stories, ideas, memories, sensations, vibrations, images, sounds, or anything else accompany this feeling of victimization? Notice if the stories transition to feelings of entitlement, or feeling that it "shouldn't be this way." Observe and feel your experiences and shoulds with kindness, not needing to judge them, get rid of them, or change them. Notice if they reside in a particular part of the body and feel those sensations.

Now ask yourself, where does it hurt? Bringing forth kindness, practice your loving-kindness phrases toward the experiences that arise. This practice supports us in coming to the present moment and accepting it. Through continued practice, it also builds inner strength to respond skillfully.

After repeating the loving-kindness phrases, share with this part of your being the following forgiveness practice: *In all the ways I may have hurt, harmed, abandoned, or neglected myself, knowingly or unknowingly, in thought, word, or deed, out of fear, pain, confusion, or ignorance, I forgive myself, I forgive myself, I forgive myself.*

Remember to breathe gently and stay with any sensations that arise, extending kindness to your body, heart, mind, and soul, as well as call on your support systems as needed.

✷ Select one identity that causes you ease, or makes you feel entitled. Take at least 10 minutes to complete the following meditation. Notice, feel, bring to awareness, and document the thoughts and emotions that accompany entitlement. What stories of "shoulds" arise? What sensations, vibrations, images, sounds, or anything else accompany this feeling?

Notice in particular if the stories transition to feelings of victimization. Observe and feel the experiences with kindness, not needing to judge them, get rid of them, or change them. Notice if they reside in a particular part of the body and feel those sensations. Now ask yourself, where does it hurt? Bringing forth kindness, practice your loving-kindness phrases toward the experiences that arise, followed by the forgiveness practice.

You can carry this exercise forward by imagining and visualizing being in the experience of other beings in the following order: a loved one who does not share your identities, a stranger, someone you dislike, and if possible, someone you loathe.

ratefulness   social cohesion   ~~homophobia~~
airness   ~~bigotry~~   gratitude   ~~hatred~~   kindness
~~enophobia~~   equity   ~~nationalism~~   collaboration
ercy   ~~sexism~~   respect   ~~transphobia~~   freedom
~~peciesism~~   inclusion   ~~fascism~~   forgiveness
ptimism   celebration
eed   ~~nazism~~
ve   joy
elon   aling
ne
op
per
fety
verty   ction
riosity   ~~eroticism~~
versity   wellness
clusion   well-being   understanding
nerosity   ~~detachment~~   tranquility   equanimity
~~tisomitism~~   serenity   liberty   ~~islamophobia~~
operation   ~~hinduphobia~~   interbeing   justice
~~sogyny~~   collective identity   oneness   ~~casteism~~
uality   ~~colorism~~   sympathy   thankfulness

PART II

THE MAKING OF BIAS

Chapter 4

STORY AND POLICIES

Your beliefs become your thoughts.
Your thoughts become your words. Your words become
your actions. Your actions become your habits. Your habits
become your values. Your values become your destiny.

— MOHANDAS GANDHI

In late 2007, I was invited to a special event with 100 other graduate students who had received a scholarship to attend Cambridge University. We gathered on a lush green lawn at one of Cambridge's majestic colleges that could very well have been a set from Harry Potter. I found myself among a handful of North Americans at a gathering of students who hailed from across the Commonwealth, from the Caribbean, South Asia, and parts of Africa to Cyprus, Singapore, and Australia. These humans were among the most outstanding in their countries for their academic achievements primarily in the natural sciences or economics, with a few students like me pursuing degrees in the social sciences or the humanities.

We weren't given any information about the affair other than to dress formally for a celebration. Fifteen minutes into the event, I heard loud applause, and many students began gravitating toward the other side of the lawn, where a red carpet was being laid out and a marching band was playing for someone whom I assumed to be a dignitary. I too walked in that direction as one of the organizers announced that we were being honored with the presence of Prince Charles, now King Charles III. We were directed to carefully line ourselves up on either side of the carpet to have "an audience with His Majesty." I suddenly observed my colleagues, whether they were from Uganda, Lebanon, or Hong Kong, at least outwardly express a slavish fascination to be around this celebrity, wanting to glimpse his face, shake his hand, or even exchange a few words.

As he approached me, the prince stopped to speak with a Malaysian student standing next to me, Abdul, who shared that he was an accomplished pilot pursuing a Ph.D. in biophysics. After learning that Abdul was from Malaysia, the prince joked about the spice levels of Malaysian curries as he walked on to greet other students. I could feel anger rise within me. The complexity of this human's dynamic intersectional humanity had been reduced to a curry. Abdul, on the other hand, didn't think much of it. He was proud to have "a story to share for the rest of my life," that he met the "heir to the British throne."

Within King Charles or Abdul's story lay many other stories of hierarchy, each embedded with concepts and *vedana* that create a particular perception of what it means to have certain biological, experiential, and social identities: British royal descent, Malaysian, Cambridge student, scholarship recipient, and one who has met a British royal. The first root cause of every identity-based bias is a story. Based on our mind's tendency to compare, stories create the conceptual scaffolding that justifies secondary identity-based hierarchies that rank human value as better-than or worse-than. These stories are generally *made up*! There is absolutely no scientific basis for them, and yet conscious and unconscious belief in these stories is the foundational cause of bias. With that said, policies, the second root cause, are what make a story come alive in societies.

THE INTERPLAY OF STORY AND POLICIES

Policies make a story about a secondary identity a lived reality for people within nations, institutions, and societies. I define *policies* broadly as "the formal and informal principles of action adopted by an institution or groups of institutions, i.e., systems." Recall that institutions are made up of humans and that institutional biases stem from the decisions, i.e., the *policies*, made by humans who have authority over an institution. The policies of institutions, corporations, organizations, and even families are regulated, monitored, and influenced by government policies.

Government policies within a centralized society serve four primary purposes:

* *To establish standards*: policies set the minimum acceptable behavior in a society, e.g., that people do not injure or damage other people or their property.

* *To guarantee liberties, rights, and resources*: in exchange for abiding by the established standards, policies guarantee people and institutions certain liberties and rights, e.g., freedom of speech, the press, and to vote.

* *To maintain order*: policies enforce the established standards and protect liberties and rights by punishing those who misbehave.

* *To resolve disputes*: policies provide a formal way to resolve disputes, e.g., the courts, to maintain order and prevent extrajudicial violence.

Policies give stories teeth. Within a society, they erect and enforce the ranking systems proffered by a story. But people within the society learn the story through culture, or the remaining three causes of bias: social contact, education, and media. Figure 4.1 shows a visual representation of how the human brain is trained in bias by the five root causes of bias. Humans are affected by the policies of many institutions, including their family, workplace, and local and national governments.

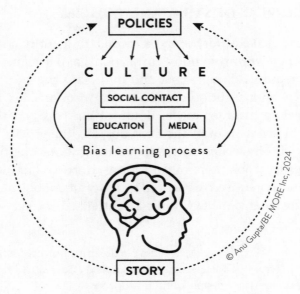

Figure 4.1

Some examples of how humans are affected by policies are the family policy that obliges humans to date and marry someone from their own ethnic or religious community, a workplace policy that obliges humans to wear their hair in a certain manner, or a government policy that bans certain books in public libraries or restricts humans from using public bathrooms because of their gender identity. Each of these policies is informed by a story and the impact of the policy is contingent on the reach, or, as we say in the law, the "jurisdiction," of a particular institution. Among humans globally, there are numerous policies that sprout from specific and context-dependent stories about different human identities.

As we continue our breaking bias journey, in this chapter I will review the first two root causes of bias for secondary identities that may vary across societies but uphold a similar hierarchy. Given the diversity of human cultures, my goal is to present you with sufficient practice so you can identify these two root causes for identity-based hierarchies in your society, and thereby, work toward breaking them!

BIOLOGICAL IDENTITY: FACIAL FEATURES

In my early 20s, I started getting two or three sinus infections a year and my doctor identified the cause: a deviated septum. She said it was a common problem and it could be surgically fixed with a septoplasty, a procedure to straighten the deviation so fluids could easily flow through my nasal passages. I consulted my physician parents, and they agreed that I should get the procedure. Then in all seriousness, they added, "While you're at it, why not get a nose job too?" This would fix my fat nose to look more "refined and pointy," they explained. They even offered to pay for it.

Though I was shocked at the proposition, for a moment I considered it. The story going through all of our minds was that small, pointy noses are beautiful and noses that deviate from that shape are not. This story created a perception, which was made up of a concept that a nose of my shape was ugly and accompanied with unpleasant *vedana*. I recall standing in my parents' living room practicing mindfulness, becoming aware of the story attached to my nose, and realizing it was up to me to decide its fate.

Since then, I have heard hundreds of similar stories from people of all colors and backgrounds. My Jewish students were tortured by their noses, black colleagues were ashamed of the wideness of their nostrils, and my partner's Filipino family admitted that they massage the nose of every newborn for a few weeks in the hope that it will help create a nose bridge like those of their former colonizers, the Spanish.

These patterns of perceptions about facial features, whether they are about noses, eye shape, cheekbones, chins, or hair texture, are far too common across cultures and societies. For example, in 32 American states, legislatures have banned humans with wavy and kinky hair from wearing their hair in locks, or courts have failed to protect them, disproportionately affecting humans of African descent.[1] Underlying such policies is a story that confers presence or absence of beauty and professionalism in certain aspects of human appearance. This is the interplay between story and policies.

PRISM EXERCISE

Pause. Take three full breaths and return your awareness to your somatic experience.

In the space below or in your journal, reflect on a facial feature you have that has caused you pain. Then reflect on one that has caused you ease.

Reflect on the underlying story and the policy connected with each of these facial features. What is the story? What are the concepts and emotions attached to it? Where did you learn or do you continue to learn this story? If your body, heart, and mind permit, go to a search engine and identify positive counterexamples of humans, historical or current, for whom this facial feature *just is/was*—neither good nor bad. Moving forward, think of these humans when you notice the thought of judgment or conceit arising with respect to this identity.

BIOLOGICAL IDENTITY: DESCENT

Descent is a secondary identity that is contingent upon our biological ancestors. In most centralized and even decentralized societies, descent was and is used to socially assign humans occupational roles and functions. Though the story and policies that design descent-based occupational hierarchies vary across societies, they share an underlying structure.

For example, from ancient to modern times, whether in China, Greece, or Iraq, with minor exceptions, humans born into a family of farmers, warriors, or the royalty inherited the occupations of their ancestors. Descent ensured economic and political stability in societies across time, whether in ancient Egypt, Aztec Mexico, Hawaii, Russia, or Japan. The Great Chain of Being was the story that justified a descent-based feudal order in premodern Europe. Modern-day royal families and monarchies in nation-states like Great Britain, the Netherlands, Saudi Arabia, Thailand, and Malaysia are remnants of descent-based systems. In addition, descent is often used to justify religious and political leadership, as is the case in many Islamic societies where those in positions of authority often claim to be or are descendants of the Prophet Muhammad.

I first became acquainted with the term *descent* as an undergraduate while interning for international human rights lawyer Smita Narula.* At the time, she was co-leading an international movement to end descent-based interpersonal and institutional bias and violence toward communities such as the Burakumin in Japan, subordinated ethnic and tribal communities in Sahelian Africa, and subordinated castes in South Asia. All these descent-based biases are rooted in a story and policies that restrict the social, political, economic, and cultural beingness of humans of a particular descent. In this section, I will discuss two forms of biases that stem from descent: casteism and antisemitism.

Casteism: Descent-Based Subordination in South Asia

Based on careful study of caste systems globally, scholar Isabel Wilkerson defines caste as "an artificial and arbitrary graded ranking of human value in a society."[2] Within the South Asian context, caste refers to a complex amalgamation of thousands of *jatis*, or occupational communities, across the subcontinent's incredibly ethnically, linguistically, and religiously diverse 2 billion people. It operates as an unequal hierarchy of social organization that explicitly and implicitly assigns concepts, emotions, and *vedana* of inherent purity or impurity to humans based on their descent.

As you know, all forms of -isms and hierarchies are founded upon a story. The South Asian caste system is founded upon a dominant interpretation of the Hindu Vedic cosmology that permanently assigns some humans one of four *varnas*, or occupational places in

---

* The author of Human Rights Watch's 1999 report *Broken People*, Smita Narula is also one of the co-founders of the International Dalit Solidarity Network (IDSN). Learn more at idsn.org.

society—scholars, warriors, merchants, and servants (or Brahmins, Kshatriyas, Vaishyas, and Shudras, respectively, in Sanskrit). However, it fails to assign some humans a *varna*; these people are labeled *avarnas* and make up incredibly diverse groups of humans known as Dalits and Adivasis today due to their shared historical experiences of marginalization and pain.*

Like the Great Chain of Being, this story labels some humans intrinsically impure and inferior, and that label historically created a policy and cultural container that justified their exclusion and oppression. In the post-independence era, even though caste discrimination is illegal across the subcontinent, informal policies upheld by humans running social institutions, organizations, and families sustain this system.

Given that I am from a dominant caste, I have not experienced any direct pain due to my caste. I was not even aware of my caste until I started working with Smita. When I was growing up in the 1990s, no one in my Indian family or schools mentioned the words *varna*, *jati*, or *caste*. So naturally I was shocked to read Smita's *Broken People*, which documented horrific atrocities and the discrimination Indians experienced due to their descent-based caste identity. Unlike race or ethnicity, you cannot see a person's caste in their appearance.

After learning about caste as a college student, I went to my mother and asked her about our caste. At first she was surprised, but then she said *Baniya*. I was confused because this word wasn't a part of the four *varnas* I had learned about in my American textbooks. I probed a bit more, and after studying caste in more depth, I realized that the Western view of South Asia's five-leveled caste system

---

* Adivasis are South Asia's indigenous people, i.e., forest dwellers, animist cultures, and Earth-based cultures. Within South Asia's legal framework, Dalit and Adivasi communities are referred to as "Scheduled Castes and Scheduled Tribes."

is oversimplified; the system is in fact a complex set of fluid and constantly evolving occupational communities.*

In fact, there are hundreds of *jatis* in each rung of the *varna* system that are organized in intricate hierarchies of better-than or worse-than based on an origin story that is region specific. My mother told me the origin story of my family's *gothra,* a sub-*jati* of *Baniyas.* I won't bore you with the details, but basically it is akin to many tribal origin stories—2 humans had 12 children and each of their *male* children became the progenitor of a sub-*jati.* What united all these *jatis* and sub-*jatis* was their occupation, which in my family's case was a very particular type of textile business. Some of my relatives in India continue to run the textile business that my ancestors started or inherited many generations ago.

The *jati* system in South Asia is rooted in labor economics and a narrative that values and demonizes humans based on the work they perform. For me, the most ridiculous part about the dominant story of *varna* is that it reviles humans that it designates *avarnas*; it links their humanity to false concepts and unpleasant *vedana* associated with impurity and builds a policy and cultural infrastructure that excludes them from resources, opportunities, and experiences.

Despite two millennia of religious and political social movements to banish *varna*-based exclusion and bias across South Asian religious traditions,† despite subordinated humans' adoption of non-Hindu faiths, and despite laws in every South Asian nation outlawing caste, a descent-based occupational *jati* system—consciously or unconsciously—remains at work. This is because after subordinated people adopted another religion, they likely changed

---

* Scholars like Nicholas Dirks (see *Castes of Mind*) have shown that *jati* systems were more fluid than the rigid caste system of modern South Asia and diasporic South Asian communities. In the 1500s, the Portuguese first applied the word *casta* to describe the *jati* system they witnessed in their conquest of southern India. The first recorded use of the phrase "caste system" to describe South Asia's *jatis* occurred in 1840 by the British. In addition, there is a misconception in the West that skin color is associated with South Asian caste. This is false; there are people from the dominant caste who are dark-skinned, like my family members, and people from subordinated castes who are light-skinned, like the people with whom I conducted my graduate fieldwork.

† Including Hinduism, Islam, Buddhism, Sikhism, Jainism, and Christianity. Wisdom traditions like Buddhism, Jainism, Sikhism, Arya Samaj, Bhakti movements, and many Sufi communities emerged from the need to end caste-based discrimination, except they too became subsumed in its labor economics.

their worshipping and eating habits, but their occupation generally remained the same.

Jyoti, one of my Indian students who happens to be of Dalit descent, shared with me countless stories of members of her community, including her academic parents, routinely using unkind words toward other *jatis* of Dalits that were historically worse off than their community. Similarly, I was sad to learn that even Dr. B. R. Ambedkar, the fierce anticaste activist, visionary behind India's constitution, and one of my inspirations, wrote and spoke poorly about Adivasi communities.[3] In such moments, I have to remember that he too was shaped by the five root causes of bias. He was educated and trained in the Western academy that looked down upon indigenous and animist humans as savages and beasts. And over time, like Mohandas Gandhi, who was also trained in the Western academy and at one point held abominable views about Africans, he reformed and changed his views by breaking his own biases.

For me, South Asia's caste system is a glaring example of exclusion consciousness that is rooted in comparing mindset and hierarchies. Though not as ruthless, blatant, or complex, similar descent-based hierarchies exist across societies, appearing as or intersecting with other secondary identities like class, family name, and descent. Just think of the aristocratic racial utopia of *Bridgerton*, where one can marry across cultures, colors, and even continents, but one wouldn't dare to cross the class line. When one investigates the story beneath what represents class in modern-day England or France, one finds descent-based occupational hierarchies similar to South Asian *jatis*.

Antisemitism: Descent-Based Subordination of Jewish People

Antisemitism is made up of two words: *anti* and *semitism*. Semitism refers to ancient Semitic people of the Middle East who are the ancestors of modern-day Chaldeans, Palestinians, Lebanese, Iraqis, Jews, and many Arab communities. *Anti-Semitism* as a term was first used in the 19th century by German racial scientists and politicians as a political statement to express their hatred of European Jews.

These humans fabricated and popularized the Aryan racial myth and anti-Jewish stereotypes that eventually became the political ideology of the Nazi regime.

Antisemitism (one word) has since evolved to describe conscious or unconscious biases directed toward humans who are, or are perceived to be, of Jewish descent. I define antisemitism as "false beliefs or habits of thought that lead us to think, speak, or act in ways that directly or indirectly harm humans of Jewish descent."

Learning and teaching about antisemitism was my entry into the work of breaking bias. Until my senior year in high school, my sole understanding of antisemitism was the genocide of European Jews by the German Nazi regime. This began to shift in 2002 when I was selected to be a part of two prestigious programs. I was an apprentice and tour guide at New York City's Museum of Jewish Heritage: A Living Memorial to the Holocaust, and I served as a summer researcher at Israel's Weizmann Institute of Science. Learning and being trained to teach Jewish history, philosophy, and traditions, as well as living in Israel, inspired me to major in Middle Eastern and Islamic studies in college, which in turn helped me recognize that antisemitism, like South Asian casteism, is one of the most ancient descent-based biases.

Like all forms of biases, antisemitism is rooted in false stories about the humanity of a group of people, in this case Jewish people. These stories date back at least to the era when Christianity became the dominant religion of the Roman Empire and subsequently across Europe.* In Christianity's 1,600 years of existence, the stories have expanded and mutated to link the humanity of Jewish people with numerous lies, which generally have at least two components.

First, **religious inferiority**. Recall the Great Chain of Being paradigm in which anything other than state-sanctioned Christianity was impermissible. That story perceived Jewish humans as less than Christians because they did not follow the teachings of Jesus. The

---

* The enslavement, captivity, exclusion, and oppression of Jewish people predates Christianity under the ancient Egyptian, Babylonian, and pre-Christian Roman Empires; however, the stereotyping that sustains modern-day antisemitism originated in Christian Europe. *See* Teter's *Christian Supremacy: Reckoning with the Roots of Antisemitism and Racism.*

story also blamed all Jewish humans and their descendants in perpetuity for the death of historical Jesus, overlooking the fact that Jesus, his parents, and all his early companions were Jewish themselves. As institutionalized Christianity supplanted pagan and animist traditions across Western and Eastern Europe during the medieval age, the consciousness of new European Christians was infected with this false story. In modernity, European colonization and missionary efforts infected humans globally—including African and indigenous Americans, Nigerians, Kenyans, Indians, Filipinos, and Koreans—with this false story.

Second, **scapegoating**. From medieval times to very recent times, the Christian European culture, entrenched in its exclusion consciousness, fabricated and proffered numerous stereotypes and conspiracy theories that made Jewish-descent humans scapegoats for various social ills (and sometimes *all* social ills). Until the 19th century, in most of Christian Europe these stories led to policies that pushed Jewish people to the margins of society.*

This shifted for some European Jews in the 19th century with the emergence of liberalism, but the shift was interrupted by the rise of the anti-Semitism that eventually became Nazism. I recall walking visitors through the Museum of Jewish History and showing them historical propaganda, from books, songs, and theater pieces to children's board games, that villainized and lampooned Jewish humans, degrading their humanity in the minds of consumers.

With Christian European settlement across the Americas, Australia, New Zealand, and other regions as well as European colonization globally, these false ideas have traveled and infected the consciousness of humans beyond Europe; conspiracy theories and scapegoating are common ways antisemitism manifests today worldwide. Just in my lifetime, I recall commentators scapegoating Jewish people for massive global events from 9/11 and the American war on Iraq and Afghanistan to the 2008 financial crisis and the COVID-19 pandemic. This is antisemitism in action, and it is especially virulent when the actions of one or a few humans who

---

* This is why most European cities have a "historical Jewish ghetto."

happen to be Jewish are used against a diverse and heterogeneous community. Like casteism in South Asia, while antisemitism is illegal in many nations, it remains a cultural reality because of the humans who continue to believe, speak, and act based on the false stories it is based on.

PRISM EXERCISE

Pause. Take three full breaths. Bring your attention to your body and recall our agreements.

Bring to mind a descent-based identity like your ethnicity, *jati*, or occupational class in your society that makes you feel victimized.

Investigate with curiosity the stories beneath this feeling. What are the concepts and emotions attached to them? Where did or do you continue to learn these stories? If your body and heart permit, identify positive counterexamples of humans, historical or current, for whom this aspect of their humanity *just is/was*—neither good nor bad. Moving forward, think of these humans when you notice victimization arising with respect to this identity. For persistent feelings of victimization, I encourage you to seek support and help. See the Communities and Practices for Support section on page 333 for some ideas.

Repeat this exercise for a descent-based identity that makes you feel entitled.

SOCIAL IDENTITIES: RELIGION AND ETHNICITY

Religion and ethnicity are secondary identities that we acquire or are socialized into by our families, our upbringing, and/or through our actions. I think of religion as a belief system that guides our actions and behavior through a set of ethical principles while offering explanations for inexplicable aspects of our human existence such as: What is the purpose of life? Why are we here? What happens after we die?

Ethnicity, on the other hand, signifies a group of humans who share a language, customs, rituals, beliefs, historical experiences and memories, and a connection to land, e.g., Armenians, Kurds, Tibetans, Quechua, Igbo, or the Irish.

Depending on context, these two social identities can be independent of each other or co-dependent. For example, one can be ethnically Slav, Yoruba, or Ethiopian while following a Christian, Muslim, Hare Krishna, or animist tradition. However, it is generally rare to find an ethnic Malay or Turk Cypriot who is non-Muslim; they may be nonpracticing, but being Muslim is part of their ethnic identity. In fact, in Malaysia, it is illegal for an ethnic Malay to change religions or profess atheism. Similarly, many Jewish people, regardless of their skin color or nationality, see their religious identity also as an ethnicity given their shared origins, beliefs, and connection to an ancestral land.

In many societies, the stories and policies attached to religious and ethnic identities uphold social hierarchies and give rise to a host of internalized, interpersonal, and institutional biases. Though the stories and policies behind such hierarchies vary across societies, like descent, they share a similar underlying structure responsible for how humans learn concepts, emotions, and *vedana* toward one another based on those identities.

Islamophobia and Other Religious & Ethnic Biases

I define *Islamophobia* as "false beliefs or habits of thoughts that lead us to think, speak, or act in ways that directly or indirectly harm humans who are or are perceived as Muslims." Today, Muslims are a group of incredibly ethnically, linguistically, and regionally diverse humans who practice one of many spiritual traditions of Islam—for example, Sufi, Sunni, Shia, Ahmadi, Ismaili—united in their reverence for the revelations of Prophet Muhammad captured in the sacred Quran.

Growing up, I heard many horrific accounts of India's partition, like the story of my grandmother's family, who were forced to flee their ancestral homes of hundreds of generations in what is now Pakistan because they weren't Muslim. In these stories, I heard various one-dimensional characterizations that pigeonholed every single one of the billions of humans who are Muslim not as who they are, but as what some Muslim humans did or continue to do in the name of Islam. Stories that Tibetan teacher Tsoknyi Rinpoche would call *real*, because they existed in the collective consciousness, *but not true*.

In post–9/11 America, I began to question these stories as I found myself being linked with them because of my appearance, i.e., brown Middle Eastern/South Asian–looking man. This contributed to my decision in college to drop pre-med for Middle Eastern and Islamic studies. Not only that, in 2004, I returned to India to study Urdu and Islam. As I studied Islam, I found a spiritual home. I found its essence to be identical to my root spiritual traditions: oneness, compassion, generosity, patience, understanding, and forgiveness. Yet as I befriended and lived with Muslims, I discovered stories some Muslims held about Hindus and other non-Muslims. Like my family's, their stories too were real, even if not true.

After graduating from college, I taught English at a rural middle school near Naju, South Korea. Outside our school, I sometimes noticed people picketing with Korean signs with large crosses. My Korean was not very good, so I generally ignored them until one day three women approached me as I was leaving school. I introduced myself in my broken Korean as they graciously invited me to come pray with them at their church. Not thinking clearly, I politely declined by making an excuse that I was Buddhist. This got them really upset as they cornered me and showed me three cards: a black card representing the darkness I was in, a red card for where I was headed, i.e., hell, unless I repented, which would then be my golden card to heaven. They clearly had a story about Buddhists, which motivated their actions toward me. Stories that were real, but not true.

In discussing the incident with my homestay family, I learned that even though South Korea is ethnically homogenous, Koreans, like many ethnicities globally, are quite divided along religious lines. I could relate to that experience. My family is Punjabi, and

Punjabis, like Koreans, are quite divided along religious lines. In our case, religion was the reason why Punjab was split into India and Pakistan, costing over a million lives, most of whom were ethnically Punjabi.

The violence following India's partition was a consequence of religious extremism. Religious extremism, whether it's Islamic, Hindu, Sikh, Christian, Jewish, Buddhist, or of another tradition, is rooted in a story of us versus them and policies that actualize a hierarchy of humanity based on people's religious identity. As a student of religion, I have found nothing in the esoteric essence of any major world tradition that condones violence, hatred, or bias, and yet religion is a flashpoint for such actions because the humans who encourage and exercise them are identified with their religious or ethnic identity, not their religion's actual teachings. Social scientist Brené Brown has termed this phenomenon *common enemy intimacy,* when seemingly disparate humans with a diversity of secondary identities come together in their shared hatred of an unreal other.[4]

The history of centralized societies from ancient to contemporary times is mired in glaring violence rooted in religious and ethnic biases that manifest as common enemy intimacy. In just the last 100 years, we have witnessed or experienced it with Armenians and Kurds in Turkey; Greeks and Turks in Cyprus; Jews and Roma in Europe; Tibetans, Uighurs, and other ethnoreligious groups in China; Catholics and Protestants in Ireland; and numerous conflicts from the former Yugoslavia, Rwanda, Iraq, Sudan, Myanmar, and Nigeria to Israel/Palestine, Lebanon, the Philippines, Ethiopia, and Ukraine. Each conflict is unique in terms of the stories about which humans did what to whom and when, but they share a story of common enemy intimacy that informs individual and collective principles of action (i.e., policies) in the form of planned or sporadic mob violence.

PRISM EXERCISE

Pause. Take three full breaths. Bring your awareness to and feel your somatic experience.

At this point, there may be many stories and anecdotes, personal, historical, or intergenerational, arising for you. Place your hands on your heart or your belly and feel your body. Take 10 full breaths and try to move your attention from your mind into your body. Become mindful of any tightness, sensations, and emotions that may be present.

Before proceeding, take at least five minutes to journal and release any thoughts, emotions, and ideas stored in your body-heart-mind about what you've read thus far, and then get embodied by doing at least 60 seconds' worth of push-ups, jumping jacks, squats, or another embodiment exercise.

EXPERIENTIAL IDENTITIES: PROFESSION AND CLASS

Profession and class are interdependent secondary identities that describe the most practical and vital aspects of our daily lives: how we earn a monetary income through a job or occupation based on our schooling, time, energy, efforts, and creativity (profession); and how we compare with others in terms of status, how much money we make, and how many possessions we own (class). Historically, in most centralized societies, we generally inherited our profession and class based on our descent, for example, through *jatis* in South Asia or feudal orders and professional guilds in Christian Europe, Islamic societies, and other centralized societies.

In the 20th century, for many humans, profession and class have become experiential identities because we can change these identities through gaining new experiences, such as education, through personal actions, and through our own will, even in societies with rigid descent-based hierarchies. This is a very recent transition in the evolution of human consciousness, credited to ideas of liberalism, capitalism, and the era of industrialization that began in Western Europe and spread globally within the last 200 years.

In most societies, the story and policies attached to professional identities are intertwined with class and shape our perceptions of ourselves and others through the lens of hierarchies and biases. Some professions, such as being a doctor, lawyer, or engineer, are highly regarded in any society, not because of the actual work but because of how someone with those professional qualifications is compensated. The perception is that in our competitive capitalist societies, these professions give people the opportunity to accumulate more money and possessions so they, and by extension their families, can enjoy greater worldly comforts. This perception is rooted in a story and policies that get enacted within ourselves, our families, and societies.

Buying into this story was why I—along with millions of other teenagers and young adults globally—dedicated most of my waking hours to preparing for and studying to excel at standardized examinations. As a high school student, I thought my performance on standardized tests such as the SATs demonstrated how smart I was, so I spent an inordinate amount of time reading test prep books on my own. I didn't know my classmates spent much less of their time preparing for this exam because their families could afford to send them to test preparation courses. When it came to the LSATs, the American law school admissions test, I had learned better, so I purchased a test prep course for myself and voilà, I learned *how to take the test.* By then, I had come to appreciate that these standardized tests measure and value a certain way of thinking that can feel counterintuitive. Instead of resisting it, I chose to master it so I could enter a profession, lawyering, that could "secure" my future material concerns.

However, it didn't go as planned. My first job out of law school paid me an annual salary of $48,000, while my classmates on average earned upwards of $200,000. I had graduated in the top 20 percent of my class, so why the disparity? Because, unlike most of my classmates, who went to work at private law firms, I chose to put my legal skills and my time, energy, and creativity toward the "public interest": human and animal rights, environmental protection, and social justice.

Built into my profession is a hierarchy that assigns a monetary value not to the caliber of one's lawyering skills, the amount of effort or time one gives to the work, or even the benefit to society it offers, but to the type of work one chooses. Underneath this hierarchy is another story about labor and its value. Upon graduation, I had to choose between my passion and values or material comfort. In the last 50 years, many professionals have been forced to make such a decision, which has a direct impact on one's class status. Why just in the last 50 years and not before then? Well, as you might be able to infer, even as ideas of liberalism spread globally, most of the world remained under the rule of European nation-states, who through institutional policies restricted entry into most high-earning professions based on a human's secondary identities.

For example, for most of the 150 years since lawyering became a profession in the United States, it was restricted to white male humans of a certain background. Professor Joan Howarth's book *Shaping the Bar* meticulously tracks how, as subordinated humans demanded entry into the profession, the requirements for entry became more stringent. Today, under the guise of "character fitness," many state bars continue to restrict humans with certain identities, such as having a criminal record, entry into the profession. This phenomenon demonstrates the interplay between the first two causes of bias that decide professional standards.[5]

Similar hierarchies exist in many other professions, including medicine, architecture, and engineering. I once asked my surgeon mother why a pediatrician earns half as much as a radiologist or anesthesiologist. She absentmindedly said because the latter "work harder and have more rigorous training." When I pressed harder, of course, this story fell flat. Upon deeper reflection, she admitted that it is because the medical boards (institutions) have decided to undertake such a formal principle of action based on a story that assigns different monetary value to different types of doctoring.

PRISM EXERCISE

Pause. Take three full breaths and return your awareness to your somatic experience.

Bring to mind your professional identity. Investigate with curiosity the underlying stories you have attached to this identity. Notice ideas, memories, and experiences of entitlement and/or victimization that arise in your mind. Observe your somatic experience. Jot down concepts, emotions, and *vedana* that arise in your mind. Then, reflect below or in your journal how these ideas affect your relationship with yourself, your family, your colleagues, and your outlook on life.

The Underlying Story of Class

Though the stories and policies that design hierarchies within and across professions vary across societies, by now you can sense that they share a similar underlying structure responsible for programming our minds with bias, including assumptions about competency, potential, and intellect. Beneath these biases is a more nefarious bias that with the rise of neoliberal capitalism in the last 50 years has come to dominate the decisions of political and economic institutions globally: class bias. This is a form of bias that is informed by a story that ranks humans based on the amount of money they have and the possessions they own.

When I was a graduate student at Cambridge, I loved to bike to a coffee shop that was a ways away from the university. For me, it was a nice reprieve from the university environment. One day, the shop's middle-aged barista, Rosie, asked me if I was a townie or a gownie. I didn't understand, so she went on to explain the difference, the former being working-class folks like herself from

Cambridgeshire, and the latter being Cambridge's elite students and faculty, distinctly identifiable by their gowns.

"Am I supposed to be offended?" I retorted playfully, at which she smiled, and we got into a lively conversation about Britain's classist public education system that prevented anyone but the wealthy or wealth-adjacent from receiving the preparation needed for admission into elite institutions like Cambridge. What she described was analogous to the American public education system, where zip codes determine school resources and hence the quality of the education that children receive.

At one point in our discussion, Rosie passionately uttered the following words, which summarize the story of class: "In their ghastly Oxbridge accents, they blame us for being poor, for being lazy, for not working hard enough, and for being responsible for our sickness, our hunger, our poverty, and our misery, when they created the systems that produce all of those things. We're just pawns in their game." In these two sentences, Rosie taught me what I hadn't pieced together in all four years of my college education.

In the 2013 documentary *Inequality for All*, there's a conversation I'll never forget between former American labor secretary Robert Reich and a white working-class man. The latter blamed himself for his poverty. His reasoning? Unlike the rich people on Wall Street, he didn't study hard enough in high school.[6] I know I don't have to tell you, but this man has all the symptoms of internalized bias, which at its foundation begins with a story—a story that falsely claims that there are equal economic opportunities and equally functioning quality schools for everyone, and if one is not economically prosperous, it is because one didn't work hard enough. This story of a self-made person who pulls themselves up by their bootstraps ignores the thousands of policies of governments and institutions that favor humans with wealth (e.g., the way taxes are calculated) and distributes subsidies to corporations in certain industries, all of which favors the humans who own those institutions. In the global financial markets, 91 cents of every dollar go to the top 1 percent.[7]

Gandhi very simply said, "Earth provides enough to satisfy every man's needs, but not every man's greed." While many forms of class hierarchies attributed to descent, ethnicity, religion, or another secondary identity have existed in settled human societies, contemporary class hierarchies and the inequalities they perpetuate are unique to our times. The story of class that Rosie articulated describes a certain worldview that forms the infrastructure of our contemporary global economic system: hyperindividualism, separateness from nature and one another, domination, commodification, competition, ceaseless accumulation of wealth, exploitation, selfishness, cruelty, and retribution—in other words, exclusion consciousness. This worldview contravenes the values of every human wisdom tradition.

PRISM EXERCISE

Pause. Take three full breaths and feel any body sensations. Recall one of our shared agreements that may bring you the most insight and equanimity at this moment.

Philosopher David Loy describes modern class systems as symptoms of our economic, political, and media systems. He calls our current economic paradigm *institutionalized greed*, our politics *institutionalized hatred*, and our media *institutionalized ignorance*.[8]

Notice the ways Loy's words land in your heart-mind, body, and spirit. With kindness, bring awareness to the thoughts, emotions, and somatic experiences that they trigger in your experience. Take a few minutes to breathe and reflect on your response below or in your journal.

THE FIRST TWO CAUSES OF BIAS
FOR ALL SECONDARY IDENTITIES

In this chapter, my goal has been to familiarize you with the first two root causes of bias for a few secondary identities that vary across societies but operate similarly. As we continue our breaking bias journey, in the next two chapters we will focus on the stories and policies of two secondary identities that have global ramifications: race and gender.

With that said, I encourage you to explore and delve deeper into the region-specific and context-specific stories and policies for different secondary identities: for example, a Kalmuck, Tatar, or Uzbek in Russia; a Buddhist, Hindu, or Shia Muslim in Saudi Arabia; a Syrian or Afghan refugee in Germany; a person who was formerly incarcerated; a survivor of genocide; a veteran; a divorced person; a person living with long COVID; an aging person; or one suffering from a mental illness.

I especially encourage you to explore these two root causes of bias against humans with disabilities. Disability encompasses a vast spectrum of secondary identities that are biological, social, and/or experiential. Humans experience a range of physical, sensory, cognitive, and/or genetic disabilities, and every single one of these experiences is perceived differently based on the story about that disability within a society and the principles of actions, or policies, that story informs within institutions like our families, organizations, and governments.

I personally witnessed just one of these stories with my Indian cousin Noni, who was born with cerebral palsy and lived until he was 16. Though my aunt gave him unconditional love, in Indian society, the story ascribed to his humanity was that it was defective—not differently abled—which is rooted in the presumption that there is a "right" way to be human. This story informed the kind of social and government services available to him, not to mention the dozens of charlatans my aunt was socially coerced to see in an effort to "fix him" when in fact there was nothing to fix. Noni's experience is not uncommon for humans with cerebral palsy in India.

As you proceed, it is my sincere hope that you will apply the tools you are learning to identify the story and policies for various identity-based biases in your society and apply what you discover to move toward breaking bias.

PRISM PRACTICES

Pause. Take three breaths. Bring your attention to and feel your somatic experience.

* Select a secondary identity that is a cause of inequity and human suffering in your society. What stereotypes exist for the subordinated humans on this hierarchy? Where did you learn these stereotypes? In what ways do these false stories affect your relationship with yourself? With others? How do they manifest in your decision-making? Investigate the origin of these stories. Reflect on some social, economic, cultural, and political policies that sustain this hierarchy.

   Then, identify at least one counterexample to these stereotypes. Moving forward, when you notice stereotypes arising in your mind about this identity, replace them with real-life counterexamples. This practice will weaken your identification with the stereotype over time.

* Take 10 minutes to complete the following exercise. Visualize being in the shoes of a human with a stereotyped identity. Imagine what it's like to be this human. What lies might they have been taught about their humanity? How do these lies influence their thoughts, words, and deeds toward themselves? Toward others? What experiential identities (e.g., trauma, disability, incarceration) may they hold as a result of their subordination? Breathe and stay with these sensations as they arise. End the exercise by extending your loving-kindness phrases toward this human, and all humans who share this identity with them.

* Take 15 to 30 minutes to complete the following perspective-taking exercise. Visualize being a nonhuman being that has been hunted or fished to extinction by humans during modernity.

Notice and feel the sensations in their bodies as a result of human actions. Breathe and stay with these sensations as they arise. End the exercise by extending your loving-kindness phrases toward these beings. Feel free to practice this exercise for multiple beings, but stay with one being during each practice.

* Complete the previous perspective-taking exercise for humans who hunted these animals. What concepts, emotions, and stories do they ascribe to themselves? To the nonhuman beings? Notice and feel any sensations of entitlement or victimization in their bodies. Breathe and stay with these sensations as they arise. End the exercise by extending your loving-kindness phrases toward these humans. You can use someone you personally know to complete this exercise.

* Imagine you are in a world without class-based biases and hierarchies. Using words, images, or any other means, visualize and describe what this world looks like. What does it feel like? How do you feel mentally, emotionally, and physically? What do you do with your time? With your energy? With your creativity? What about those you love? How do they spend their time? Let your imagination run wild. There is no right or wrong way to imagine. Just imagine.

Chapter 5

RACE

In order to know who we are,
we have to know what we've done to one another.

— OCEAN VUONG

I immigrated to the United States when I was 10 years old. Three days after we arrived in snowy Queens, New York, my mother enrolled me in elementary school. Per the Department of Education policy, each new student was required to identify their race based on three choices: Caucasian, African American, or Other. My mother left the question unmarked. When the school administrator noticed, he reasoned, "Well, you're not Caucasian or African American, so let's check 'Other.'" That moment was my first encounter with race and with being "other" on the race hierarchy. At that time, I was oblivious to this simple question's implications for the lives of billions globally.

Before you turn the page, I'd like you to define race in your own words below. What exactly is race? What does race mean to you?

Race is:

Over the last two decades, I've posed this question to thousands of people. I generally receive three responses, and your answer likely falls into one or more of them:

1. Race is a social construct. In other words, it's made up, i.e., it is a **story** that a few humans made up and told to others as if it were true.

2. Race is something we see in people's **appearance**, like skin color or hair, facial, eye, nose, or lip structure, and so on. We have no control over these biological identities. We each inherit them through **descent**, that is, from our biological ancestors. Isabel Wilkerson accurately calls race a *metric*.[1] The moment a human's appearance makes contact with our visual senses, our minds assign this thing called *race* to them, and we're shocked when we're wrong.

3. Like many secondary identities, race is a social **hierarchy**.

Based on these three elements, I define *race* as "a story that ranks humans on a hierarchy based on descent and appearance." You'll notice that there is no mention of a natural, scientific, biological, or genetic basis for race anywhere in this definition. This is because one does not exist. In Chapter 2, you learned today's humans share common ancestors who spread across our planet between 315,000 years ago and the present day.

In 2000, after successfully decoding the entirety of human DNA, the Human Genome Project went a step further by showing definitively that race has no genetic or scientific basis. It demonstrated that the genes for our skin color have nothing to do with the genes for hair type, eye shape, blood type, musical talent, athletic skill, or cognitive abilities. Not only that, it also showed that within the 0.1 percent genetic difference between humans, the vast majority of variation occurs *within* groups of humans who share a country or an ethnicity, such as Persians or Nigerians, not between one group and another. This means that two random Italians may be as genetically different as a Korean and an Italian.[2]

In 2014, Nobel laureate Toni Morrison reiterated this truth on *The Colbert Report* when she said, "There is no such thing as race. None. There is just a human race—scientifically, anthropologically."[3] With that said, when author Gary Zukav repeated this truth to Oprah Winfrey on her 2017 *Super Soul Sessions*, she astutely responded, "Race may not be real, but racism is very real." This somatically felt truth about racial bias resonated with thousands in their audience.

To our minds, racism is what explains the murders of George Floyd, Sandra Bland, Vincent Chin, and countless others killed for no reason other than their *being*. Racism explains apartheid and Jim Crow segregation, slavery, colonization, and why absolute strangers can address me as Osama bin Laden. As someone who is harmed by and is a witness to racial bias on a daily basis, regardless of what the science has found, in my lived experience, race *feels* very real to me.

This feeling of cognitive dissonance, of knowing one thing at the absolute level and experiencing another at the relative level, is what led me to understand how the story of race originated and spread like a virus throughout our global human consciousness. Contrary to popular belief, racial bias is a very recent development in human history, and in this chapter, we'll delve into its first two causes and conditions. But before we get into it, I want to offer you the following cautionary words from biological anthropologist Alan Goodman:

> To understand why race is a biological myth requires an absolute paradigm shift in perspective. It's like seeing what it must have been like to understand that the world isn't flat. Perhaps I can invite you to a mountaintop and you can look out the window and at the horizon and see, "Oh, what I thought was flat I can see a curve in now," that the world is much more complicated. In fact, that race is not based on biology, but race is rather an idea that we ascribe to biology.[4]

RACE AND A CHRISTIAN GOD

The simplest way to understand the story of race is to read the 1967 American Supreme Court decision *Loving v. Virginia*. The case involved Mildred Loving, a dark-skinned woman of mixed African, Cherokee, and European descent, and her husband, Richard Loving, a light-skinned man exclusively of European descent, who were thrown in prison for marrying each other. They had violated Virginia's Racial Integrity Act, a legal policy that forbade marriage between humans the law classified as "white" and "colored."

Until very recently—1994 in South Africa and 2000 at Bob Jones University in the U.S., for example—such policies were the norm in societies and institutions colonized, settled, or influenced by humans of European descent. These policies classified "colored" as the many people we consider black and brown today, e.g., African; Native; East, Southeast, South, and West Asian; Middle Eastern; North African; Central Asian; mixed; Pacific Islanders; and Roma, among others.

The *Loving* decision overturned this legal policy in the United States, but it did not respond to the Virginia court judge Leon M. Bazile's reasoning for upholding this policy and declaring Mildred and Richard's marriage illegal.

> Almighty [Christian] God created the races white, black, yellow, malay, and red, and he placed them on separate continents . . . The fact that he separated the races shows that he did not intend for the races to mix.

These two sentences summarize the story of race. When I first read these lines, I had to reread them several times. Naturally, my mind asked, *What about me and the over 2 billion brown humans of South Asia?* Then I reflected on his attribution of race to his understanding of God.

I had been introduced to Christianity by my brown caretakers, Mary and Josephine, in India. They were Malayali Assyrian Christians and their ancestors adopted Christianity in the 1st century C.E. when Saint Thomas arrived in modern-day Kerala. Just for the record, this was 2,000 years ago, before Constantine's conversion to Christianity, before the Catholic Church was established in Rome, and many centuries before the ancestors of most humans who identify as white or black today adopted Christianity. Mary and Josephine taught me many things about the Christian faith, but nothing about race.

In my gut, when I read the Virginia law, I knew there was something fishy happening here. When I dug deeper, I learned that the law classified as *white* a person "who has no trace whatsoever of any blood other than Caucasian" and as *colored* anyone with any traceable African, Native, or Asian "blood," a policy popularly known as the "one-drop rule."

PRISM EXERCISE

Pause. Take three full breaths. Bring your attention to your somatic experience, recalling our shared agreements.

In the space below or in your journal, reflect on the phrase *purity of blood* to refer to a human's descent. What images, memories, concepts, or emotions accompany that phrase for you? With respect to of race, what do you think "purity" indicates?

Policies like Virginia's Racial Integrity Act didn't hide their bigotry. They defined *purity of blood* as the absence of human ancestry from non-Christian and non-European indigenous, African, and Asian cultures, communities, and nations. The notion of purity of blood goes to the core of the racial hierarchy. It makes humans with the intersectional identity of "white" (i.e., nontraceable Native, African, or Asian ancestry) *and* Christian religious beliefs the dominant in-group; those without that intersectional identity are the subordinated out-groups.

Perhaps surprisingly, this hierarchy plays out even among the subordinated, where the closer one is to the dominant white Christian ideal through one's descent, appearance, accent, mannerism, or religious beliefs, the more privileges and ease one experiences socially in comparison to subordinated groups who are farther from that ideal. For example, race plays out as appearance-based colorism in every ethnic community globally, regardless of color, whether Brazilian, Dominican, Nigerian, Punjabi, Korean, Jewish, or Filipino. And it plays out as religion-based Christian superiority in its treatment of humans who subscribe to animist, shamanistic, African, or Asian spiritual traditions, as well as the treatment of Jews, Muslims, and those who hold other religious beliefs in societies where Christianity is the dominant religion.

We now know the story of race has no scientific or even religious basis. We also know that most of the humans mentioned in the Bible would be considered black or brown by Bazile's own standards. So what I found most curious was that no one in my legal classroom, including my professor in the constitutional law course where we read this decision—the legal scholar Kenji Yoshino—corrected or refuted Bazile's false story.

After teaching the story of race to thousands of professionals for over a decade, I've come to realize that this is not because of malevolent intent or even a conscious belief in this story, but because outside of academics in anthropology, history, and sociology, very few of us are taught that this story came to infect our global consciousness through a very specific interpretation of Christianity and science. When I first pieced this story together as a law student, I kept asking how a made-up story that is less than 300 years old could so powerfully infect the human imagination globally. The answer lay in the very reason I went to law school: policies—the second root cause of bias—that violently disseminated, policed, and enforced this story and violently suppressed any alternatives.

Policies were and are the mechanism of control. They are drafted, defended, and enforced by certain humans and they shape the perceptions and regulate the behavior of all humans who come under their jurisdiction. Policies make the story of race a lived reality for billions of people globally. They define and enforce all aspects of human life based on how a human is racialized, from land ownership, housing, education, marriage, employment, and political office to freedom of movement, bodily autonomy, and religious liberties. Recall that policies are a *principle of action* that binds people and institutions together within a society for four purposes: *to establish standards, guarantee liberties and rights, maintain order,* and *resolve disputes.*

As we get into it, I want to acknowledge that race has caused and continues to cause horrific human tragedies, pain, and suffering globally. My own entry into this work was a result of the tremendous marginalization and pain I suffered based on the story of race. There is expansive scholarship on the atrocities humans have committed against other humans because of their belief in this story. My goal in this chapter is to give you enough context to understand the first two root causes of racial bias: the origins of the story that associates human descent and appearance in a hierarchy our minds perceive as race; and the way policies informed by that story have built a cultural container that programs the human mind with false concepts and *vedana* that make this fake story real.

THE FOUR PHASES OF RACE

The secondary identity that we understand as race was invented in the age of capitalist modernity. Never before in human history did humans place one another on a permanent descent- and appearance-based hierarchy. Before race, phenotype-based hierarchies were marked by how humans adorned their bodies—the types of clothes and jewels they wore, how they wore them, and facial or bodily markings, among other things, but not their skin color or appearance.

The word *race* arrived in the English language around 1580, 88 years after the Spanish conquest of the Americas began, 62 years after the Portuguese began transatlantic human trafficking, and more than 1,500 years after the historical Jesus. Etymologists do not definitively know the origins of *race*, but they suggest it came from the Old French word *rasse* or the Italian *razza*. An analogue to *type*, *sort*, or *kind*, race was meant to identify the group a human belonged to based on qualities that are easy to discern just by looking at someone. For example, it was first used in English literature in the Shakespearean era in reference to "the race of nobles" or "the race of bishops."

Race transitioned from a marker of outer difference into a hierarchical classification system of humans in four phases: (1) a **descent**-based purity of blood hierarchy; (2) an **appearance**-based caste hierarchy; (3) **a made-up story** that attributed the creation of race to God and science; and (4) a **codification** of this story by Western Christianity, science, and policies (see Figure 5.1 for a visual map of this evolution). Let's uncover each one of these four phases.

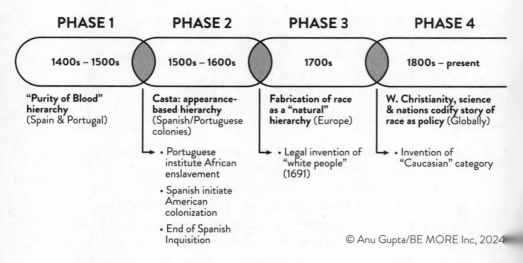

PHASE 1	PHASE 2	PHASE 3	PHASE 4
1400s – 1500s	1500s – 1600s	1700s	1800s – present
"Purity of Blood" hierarchy (Spain & Portugal)	Casta: appearance-based hierarchy (Spanish/Portuguese colonies)	Fabrication of race as a "natural" hierarchy (Europe)	W. Christianity, science & nations codify story of race as policy (Globally)
	• Portuguese institute African enslavement	• Legal invention of "white people" (1691)	• Invention of "Caucasian" category
	• Spanish initiate American colonization		
	• End of Spanish Inquisition		

© Anu Gupta/BE MORE Inc, 2024

Figure 5.1

1400s–1500s: Phase 1, Descent-Based Hierarchy

I encountered the concept of *limpieza de sangre*—a literal synonym for the "purity of blood" we talked about earlier in this chapter—in an undergraduate Islamic studies seminar called "Interreligious Encounters." The phrase was coined during the bloodbaths of the Spanish Inquisition that ended 700 years of Islamic rule on the Iberian Peninsula in 1492. Under Europe's exclusion paradigm—recall the Great Chain of Being (GCB)—humans across Spain or Portugal could no longer practice any faith other than Catholicism. As with animist and pagan traditions across Christian Europe, this left Iberian Jews and Muslims to be killed, to flee, or to convert to Catholicism, at least outwardly. Those who chose the latter path became known as New Christians—*conversos* if they had previously been Jews, and *Moriscos* if Muslims. By converting, New Christians were able to retain or grow their influence and power in business and the Church. To temper their influence and status, the Old Christians devised *limpieza de sangre*.[5]

The new Christian regimes of Spain and Portugal claimed that New Christians lacked true Christian "purity of blood" because of their "impure" ancestry. They adopted institutional policies that limited New Christians from accessing positions of power in the Church, government, education, and other institutions. They defined a New Christian as anyone who had a single Jewish or Muslim ancestor in the previous five generations—that's 32 great-great-great-grandparents! The authorities enforced this regime by issuing written "purity of blood" certificates to Old Christians to prove that particular human was not part of the inferior group.[6]

This was the first time in recorded human history that a regime adopted a policy that tracked with written records the ranking of humans' value based exclusively on their descent. Prior to this time, Christians, Hebrews, Egyptians, Muslims, Greeks, and even the *jati*-obsessed Hindus permitted out-groups to overcome their alleged inferiority by converting to the "superior" group through a process of assimilation over a period of time. The Greeks, for example, permitted the Berber peoples they conquered in North Africa (whom they pejoratively called *barbarians*) to speak, write, think, and live as Greeks.

With the "purity of blood" doctrine in place, however, the New Christians could not change their status. Their standing in the social hierarchy became hereditary and fixed, which the Lovings confronted in Virginia's "purity of blood" law five centuries later.

Policy of Human Trafficking, Land Theft, and Colonization

Before moving to the second phase, imagine the situation of Europeans in the medieval age. They found themselves in hierarchical and impoverished feudal kingdoms under the thumb of the Catholic Church and Church-backed corrupt monarchs who were, purportedly, divinely ordained. The ruling monarchs were constantly at war with one another for more land, power, and wealth. The masses were reared in cultures of fear, self-hatred, shame, and guilt and told that the Earth was flat. Anyone who didn't practice the official form of Christianity risked being killed for being a heathen, pagan, or savage.

Church officials and European monarchs didn't know about the faraway cultures and humans of the Americas, sub-Saharan Africa, Australia, or the Pacific Islands, but through their encounters with the Islamic world, they had heard of the riches of the Indies, or present-day South and Southeast Asia. But traveling to the Indies over land was tough. One had to safely traverse the difficult terrain, the numerous warring kingdoms of Europe, and the "infidel" Muslim territories of North Africa, the Middle East, and Central Asia. The greed for gold, wealth, land, and control of the spice trade of the Indies motivated European monarchs to commission explorers to get to the East by sea instead. Spanish and Portuguese explorers were the first known Europeans to successfully do so.

Starting in 1452, the pope instituted a policy through papal directives that granted the Portuguese, and later the Spanish, French, and other Christian monarchs, the right to "dominate" all territories that were not under Christian rule and to subjugate all non-Christian humans, whom they called "Saracens [Muslims] and infidels," for "perpetual servitude." These directives evolved into policies that European kingdoms and nations held for centuries, throughout modernity. These policies established the standards for (1) who was human, i.e., European Christians, and who was not, i.e., the remainder of humanity; (2) who could be enslaved and colonized (non-Christians); and (3) how European Christians held the right over non-European Christians to steal and "dominate" land.[7]

Once European nations began to enact policies based on this secondary identity-based standard, they reserved rights and liberties granted by their state only to those who were considered humans according to those standards. Anyone, including European Christians, who rebelled against this established order was met with terror and brutal force to maintain order. Those who sought justice through legal means generally lost their claims because the underlying mechanism for resolving disputes didn't acknowledge the humanity and legal standing of non-Christian Europeans.

These papal directives were incredibly powerful because they supplied European Christian monarchs, enraptured by exclusion consciousness, with a moral and religious justification for their ruthless plunder of humans and nonhuman beings. In particular, European monarchs used these directives to derive their national policies for three crucial actions over the course of modernity: human trafficking, land theft, and colonization.

Human trafficking: The Portuguese were the first to begin West African enslavement in 1453 and their descendants were the last to abolish it in 1888 in Brazil.[8] The Spanish, British, French, Dutch, and their white descendants across the Americas engaged in the brutality of African enslavement for the vast majority of capitalist modernity (more than 400 years) for the exclusive purpose of wealth creation and accumulation. At least 15 million humans from Africa were forcibly kidnapped, captured, and transported across the world, relegated to be property and a fixed capital line item on the accounting systems of European colonial enterprises.* Why? Because they were "infidels." The desire to profit from slavery

---

* Listen to historians Anita Anand and William Dalrymple's podcast *Empire: Slavery* for an abridged overview of the origins, brutality, and consequences of African enslavement.

and accumulate wealth through free labor required a story of race that would allow for even converted Christian Africans to remain the enslaved property or servants of European-descent humans. Non-African humans who were European colonial subjects in China, India, and Indonesia were also trafficked to serve as free labor in European colonies. The descendants of these enslaved and indentured humans remain scattered globally from Suriname, Guyana, and the Caribbean to Mauritius, South Africa, Réunion, and Fiji.

Land theft: The papal directives transmuted into a legal policy known as the Doctrine of Discovery. This doctrine justified European Christian kingdoms in stealing lands inhabited by animist, indigenous, and non-Christian humans, labeling them *terra nullius* or "nobody's land." The Portuguese and Spanish monarchs first used this policy to justify the colonization of West Africa, the Caribbean, the Americas, the Philippines, and other parts of the world, and the principle soon entered the legal policies of the remaining powers around the world. For example, the doctrine entered American jurisprudence in 1823 in the landmark *Johnson v. McIntosh* Supreme Court case that deemed indigenous humans incapable of owning land title because of their "savage ancestry."[9] This rationale evolved into policies allowing governments to dispossess hundreds of indigenous nations of lands they had stewarded for thousands of years and grant it instead to European Christian settlers across not only the Americas but Australia, South Africa, Algeria, New Zealand, and other parts of the world.

Colonization: In 1492, the year the Spanish Inquisition ended, Columbus and his crew landed on what they thought was India; in fact, it was the modern-day Bahamas and the Dominican Republic. Empowered by the papal policies, they proudly called themselves *conquistadores* and mislabeled the indigenous people *Indios*, or Indians, a name that has remained with those people to this day. Ferdinand Magellan reached and colonized the coveted spice islands in 1521, naming them the Philippines after King Philip II of Spain. Motivated by the greed for gold and land, the *conquistadores* introduced the bloodbaths of the Inquisition and Christian Europe across the Americas, Africa, the Philippines, and other places they resolved to colonize. In 1526, the Portuguese scaled their human trafficking business by establishing the transatlantic slave trade. The *conquistadores* justified the mass slaughter of indigenous peoples and African enslavement just as the treatment of non-Christians was justified in Europe: based on their inferior non-Christian "infidel" status, not on their race. *Race* was not yet a word and the story of race was not yet formed.

In the 17th century, other European powers joined Portugal and Spain in their global domination and empire-building projects by engaging in these three interdependent and interconnected actions. All of them placed the diverse humans they encountered into their GCB mental model, designating them heathens, pagans, and savages. I mention this not to justify what the European powers did, but to remind you of the state of their consciousness and how divorced they were from their own humanity and the humanity of those they dominated.

PRISM EXERCISE

Pause. Take three full breaths and return your awareness to your somatic experience.

Before you continue reading, take a few minutes to feel your body. Notice the sensations and their *vedana*. If you notice an active mind, see if you can move or shake to circulate energy from your head to your body.

Regardless of whether what you will read next in this chapter is familiar to you, it will trigger emotions, feelings, and possible discomfort. In those moments, I invite you to get out of your head and feel your body. If states like anger, sadness, or grief, or body reactions like tears, coughing, or a clenched jaw arise, acknowledge, feel, and release them with deep nourishing breaths. Then take a break and engage in a self-care activity that feels nourishing to your body, heart, and soul. You may also want to call on your support system.

1500s–1600s: Phase 2, Appearance-Based Hierarchy

As the *conquistadores* violently pushed as far as modern-day Colorado, Chile, and the Philippines, the Spanish pioneered the age of modernity's empire-building project by establishing New Spain. This was exclusion consciousness at work. The project's goal? Conquest of land and people for wealth and status to become the most powerful kingdom in the world by any and all means necessary, nominally in the name of Christianity.

You don't need to have a doctorate in the Christian faith to know its most basic ethical principles: thou shall not kill, thou shall not steal, and thou shall not be covetous. So how does one justify stealing land and spilling rivers of human (and nonhuman) blood? Calling humans "infidels" and "savages" will only go so far until the human consciousness hears the wails, sees the suffering, and feels the pain the unconscionable brutality is causing.

Thus, the exclusion consciousness covers its greed-driven ambitions for empire with an outwardly noble and selfless narrative of "civilizing the savage" and "saving their souls" by bringing them Christianity. Paraphrasing a famous quote from Kenyan leader Jomo Kenyatta, Desmond Tutu beautifully described this process as follows: "When the missionaries came to Africa, they had the Bible and we had the land. They said 'Let us pray.' We closed our eyes. When we opened them, we had the Bible and they had the land."

As the *conquistadores* built New Spain by slaughtering indigenous humans and trafficking humans from Africa, the missionaries arrived with the explicit objectives to entrench domination by colonizing the minds of the surviving indigenous and African humans under the guise of "saving their souls." In this early period of conquest, as more and more indigenous and African people succumbed to Spanish rule, new groups of Christians of mixed descent, who had likely never existed before, came into being.

In Spain and Portugal, Old and New Christians were virtually indistinguishable when it came to appearance. In New Spain, however, mixed people could be distinguished based on their appearance, such as their skin color, hair texture, and facial and other body features. This is how the Iberian Peninsula's *limpieza de sangre* became *casta*, or caste. Despite *caste's* association with India, which you learned about in Chapter 4, the word actually comes from the Spanish and Portuguese word *casta*, meaning "breed."

Through policies, the Spanish authorities fabricated and assigned humans to more than 40 castes based on descent and appearance, including *peninsulare, criollo, mulatto, mestizo, castizo, zambo, indio, negro,* and others, many of which exist to this day. These categories ranked people based on their purity of blood, i.e., how much Spanish Christian ancestry they had, which, because humans inherit their physical features from their ancestors, also manifested in their appearance.

As in their home countries, colonial Spanish authorities kept meticulous written records of each human's caste and, through policies, restricted the social, economic, cultural, and political privileges and rights of humans based on their caste. Simultaneously, these policies promulgated an appearance-based human hierarchy that valued light skin and European physical features and devalued darker skin and bodily features associated with African and indigenous humans. They made *caste* synonymous with color, descent, and appearance as well as class, a legacy that remains across the former Spanish and Portuguese colonies globally.

I bore witness to this caste system firsthand while studying abroad in Mexico as a college senior. I lived in Merida, a city that is 90 percent Mayan, where 100 percent of advertising used images of humans with light skin and European appearance. Today, two decades later, this legacy continues in Latin American and Latine diasporic media. Even my Mayan homestay family distinguished themselves as *cristianos*, i.e., civilized and educated, versus the *indios*, a pejorative slur in Mexican Spanish that means "savage" and "primitive."

To recap, in the 17th century, race as an idea is beginning to form based on "pure" Christian ancestry and European appearance, but it's not called *race* yet. In the Spanish and Portuguese colonies, it is called *caste*, and in other European colonies, the divide is still rooted in Christian versus non-Christian status.

1691: The Legal Invention of Whiteness

By the 1600s, after witnessing Spain's and Portugal's economic success, the English, Dutch, and French commissioned companies to start their own human-trafficking and land-stealing colonial enterprises to settle different parts of the world. Companies like the Dutch, French, and British East/West India Companies, the Royal African Company, the Hudson Bay Company, the Levant Company, and the Plymouth Company were set up with the deliberate plan to trade, traffic humans, steal land, and compete with Spain and Portugal in empire building. In their missions to settle and colonize faraway places, these companies took the most undesirable of their persecuted minorities, like the Puritans, Quakers, French Huguenots, criminals, and prisoners, who were willing to risk going to an unknown foreign place because they couldn't freely be who they were at home.

In 1607, the Virginia Company of London landed in the Americas to establish Jamestown in modern-day Virginia. The first enslaved African was brought to what is now the United States in 1619, one year before the Plymouth Company landed in Massachusetts. The establishment of English, Dutch, and French colonies in North America, the Caribbean, and other parts of the world sparked numerous wars with indigenous nations, akin to the Spanish conquest in the Americas.

Like the Spanish and the Portuguese, these European colonists were also invested in the GCB worldview and perceived the indigenous, African, and Asian people they encountered as heathens and savages. They too used Christianity—whether Catholicism or the newly emerging Protestant denominations—to justify land theft and genocide.

Unable to enslave large numbers of local indigenous humans, they trafficked humans from Africa to serve as free labor to build and grow their empires. In the process, they dominated African humans physically, emotionally, psychologically, and sexually. In the English colonies, the routine rape of African women introduced a group of mixed people, akin to the *casta* of mulattos in the

Spanish colonies. In 1656, less than 50 years after the English began settling in the American colonies, one of these mixed people, Elizabeth Key Grinsted, the daughter of an aristocratic Englishman and an enslaved African woman, used English law to win her freedom on the grounds that she was a baptized Christian. Winning one's "freedom," particularly as a woman, in a court like this, was rare; many people tried to do this but were blocked in various ways.

Within a few years after Grinsted won her freedom, the Spanish logic of purity of blood and appearance-based caste entered colonial English institutional policies. For example, Virginia passed numerous decrees restricting the freedom of anyone with any African ancestry, regardless of their appearance or religion. In 1676, an armed rebellion against the colonial authorities known as Bacon's Rebellion showed the English authorities the dangers of cooperation between Europeans and Africans.

The British colonial administrators began to see that the Spanish-style caste system would be insufficient for them to remain in power. In their view, as more African and indigenous humans adopted Christianity, they would be forced to share some power with mixed peoples, as had happened in many Spanish and Portuguese colonies. With this fear in mind, in 1691, Virginia passed a law that legally created a group of humans called *white people*, consisting of "pure Europeans," and prohibited them from intermixing with or marrying anyone with traceable African or indigenous ancestry. How did it define *traceable*? Through five generations, just as New Christians were defined in Spain. I am not making this up. I remember sitting at the NYU Law library reading this statute, being stupefied, and thinking, *Wow, humans operating from* wetiko *just imitate one another.*

This Virginia policy created, for the first time in recorded human history, a pan-European "white" identity. In New Spain, while the castes of *peninsulares* and *criollos* were also what we understand as white today, they weren't labeled *blancos/brancos* yet. The Spanish justified their superiority on the basis of their descent, i.e., the purity of their Spanish Catholic blood, and in the case of *peninsulares*, being born on the Iberian Peninsula. In the English colonies, however, diverse ethnic, religious, linguistic, and cultural groups such as the English, French, Dutch, Danes, and Scots, who were and remained enemies in Europe, were placed under a singular umbrella of "white" based on their descent and appearance in opposition to anyone with African or indigenous—and later Asian—ancestry.

This law became the basis for all other laws that conferred social, political, economic, and cultural rights exclusively upon these newly named "white" humans. Through numerous other legal policies, European-descent humans constructed a dominant "white" secondary identity, subordinating all others. These institutional policies became the prototype for our modern understanding of race. They birthed the descent- and appearance-based metric that would become the basis of race in the 1700s. Although white American colonists would throw out the British monarchists to form the United States within the next 80 years, the American nation builders would retain this tradition in their system of laws, and the English, Dutch, French, and other European nations would transport it globally to their empires across Canada, the Caribbean, Asia, Africa, Australia, New Zealand, and the Pacific Islands.

The Need for a Story of Race

By the early 1700s, a descent- and appearance-based social hierarchy was institutionalized across the European colonies. However, as Western Europe was ushered into Enlightenment thought through exposure to new ideas from indigenous, Islamic, and Asian cultures, Christianity alone could not justify the unspeakable horrors of enslavement, genocide, plunder, and pillage being committed in the name of God, not only against converted Christians, but against white people's own mixed-descent children. A story was needed to fill this gap.

PRISM EXERCISE

Pause. Take three full breaths and bring your attention to your body, staying mindful of our agreements.

I'm going to ask you to practice perspective-taking and imagine that you are one of the humans who coined the legal construct of "whiteness" and identified as "white." Imagine being in their body, heart, and mind. Imagine being in their experience as they humiliated, demeaned, beat, killed, raped, and even sold their own children into enslavement. Imagine being a human who drafted policies that incentivized rape, indemnified perpetrators, and permitted the sale of one's own children for profit.

What mind-states enable humans to commit such cruelty above the wails, cries, tears, and screams of fellow humans? Please take a moment to feel and document such heart-mind states in your body right now. Remember to breathe and feel your somatic experience.

I've contemplated this PRISM exercise for years after reading accounts of humans who undertook such actions. I have felt such mind-states in my body and imagined nothing short of a depraved heart. But the evidence reveals that this sort of depraved consciousness wasn't limited to people with pathological mental illnesses; it was actively encouraged by European and white American policies and administrators globally. In Australia, India, Kenya, Indonesia, South Africa, Cuba, or Peru, colonial policies set the stage for merciless pillage, rape, murder, and destruction of the other—and even one's own kin—in the interest of wealth. Such depraved acts are not only unimaginable in any Christian doctrine, but also deeply against our human mammalian biology. A narrative was needed to condition generations of newly minted, legally constructed white people to exercise such unimaginable forms of cruelty.

Against this backdrop, many of the same humans leading the scientific thought experiments of liberalism, free markets, property rights, and rationality in Europe also supplied the narrative needed for the horrors of African enslavement, land theft, genocide, theriocide, and global colonization. By the mid-18th century, many competing fictions supplied by various highly respected European men culminated in a singular story of race that remains intact in administrative and legal policies globally, as you read in the *Loving* decision.

The Western academy continues to honor these men as prolific scholars, but for me, unlike the indigenous and non-Christian humans they dominated and attempted to eliminate, these men exhibited each and every symptom of entitlement: narcissism, pride, and/or megalomania. I couldn't possibly list all of them, but they include men like Carl Linnaeus, Henri de Boulainvilliers, Petrus Camper, Georges-Louis Leclerc, Immanuel Kant, Johann Friedrich Blumenbach, Georges Cuvier, Samuel Morton, Louis Agassiz, and Francis Galton. You'll read some specifics about these men in the next section. Feel free to research any of them in combination with "race" to read more about their contributions to sustaining racial hierarchies.

In brief, they used the guise of science to craft a completely nonsensical story of race. They concretized the Spanish notions of "purity of blood" and caste as race globally. In the name of progress and "civilization," colonial policymakers worldwide used their story to justify the plundering of our planet and causing unimaginable suffering to humans and nonhumans globally. Worse, they attributed the fictions of their own depraved minds and *wetiko* consciousness to God and nature. Think of the story of race as a child of two parents: Western European Christianity and Western science.

Before we move to Phase 3, I want to acknowledge that this information *feels* heavy. I certainly felt angry, betrayed, disgusted, and even numb when I read what men like Walt Whitman, Ralph Waldo Emerson, Immanuel Kant, and Jean-Jacques Rousseau—men whose quotes are plastered across modern thought—thought about black, brown, non-Christian, and animist people.

PRISM EXERCISE

Pause. Take three full breaths.

I encourage you to return to our shared agreements and become mindful of your somatic experience. Take a few minutes to notice how this information is being received by your body, heart, and mind. Feel free to release any thoughts, emotions, and memories below or in your journal.

1700s: Phase 3, Racializing Humanity with the Story of Race

At this point, you have some idea of the story of race; recall Judge Bazile's *Loving* decision. In this section, I will share with you where these five made-up categories—black, white, yellow, red, and malay—came from, and how they came to infect our global consciousness, and why.

As we've seen, the Spanish, Portuguese, and later other Christian Europeans perceived the non-Christian humans of the Americas, Africa, and Asia through their GCB exclusion paradigm and its very specific biblical interpretation of the origins of humanity. Having been in a completely closed society for all of the medieval age, the GCB offered no explanation for how thousands of diverse cultures originated.

As a result, in learning about these cultures from the travelogs of *conquistadores* and missionaries, the wealthy Christian men of Europe landed on two made-up theories about the origins of black and brown non-Christian humans: the multiple origins or *polygenism* theory and the degeneration or *monogenism* theory. The polygenists believed that non-Christians were a different species of humans who didn't share their origins with Adam and Eve. They used this logic to conclude that these beings were beasts, monsters, and demons.

The monogenists claimed that all humans descended from Adam and Eve but that Christian Europeans like them were the original form of humans as God intended them to be. They saw the rest of humanity as a degeneration of the ideal human due to "climate differences." They claimed that lightness of skin, hair, and eye color made one divinely endowed with biological superiority. Mind you, as you know by now, all these self-proclaimed brilliant men were descendants of humans who, at some point, were animist, pagan, Jewish, or Muslim!

Yet, immersed in their own superiority, they argued that their ethnic group—Anglo-Saxon, Gaul (French), Swede, German, etc., depending on the ethnicity of the theorist—was the apex of "civilization"; all other humans must have degenerated from the perfection of their ancestors when they migrated to tropical and arctic climates globally. I remember reading about these bogus ideas in Stuart Ewen and Elizabeth Ewen's *Typecasting* and being absolutely shocked that our society continued to honor many of these entitled, narcissistic, and hateful men through monuments, universities, and ongoing scholarship. I felt so angry that I had never learned about this in grade school, that I was instead being asked to identify my race at registration. Well, it doesn't stop there.

In 1758, Swedish naturalist Carl Linnaeus, the person responsible for naming more than 4,400 species based on physical characteristics, including our own, *Homo sapiens*, published the 10th edition of *Systema Naturae (The System of Nature)*. In it, he named four *varieties* or *races* of humans based on location and physical features: European white, American reddish, Asian tawny, and African black. But he didn't stop there. He went on to assign aesthetic, moral, and intellectual stereotypes to each group as *inherent.* Hiding his exclusion consciousness and entitlement behind science by claiming to draft the "system of nature," these stereotypes, listed word for word in the table below, ascribed intrinsic superiority to white people and intrinsic pathologies to all the other people we understand as black and brown today.[10]

Human "Varieties" or Races According to Carl Linnaeus					
Human Varieties	Skin Color and Body Type	Body Description	Temperament	Manner of Clothing	Form of Government
Americanus	Red, choleric, and straight	Straight, black and thick hair; gaping nostrils; freckled face; beardless chin	Unyielding, cheerful, free	Paints himself in a maze of red lines	Governed by customary rights
Europaeus	White, sanguine, muscular	Plenty of yellow hair; blue eyes	Light, wise, inventor	Protected by tight clothing	Governed by law
Asiaticus	Sallow, melancholic, stiff	Blackish hair, dark eyes	Stern, haughty, greedy	Protected by loose garments	Governed by opinions
Africanus	Black, phlegmatic, lazy	Dark hair, with many twisting braids; silky skin; flat nose; swollen lips; women with elongated labia; breasts lactating profusely	Sly, sluggish, neglectful	Anoints himself with fat	Governed by caprice

Table 5.1

I want you to pay special attention to the way he described black people. Having likely never met or spoken to a black person, he reduced the thousands of diverse cultures, communities, and traditions of the huge continent that is Africa to negative adjectives. Even 15 years after I first came across this table, I still viscerally want to vomit reading his words that objectify the body parts of human beings, particularly black women.

This man is lauded as the father of the modern-day discipline of biology, but what he conceptualized was the common way wealthy European men thought, spoke, and wrote about black and brown people. Linnaeus's false and reductionist schemata of human races justified and immunized the horrendous acts of Europeans as natural under the laws of God and science. The founding fathers of America and all other nations colonized and settled by Europeans were influenced by these ideas.

Sadly, his simplistic framework has trickled across disciplines where even well-intentioned scholars and advocates use his schemata of white, black, yellow, and red humans as a way to unite humanity, even though race is a complete fiction and no human is actually the color yellow or red.* Linnaeus created a system that classified humans and connected our descent, physical features, ways of adorning our bodies, and ways of being with beauty, temperament, behavior, and intellectual capacities as science. Given his influence in the West, his false story was unquestioningly adopted and introduced into European sciences, policies, and culture at home and in their colonies globally. Remember when my parents encouraged me to get a nose job? Well, Linnaeus's designation is one of the origins of how the story of our biological features become *global* markers of beauty.

If you are a stickler for details, you're probably wondering why Linnaeus mentions only four categories; what about the fifth category—malay—that Bazile mentioned? Well, what Linnaeus created was only the draft for the story of race. It was revised by his devoted German student Johann F. Blumenbach a few decades later.

Inventing "Caucasians" and the
Story of Race Sold as Science

In 1790, in his international bestseller *On the Natural Varieties of Mankind*, Johann F. Blumenbach built on Linnaeus's distorted way of thinking by adding a fifth category of "Malays," completing the simplistic scheme that Bazile would list in the *Loving* decision 177 years later. There was nothing scientific about this addition, other than the fact that since Linnaeus's *System of Nature*, the Brits had come to know about and wreak havoc on more human cultures in

---

* For example, *The Seat of the Soul,* one of my favorite books by Gary Zukav, still uses outdated racial terminology like *negroids* and *mongoloids* in discussing humanity.

the Indian and Pacific Oceans, like those of Hawaii, Polynesia, Australia, and Micronesia. Blumenbach lumped the diverse humans of these regions into their own independent racial category of Malays. However, he didn't stop there either.

Blumenbach was a skull collector and he had a reputation across Europe for having the largest collection of human skulls. In total, he amassed 245 skulls from around the globe. Among these, he prized one particular skull—that of an enslaved woman who was from the Caucasus, the modern-day country of Georgia, sent to him by the Russian czar. Blumenbach called this skull the pinnacle of human perfection, possessing a symmetry and beauty that was simply and viscerally captivating.[11] Quick reminder: we are talking about a skull here!

From this most beautiful skull, using the folklore created by European intellectuals before him, he wove a fanciful tale about the origins of humanity, its noble roots, and its subsequent degeneration. He claimed the Caucasus were the starting point of humanity, the location where *Homo sapiens* first appeared in its pristine and perfect form. He anointed this skull with the "scientific" name of *Caucasian*, a term that continues to be used as the "scientific" name for white people. He claimed that Caucasians—all original Christian people with white skin like him—possessed "the most beautiful form of skull," which was a mark of their superior status among all humans. From this he fabricated the story of race and human hierarchy with five races that descend from the Caucasian ideal:

> All mankind . . . seems to me . . . divided into five varieties. . . . Caucasian, Mongolian, Ethiopian, American, and Malay. I have allotted the first place to the Caucasian . . . which make me esteem it the primeval one. This diverges in both directions into two, most remote and very different from each other; on the one side, namely, into the Ethiopian, and on the other into the Mongolian. The remaining two occupy the intermediate positions between that primeval one and these two extreme varieties; that is, the American between the Caucasian and Mongolian; the Malay between the same Caucasian and Ethiopian.[12]

In defining Caucasians, he gave the legal fiction of whiteness, created by English colonists a century before in 1691, a location-based origin, i.e., the Caucasus. He also excluded Europe's light-skinned Jews and non-Christians like the Sami and Roma people, whom he categorized as "uncouth Asiatics," but curiously included the dark-skinned people from the Middle East and North Africa. Why, you may ask? To ensure that Jesus, early Christians, the Greeks, and the Romans, the incubators of Western civilizations according to European thought, were white like him.[13]

Pseudoscientists after him would go on to scientifically create hierarchies within the "white race," i.e., Nordics, Alpines, and Mediterraneans based on location and physical appearance, stories that would enter the immigration policies and cultures of Europeans and their descendants in nations like the United States, Canada, and Australia.

These fantastic stories circumvented the possibility that any people other than a very particular type of "Caucasian" could achieve significant social, political, and cultural accomplishments, a sentiment that pervades the academy and public opinion globally to this day. The irony of this phenomenon is not lost on the olive-hued and very mixed humans who are actually from the region of the Caucasus.

1800s—Present: Phase 4, Christianity Codifies the Story of Race as Religion

In my experience in the Western academy, I have noticed that while most of the fabricators of the story of race are lauded as "scientists," the establishment rarely acknowledges their motivation for theorizing around human "races": to organize and understand God and the natural world through the hierarchical lens of the GCB. At least outwardly, they dedicated all of their scholarship to doing God's will. Until the 20th century, in the minds of most Europeans and their descendants, there was rarely a division between science and religion, and anyone who spoke up against the institutionalized Christianity was imprisoned or even killed for being a heretic.

So naturally the discoveries in Western science were also discoveries in Western European Christianity.

And this is how white missionaries and theologians, particularly in the colonizing nations, adapted the story of race into their biblical cosmology. In particular, they used the Curse of Ham to justify African enslavement. For those of you who don't know this story, here's how it goes: In a region that is likely ancient Iraq, Turkey, or the Levant (think: brown people), Ham saw his father, Noah, drunk and naked (possibly also masturbating), and scoffed at him. In response, Noah cursed Ham's son, Canaan, and his descendants to be ruined by slavery. Now, why Canaan was the one cursed when Ham was the one who saw Noah naked, or when Noah was the one who was drunk and naked in the first place, or why it is such a big deal to see another person drunk and naked, is not clear. But regardless of who did what to whom, the question I ask is, How did this curse become connected to skin color and the incredibly diverse peoples of the African continent?

The story of race! European Christian theologians who profited from African enslavement applied the story of race to the curse of Ham, claiming that all Africans (and other people with dark skin) are Canaan's descendants. They attributed their dark skin to a form of "degeneration" from the "pure" white skin of the fictional Caucasian people. This biblical reinterpretation of the story of race was used to enslave and then exclude black people from civil society across the Americas and European colonies globally.

Scholars of race have repeatedly indicated that the use of the word *race* in translating biblical passages is a mistranslation of the original texts in Aramaic, Greek, and Hebrew.[14] These texts rarely describe people by their skin color. The idea of black or white people or five human races did not exist in biblical times. In fact, recall that *race* as a word didn't even exist until the 1580s. For all we know, every one of the biblical characters, including Jesus, had brown skin like the people of the Middle East today.

Yet this enterprising and false interpretation of the Curse of Ham was globalized through Catholic and Protestant missionaries and church policies that for generations taught black and brown people about their inherent descent-based inferiority because of Ham's apparent "sin" thousands of years ago. The 1895 painting *Ham's Redemption* by white Spanish-Brazilian eugenicist Modesto Brocos is a classic example. This racially biased painting shows an Afro-Brazilian woman with dark skin expressing her gratitude to God for a grandchild with light skin as a lifting of the Curse of Ham. Such narratives and stories were used as propaganda in support of "whitification" or *blanquimiento/branqueamiento* policies across Latin America from the 19th to the mid-20th centuries. Such visual representations taught the story of race as science and religion and justified race-based subordination and hierarchy, including segregated Christian worship, globally.

More recently, my friend Sherry shared a haunting story with me. I met Sherry after participating in Oprah Winfrey's eight-episode special with Isabel Wilkerson on her book *Caste: The Origins of Our Discontents.* Our shared interest in pop culture, spirituality, and racial healing made us quick friends. In one of our conversations, Sherry shared her struggle in supporting Ruth, a devoted Christian friend of hers. Ruth often expressed to Sherry how she hated herself because of the Curse of Ham. This is internalized bias in action. Ruth's mind has been programmed with a false story. The concepts and *vedana* of this false story have become the lens through which she views herself and other black people. While it is easy for Sherry and me to know this intellectually, this experience remains *real*, even if not true, for Ruth and millions like her globally.

The story of race continues to be used by missionaries of all colors to "convert" and colonize the hearts and minds of millions of indigenous and non-Christians globally by teaching them self-loathing and hatred for themselves and their own ancestors. Scholar Audrey Smedley, after decades of careful research, determined that "the Bible played no role initially in the construction of racial inequalities . . . it's people who have misused and misinterpreted the Bible to justify one way or another their racism."[15]

For me, the Bible is a source of wisdom that can be applied for different purposes. In the hands of bridge-builders like the Rev. Dr. Martin Luther King, Jr., Dietrich Bonhoeffer, Thomas Merton, the

Rev. Dr. Jacqui Lewis, the Rev. Dr. William Barber II, Sister Simone Campbell, and countless others, it spreads the promises of inclusion consciousness: compassion, generosity, and love toward all beings. In the hands of segregationists like Judge Bazile and Modesto Brocos, it is used to justify separation, selfishness, entitlement, and hatred through enslavement, land theft, genocide, colonization, and forced assimilation.

Western Scientists Codify the Story of Race as Science

After the completion of the Human Genome Project in 2000, President Bill Clinton famously remarked, "We are all, regardless of race, genetically 99.9 percent the same . . . Modern science has confirmed what ancient faiths have always taught: the most important fact of life is our common humanity."[16]

PRISM EXERCISE

Pause. Take three full breaths and return your awareness to your somatic experience.

Before proceeding, I'd like you to reflect on *why* modern science was needed to confirm this ancient truth. Close your eyes and ask yourself why scientists and governments spent billions of dollars, time, resources, and energy over decades to confirm what humans have known for millennia. Trust what arises for you and document it below or in your journal.

My mind continues to ask similar questions whenever science "proves" some of the most commonsense truths: the negative mental health effects of police violence on black people; the prevalence of higher rates of diseases among black and brown people due to presence of toxic waste sites in their neighborhoods; the high rates of addiction, obesity, poverty, and suicide among indigenous people across North America, Australia, and elsewhere due to genocide, forced displacement, and assimilation policies that separated people from their ancestral lands, families, communities, spiritual traditions, and languages for generations. I don't know about you, but to me, all these correlations and/or causations are common sense.

For example, if someone burns my home, forcibly removes me from my ancestral land, separates me from my family, beats me, tells me I am ugly and stupid, forbids me to use my language, bans my spiritual practices, and force-feeds me commodity foods*—as has been the case for many indigenous humans—of course it's going to impact my physical, mental, and spiritual health! So why do scientists, whether they are in the natural or social sciences, need to spend an inordinate amount of their time, effort, and resources in writing about what's most obvious instead of putting those same efforts toward alleviating the suffering? I ask this as a rhetorical question, because for more than a decade, I have been one of those scientists. As I mentioned in Chapter 3, this is the Western scientific paradigm, and when it comes to our humanity, its foundations are entrenched in the story of race. Let me explain.

Remember Blumenbach, the skull collector who fabricated the story of race and sold it as science? Well, in order for a sale to be successful, there have to be buyers. And there were millions of buyers of Blumenbach's story among European descendants. Over the next century, Blumenbach's "natural" varieties of man became the foundation of numerous scientific disciplines such as craniology, physiognomy, physical anthropology, phrenology, eugenics, and genetics that claimed to further "prove" the hierarchy of race based on the "inherent tendencies" of black and brown people. Studying "savages and primitives" became an industry.[17]

In their deeply entrenched classist European societies, these mostly wealthy Christian white men wasted millions of hours

---

* These are the canned and highly processed foods the U.S. Department of Agriculture distributes on indigenous reservations, which are historically responsible for numerous disparities in health and nutrition outcomes in impoverished Native communities.

administering thousands of horrifying experiments breaking apart black and brown bodies, measuring our brains, ears, noses, hearts, genitals, and interior organs to try to find the single cause of our inferiority. Of course, they didn't find anything, because there isn't anything to find! The problem has always been in their minds—in their belief that they are somehow superior to all others and have dominion over all of creation. Yet, in this process, they entrenched the narrative of race and built a body of "scientific" evidence that continues to build upon the falsehoods of previous research, all to prove their own superiority as the "master race."

For generations, colleges and universities taught the story of race as natural; the scientific establishment confirmed it; clergymen preached it; tycoons like John D. Rockefeller, Andrew Carnegie, and Henry Ford funded it; and even conservationists and American social reformers like Margaret Sanger, Madison Grant, Helen Keller, and Teddy Roosevelt championed it.

This tradition continues into contemporary times with misguided scientists trying to identify the single gene, neurotransmitter, or cultural element in black and brown humans that makes us more susceptible to disease or poverty. When I was developing the PRISM Toolkit with funding from the U.S. National Science Foundation, I discovered hundreds of millions of dollars of flawed government-funded research that stands on the false premises of "purity of blood" and the one-drop rule. Even some of the most celebrated scientists are not immune to defending the story of race. In 2007, James Watson, one of the scientists who discovered DNA's double helix, expressed that he is "inherently gloomy about the prospect of Africa" because "all our social policies are based on the fact that their intelligence is the same as ours [i.e., white people]—whereas all the testing says not really."[18]

This legacy equally influenced Western social sciences, arts, and humanities, and it is premised on the false assumption that Western *civilization* is the superior evolution of humanity. In 2016, philosophy professors Jay L. Garfield and Bryan W. Van Norden wrote a *New York Times* op-ed arguing that philosophy departments ought to include African, Asian, Islamic, Jewish, and Native philosophical traditions in their curricula or rebrand themselves as European and American philosophy departments.[19] In response, they received tremendous backlash from countless classicists, philosophy enthusiasts, and online trolls who refuted their plea with two counterarguments: (1) no other human culture has a history of "civilization" that is worthy of study, and (2) Western civilization is the best.

The epistemology and knowledge production of European colonial enterprise in the 19th and 20th centuries was so all-encompassing that when it comes to how we perceive ourselves and other humans, no modern discipline is untouched. This is why the Human Genome Project had to make a statement that race has no genetic basis because, as we'll learn in the chapters on education and the media, academia and the global education system are entrenched in Eurocentrism and the story of race that has trained our brains to perceive race—and many of its accompanying stereotypes that Linnaeus first sold as science—as biological, genetic, and natural.

Beneath the logic of all racial science is what social psychologists call *confirmation bias*, or searching for evidence that supports previously held beliefs and stereotypes. John Sender, my economics professor at Cambridge, had a better phrase for it: "Garbage in, garbage out."

Western Nations Codify the Story of Race as Policy

Modern democracy and nation-states were birthed after Linnaeus drafted of the story of race: the first French republic and the American democracy were established between 1788 and 1792. Thomas Jefferson, in his *Notes on the State of Virginia*, expressed his views about the "natural" inferiority of black humans and the savagery of indigenous humans, ideas advanced by Linnaeus that justified the brutal policies of slavery and genocide.

Against this backdrop, Blumenbach finalized the story of race by inventing the superior "Caucasian" category, providing the legal fiction of "whiteness" a scientific backing. Immediately, the story of race was codified into the policies of every nation ruled or colonized by Europeans—in other words, our entire planet—and whiteness became the established standard for humanity.

In one of my first antiracism trainings in the 2000s, Margery Freeman, an ardent antiracist educator, brought this fact home for me: race is not about being black or brown, but about being as close as possible to this idealized, made-up fiction of whiteness. From the late 18th century onward, as the newly minted "white" thinkers put forth ideas for new political systems to address human equality and well-being, they restricted the application of those systems exclusively to "white" people, i.e., pure European Christians without any traceable Native, African, or Asian ancestry.

For example, the American Naturalization Act of 1790 restricted American citizenship exclusively to "free white person[s]," a policy that more or less remained on the books until 1965.* The French adopted a similar policy of *Français de souche*, "purebred French," when they began settlement of Algeria in the 1830s. The British, Dutch, Belgians, and policymakers from other European nations codified the story of race for citizenship in their settlement and colonization of societies globally, from Canada to South Africa to Australia. The story of race also replaced the lexicon of *casta* across the Spanish- and Portuguese-dominated world. Until the mid- to late 20th century, whether a human was in Australia, Argentina, Canada, Zimbabwe, Kenya, Cambodia, Algeria, or India, fitting the definition of whiteness became the prerequisite to enjoy the political, social, economic, and cultural rights and liberties guaranteed by all emerging Western political systems and to be protected by their laws.

Take a minute to understand the application of these rights and liberties in Table 5.2 below.

---

* *See* Haney López's excellent book *White by Law*.

The Four Types of Rights & Liberties Guaranteed by Policies	
POLITICAL rights and liberties: protect human participation and engagement in political processes and decision-making. They include: * the ability to vote * freedom of speech * freedom of assembly * freedom of movement * freedom of association * freedom to run for office	**SOCIAL** rights and liberties: promote social welfare, reduce inequalities by providing equal opportunities, and ensure access to essential social services necessary for a decent quality of life. They include access to: * food * clean water and air * education * health care * housing * sanitation
ECONOMIC rights and liberties: ensure equal opportunities to participate in and benefit from economic activities, to enjoy a fulfilling standard of living, and to be free from economic deprivation and discrimination. They include access to: * work and employment opportunities * fair wages * safe working conditions * protection from physical, mental, emotional, or sexual exploitation * social security	**CULTURAL** rights and liberties: protect and celebrate diversity, and the freedom to preserve, practice, and enjoy one's cultural, spiritual, and religious identity, language, and heritage. They include the ability to: * participate in one's cultural and religious activities * freedom to access and enjoy one's heritage * protection of one's heritage from discrimination, exclusion, and violence

Table 5.2

In this policy environment, many of the rights and freedoms people take for granted today, such as voting, speech, assembly, political participation, education, health care, social services, employment, fair wages, safe working conditions, food, water, and the ability to practice cultural traditions, language, and spirituality were by law only available to white Christians of European descent. This did not change until the era of the civil rights and global freedom movements from the 1950s to the 1990s, and it still has not changed for humans living in zones of conflict, war, or under authoritarian regimes, as well as humans with subordinated identities in democracies.

In 1937, British prime minister Winston Churchill justified the British forced removal policy of Arab-descent Christian, Muslim,

Druze, and Bedouin Palestinians from their ancestral lands with the following words:

> I do not admit . . . that a great wrong has been done to the red Indians of America or the black people of Australia. I do not admit that a wrong has been done to these people by the fact that a stronger race, a higher-grade race, a more worldly wise race to put it that way, has come in and taken their place.[20]

These words exemplify the standard of humanity undergirding policies that came to regulate and define humanity in the age of capitalist modernity. Resmaa Menakem refers to this policy environment that spread globally over 500 years as humanity's socio-political and psychological training in *white Christian body supremacy*, i.e., the intersectional identities of white Christian humans that are the human ideal.[21]

The way policies institutionalized the hierarchy of race in different societies and nation-states depended on the self-aggrandizing narrative of the European nation that colonized and controlled them: Spain, Portugal, Britain, France, the Netherlands, Denmark, Italy, Belgium, Germany, the United States, or Japan. Think of these colonizing nations as the control centers that designed a unique brand of hardware and software for racial bias using administrative policies and violence.

PRISM EXERCISE

Pause. Take three full breaths and feel your body. Perhaps go for a walk, stretch, or do yoga before returning to the next exercise.

Imagine being in the shoes of the male humans in the societies listed below in the 1920s. For each identity, reflect on how the standard of whiteness affected your political, social, economic, and cultural rights and life experiences in your society. Feel free to add any other intersectional identities without changing the "racial" identity. Last, research using a search engine of your choice how you may have experienced life in these places at that time. I hope that by doing this exercise you'll begin to appreciate the all-encompassing nature of racism and how policies constricted and restricted the ability of anyone but a specific kind of human to *be*.

* I am African American in Mississippi

* I am Maori in New Zealand

* I am Berber in French Algeria

* I am Bengali in British India

* I am Zulu in South Africa

* I am Javanese in Dutch Indonesia

* I am Quechua in Peru

* I am Anishinaabe in British Canada

* I am Chinese in California

For years, I was astonished at how the story of race could infect the human consciousness in just a few centuries of history. In 2012, during a stay on the White Earth reservation in Minnesota, I posed this question to scholar and activist Winona LaDuke and her Anishinaabe family. One elder plainly said: colonization of our minds with lies and state-sanctioned terror and cruelty. In one sentence, she captured the history of modernity.

There you have it. This is how the story of race, a descent- and appearance-based human hierarchy, became a "natural" part of human existence under the guise of religious, scientific, and legal policies. The impact of this story is so far-reaching that most of us don't even question it. As anthropologist Alan Goodman put it, it's like believing the Earth is flat when in fact it is a sphere.

PRISM EXERCISE

Pause. Take three full breaths and return to your body.

Investigate internally why, despite nondiscrimination policies and decades of noble efforts for equity, racial inequality, injustice, and colorism persist in your society or industry. Take a few moments to write your thoughts below or in your journal.

1970s—Present: Race in the Era of Inclusion Consciousness

In this chapter, I gave you a 500-year tour of the first two root causes of racial bias: a fictional story and principles of actions (i.e., policies) based on that story. Thankfully, in the last seven decades, humans globally have succeeded in repealing and changing many such policies. Despite policy changes, however, race-based inequity and injustice persist in every nation because the underlying mental model rooted in the false story of race remains intact in the hearts and minds of humans making decisions across our societies. This is because despite policy changes, culture remains intact in institutions and systems that were set up by white colonial powers.

I witnessed this firsthand while working in the criminal justice and health care systems in the United States, where I came into contact with judges, prosecutors, doctors, nurses, and other operatives who respected racial equality as enshrined in the law, but still held abhorrent and false beliefs about black, brown, and indigenous humans. While religious, scientific, and government institutions have changed their policies, the people who enforce such policies continue to harbor the views stemming from the story of race.

I have witnessed similar views from black, brown, and indigenous humans toward one another and even toward members of their own groups in places as diverse as Mexico, Morocco, India, and Singapore. It is the daily micro-decisions of these humans when multiplied over a lifetime and aggregated across institutions and systems that create race-based inequity, harm, and suffering. Dr. Bonnie Duran, the indigenous public health expert I mentioned in the Introduction, calls this phenomenon the neuro-colonization of our hearts and minds with the idea of race.

This is why, despite being perceived as a scourge globally, white-supremacist and race-based violence is on the rise across Western societies. Similar violence persists in the global south in racial animosities based in color, religion, or ethnicity that were seeded by European powers during the era of colonialism, such as the conflicts in Rwanda, East Timor, the Levant, and beyond. In the age of disinformation, these conflicts are being fueled further by opportunistic humans so they, in the words of Carl Sagan, can "become the momentary masters of a fraction of a dot," creating a lose-lose environment of dog whistle and drained pool politics and an absence of kindness.

For me, the time has thus come for us to discard the story of race and replace it with stories that dignify all human and non-human beings. This is our work together as we continue on our breaking bias journey.

PRISM PRACTICES

Pause. Take three breaths and bring your attention to observe your somatic experience.

* Become mindful of the stereotypes about different racial or ethnic groups that you learned while growing up from your loved ones, friends, education, media, and religious or scientific training, if any. Reflect on ways the humans in these five categories

were shaped by the social, economic, cultural, or political policies of their surroundings. Identify at least one counterexample to each of the stereotypes you've brought to mind. Moving forward, when you notice a stereotype arising in your mind, replace it with real-life counterexamples.

* Investigate with curiosity the ways in which the stereotypes created by the story of race influence your relationship with yourself. In what ways does it manifest as entitlement, victimization, undercompensation, overcompensation, self-doubt, grandiosity, narcissism, or another afflictive emotion associated with the comparing mind? Notice and feel the underlying *vedana* connected with your sensations, stories, memories, and ideas.

* Recall an instance from your life when racial stereotypes influenced your thoughts, words, or actions toward another human in an interpersonal situation. List the stereotypes you consciously or unconsciously believed in that moment that influenced your perceptions and actions. With mindfulness, breathe, observe, and feel the emotions and sensations that arise as you reflect on this experience. Then, practice loving-kindness toward yourself, the harmed human, mentally practice forgiveness for yourself, and mentally seek forgiveness from the harmed human.

* Reflect on a decision you've made in a professional or personal setting that was tinged with racial stereotypes. List the stereotypes you consciously or unconsciously believed in that moment that influenced your decision-making. Imagine the ripple effect of your decision on the lives of humans impacted by this decision. Visualize these humans. With mindfulness, breathe, observe, and feel the emotions and sensations that arise in your experience as you reflect on this experience. Investigate what actions you can take today to repair the harm.

* Take 10 minutes to complete the following exercise. Visualize being in the shoes of a black or brown human you know (who's not you, if you are one). Imagine what it's like to be this human. Reflect on ways the story of race may impact their society's policies; their experience as a human; their thoughts, words, and deeds toward themselves and others. What experiential identities may they hold as a result of their subordination? Breathe and stay with these sensations as they arise. End the exercise by extending your loving-kindness phrases toward this human and all humans who share this identity with them.

* Imagine you are in a world without racial bias and racial hierarchies. Using words, images, or any other means, visualize and describe what this world looks like. What does it feel like? How do you feel mentally, emotionally, and physically? What do you do with your time? With your energy? With your creativity? What about those you love? How do they spend their time? Let your imagination run wild. There is no right or wrong way to imagine. Just imagine.

GENDER

Emotional neglect lays the groundwork for the emotional numbing that helps boys feel better about being cut off. . . . Patriarchy both creates the rage in boys and then contains it for later use, making it a resource to exploit later on as boys become men. As a national product, this rage can be garnered to further imperialism, hatred and oppression of women and men globally. This rage is needed if boys are to become men willing to travel around the world to fight wars without ever demanding that other ways of solving conflict can be found.

— BELL HOOKS

If you've made it this far, I want to first thank you for your patience. I am sure there were dozens of places where you thought, *What about gender?* We've waited this long because gender is a *very* complex identity and I approach breaking gender bias after my students have an in-depth understanding of identity, bias, and race. This is because, unlike race, the origins of gender are not so clear and go back at least all of recorded human history, i.e., 5,000 years.

My inquiry into gender began a few months after my family immigrated to New York when I met my classmate Rosa. Like me, Rosa was a recent immigrant, but from Colombia. She was thin, almost a foot shorter than I was, with an irascible tongue. She used to tease and pick on me, probably to deflect attention from herself. Given her size, and, more important, the fact that she was a girl, my mind always thought of her as harmless. One day she dared me to arm wrestle. My tween mind went into it confidently, ready to defeat this annoying opponent, until her bony arm pinned my right hand to the table. The somatic experience of losing this simple game, especially to someone my mind imagined as a *girl*, and a bony, scrawny one at that, threw my young worldview into a tailspin.

Raised in an Indian patriarchal culture, I had unquestioningly learned that there were two genders, boys and girls; that boys were stronger, smarter, and more valuable than girls; and that this was just the way it was. Until that day, I hadn't even questioned these learned ideas, but losing to Rosa piqued my interest.

Gender as a secondary identity forms the infrastructure of human relations across cultures and societies. It's one of the first identities we notice about another human. It dictates how we view ourselves; how we expect others to view us; what roles and functions we play in our various social environments; how we speak, walk, carry, and adorn our bodies; and numerous other aspects of our human beingness and doingness. I'd like you to take a few moments to reflect on the meaning of *gender* for you.

Gender is:

As we dig in, I want to start by stating that I am a human in a queer male body and that I feel and mostly identify as a cis man. Over four decades of my life, I have witnessed, experienced, enacted, and performed gender differently in various heteronormative and queer contexts, from my native India and the diasporic South Asian communities of many ethnoreligious backgrounds to Western democracies like the United States and the United Kingdom, as well as Islamic, Hindu, Buddhist, Christian, East and Southeast Asian, and indigenous spaces. My lived experiences of gender are unique and they inform my understanding of the first two causes of gender bias.* The same is likely true of you. With that in mind, your understanding of gender likely spans one or more of the following three responses.

---

* If what I describe in this chapter does not match your embodied experiences, particularly if you're from a subordinated gendered identity, i.e., a woman or a human on the gender and sexuality spectrum, I request that you be curious with me, but ultimately trust the experiences of your body, heart, and soul.

First, gender is a social construct. In other words, it is a story that humans made up and shared with others as if it were true. Unlike the singular story of race, however, there are multiple stories of gender that vary across cultures, regions, and societies. As a result, I see gender as a layering of multiple stories. In modernity, the meta-story of binary gender—with the dominance of cis hetero males and subordination of cis hetero females, and the exclusion of all others—was layered on top of culture- and region-specific stories of gender globally. Today, most humans experience this meta-story internally and externally alongside preexisting gender stories based on context, space, and place. In addition, in the era of inclusion consciousness, humans are layering new stories of gender into the mix, such as being nonbinary or genderqueer, among others.

Second, all stories of gender are based on a human's three biological identities—sex, gender identity, and sexual orientation—and on other secondary identities, most prominently race, ethnicity, class, and religion, but also disability and age, among others. For example, in Latin America, the gendered experience of cis humans varies based on whether one is Christian, non-Christian, indigenous, black, white, mestize, mulatte, or Asian of a particular class background. In her scholarship, bell hooks often reminded readers that the experiences of gender are not the same for all individuals. The intersection of gender with race, class, and sexuality adds layers of complexity and shapes our lived realities.[1]

Third, gender assigns, coerces, empowers, expects, and/or forbids humans to perform specific **social roles** derived from a human's sex, gender identity, sexual orientation, and other intersectional social identities. For most of human history, these roles and functions differed based on cultural contexts, spaces, and places, but they were standardized globally in modernity. In the era of inclusion consciousness, humans have and are organizing to shift and transform these roles.

Based on these three elements, I define *gender* as "a layering of stories that assign and expect humans to perform specific social roles based on the intersection of sex, gender identity, sexuality, and other secondary identities within families, institutions, and societies."

You'll notice that I don't include the word *hierarchy* in the definition of *gender*. This is not to absolve or ignore the tremendous harm that cis men in particular have inflicted and continue to inflict on women, queer, and gender-diverse humans; it's because gender by itself is not a hierarchy. To me, the biological basis of what we call gender *is*. Each human is born either with a womb or without a womb; they are born with a combination of X and Y chromosomes, sexual and romantic desires, and an inner sense of gender identity based on the interplay of intrinsic temperaments and energies that cultures have labeled as masculine and feminine.

Many humans in varying cultural contexts feel absolutely at peace with the roles and expectations their gender places on them. Some examples of this are the roles many nonbinary and queer humans have historically played and continue to play as religious and spiritual healers in animist cultures, and the role of mother or father played by women and men, respectively, in most human cultures. All these roles are what they are. There is no hierarchy intrinsic to them. Gender is made into a hierarchy through patriarchy.

PATRIARCHY, MISOGYNY, AND THE GENDER HIERARCHY

As you can imagine, patriarchy is a vast and complex topic. In simple terms, I have found it to have three features. First, it is steeped in systems and institutions based on a story or stories of gender that claim a particular type of man, specifically cis and hetero, is superior to women, queer, and gender-diverse humans. It is also steeped in *misogyny*, a deep-seated hatred, contempt, sexual objectification, and distrust of women and feminine energies.

Second, patriarchy assigns rigid gender roles and expectations to humans based on the intersection of their three biological and additional social identities, creating a hierarchy of humans, with cis hetero men of certain social identities (wealthy, dominant racial, ethnic, religious group, etc.) on top. These policies aim to control female bodies and sexuality, often permitting and immunizing their sexual and physical exploitation; they expect humans of all genders to perform particular social roles usually within the gender binary; they restrict many humans from loving who their bodies want to love; and they control the familial and professional pursuits of humans of all genders.

Third, patriarchy across cultures is enforced by policy and culturally sanctioned physical, emotional, psychological, and sexual violence, terror, cruelty, and discrimination toward females and all genders, including cis hetero men, who question or desire to reform it. In modernity, human cultures globally are shaped by various systems of patriarchy that train everyone within those cultures in gender bias via the avenues we'll discuss in Part III.

Recall that bias is learned false beliefs or habits of thoughts that distort how we perceive, reason, remember, and make decisions. Gender bias manifests as those learned beliefs or habits, and it affects every human, including women, queer, and gender-diverse humans, as well as cis hetero men who rebel against traditional gender roles and expectations and those who uphold them. To me, *gender bias* is the umbrella phrase for sexism (bias toward women and men who breach gender roles), homophobia (bias toward queer humans), and transphobia (bias toward trans, nonbinary, and gender-diverse humans).

As you can imagine, the roots of gender-based biases are many and complex. I could not possibly describe (or even know) the myriad ways humans have imagined and enacted gender across cultures. Throughout most of human prehistory and history, we have evidence from many indigenous cultures that human genders varied beyond the man/woman binary.[2]

The gender binary, rooted exclusively in human anatomy and body parts (i.e., biological sex), was globalized in modernity through policies, and it remains the dominant way that humans relate to one another. What I will present to you in this chapter is one way of understanding how humans enact and experience gender bias. As we delve deeper, I'd like to use the wise words of our elder Gloria Steinem as our guide:

While gender can be a source of inequality and oppression, it can also serve as a source of identity, connection, and empowerment when recognized and celebrated in all its forms.[3]

This is the tension that the layered stories of gender create in our lives. I hope that our exploration in this chapter will enable you to recognize and celebrate the *is-ness* of gender within yourself and across the human gender spectrum.

FEMININE AND MASCULINE: THE *IS-NESS* OF GENDER

I spent my childhood in northern India with an absolutely doting grandmother whom I called Amma. As in many Indian families, my father's parents lived with us, and I remember spending hours with Amma playing card games, learning about Hindu deities, and eating delicious Indian sweets. From the time I was young, Amma made me feel that I was extra-special. She would say, "Your sisters will go away to their real homes after getting married, but you will forever be mine." This differential treatment of girls based on a marriage to a member of the opposite gender decades away was the reason why I, a boy, came first.

This narrative was ubiquitous in my surroundings in subtle and overt ways. The men in the family were served and ate their meals before the women. Men would work only outside the home. If the women worked outside, as my surgeon mother did, they were expected to work inside the home as well, while men were forbidden from doing housework or anything else perceived as feminine.

One day when I was six, we were holding a social gathering at our house and a famous Hindi song came on the television. I started dancing freely to it, imitating the moves of Karishma Kapoor, a well-known Bollywood actress. Witnessing my antics, Amma rebuked me harshly in front of all our guests. Not only that, she took me aside and made me promise that I would *never* dance "like a girl" ever again while she was alive because that was feminine and "you are supposed to be masculine." And I did not dance freely like that until after her passing 25 years later.

PRISM EXERCISE

Pause. Take three full breaths and bring your awareness to your somatic experience.

Take a few more breaths and recount your earliest memories of gender. How are they related to notions of masculine and feminine? Boy and girl? What are some concepts, emotions, and *vedana* attached to these concepts? Record your reflections below or in your journal.

I'd like you to keep these memories at the forefront as you proceed through the chapter. Add to them as more memories and stories emerge, always tracking your somatic experience.

Returning to my Amma, the same woman who forbade me from being feminine also taught me many Hindu creation stories. In one story, an all-pervasive, non-dualistic, genderless, singular energy known as Brahman, whom many traditions call God, Allah, Ahura Mazda, Consciousness, the Tao, or the Great Mystery, manifests in the complementary and oppositional duality of mind and matter or spirit and nature. Through this split arose feminine and masculine energies that together form the Divine. My grandmother explained that every animate being is a blend of these two energies, which she termed *Shiva and Shakti* or *Radha and Krishna*. Neither is better or worse. They both inter-are.

Most ancient wisdom traditions that are rooted in inclusion consciousness share a similar essence. For example, the Taoist interdependent forces of yin and yang and the concepts of the Divine Feminine, i.e., Shekinah, the Sacred Feminine, and *Umm-al Kitab* ("Mother of the Book") in the mystical Jewish, Christian, and Islamic traditions, as well as all animist traditions I have encountered, including the Hawaiian, Navajo, Yoruba, Zulu, and Lakota, among others.

Amma explained that what we called *man* and *woman* was just the clothing over our soul's unique composition of masculine and feminine energies. She always pointed out that there are humans who are born male with more feminine energy, whom our Indian society called *hijras* or the "third gender," a community that has existed in South Asian cultures for millennia. As a young gay boy who didn't even have a word to describe how he felt, I used to ask her—using her logic—if we were all just souls with these energies, why couldn't I dance like a girl and why couldn't boys marry boys? In all her wisdom, she would pointedly answer: *samaj ke niyam hain*, or "there are rules in our society."

Fifteen years after such conversations, while advocating for black, brown, immigrant, and LBT women at the United Nations,* I realized that my Amma, whom many in my Indian community perceived as uneducated and illiterate, knew what many educated Westerners are now coming to terms with, that gender is a story enforced by policies. And despite knowing this truth from both her spiritual practice and lived experience, she upheld and enforced these policies.

Like the vast majority of women in the world, she carried, in her body and mind, psychological and physical scars of physical, sexual, and emotional violence from the numerous conscious and unconscious attempts she made to transgress her society's gender rules. She wasn't alone. Her eldest son, my uncle, died by suicide almost a decade before I was born because the rules of his society did not permit same-sex-loving people to exist. For almost 50 years since, my father has been emotionally numb because the rules of sexism wouldn't permit him, as a cis hetero man, to fully mourn and grieve the loss of his older brother.

In the words of the poet Nayyirah Waheed in her poem "masculine":

---

* Lesbian, bisexual, and trans women, through the international human rights legal mechanisms of the Convention on the Elimination of All Forms of Discrimination Against Women (CEDAW).

there have been so many times
i have seen a man wanting to weep
but
instead
beat his heart until it was unconscious.[4]

I have been that man, and I almost lost my life being that man. This is patriarchy, or the gender hierarchy in action. There are *no winners* in patriarchy.

The gender hierarchy is *wetiko*'s earliest human hierarchy, and it remains the dominant one globally. It shows up as discrimination; physical, emotional, psychological, and sexual violence toward those subordinated on the gender hierarchy; the exclusion of girls, women, and queer and gender-diverse humans from access to rights, resources, and opportunities globally; a lack of physical safety for them in public spaces; defining the very existence of queer and gender-diverse humans as illegal in most societies; and socializing boys and men globally in an unhealthy form of masculinity that suppresses their feminine temperaments, like *all* men on both sides of my family.

Before we dig into how such a reality came to be, I want to speak to the *is-ness* of gender. What I mean by its *is-ness* is that it is a part of existence and, as my Amma explained, gender consists of qualities, energies, and temperaments our societies label as masculine and feminine. These temperaments accompany our sex with gender identity and sexual orientation. Before modernity, cultures across the world had unique ways of expressing and defining gender based on these energies and temperaments.

In our globalized times today, most humans in the English-speaking world experience and enact the social identity of gender as nonbinary, cis or trans woman, or cis or trans man. At a personal level, how we each perceive, enact, and experience gender can also depend on our sexuality, including being gay, lesbian, straight, bisexual, asexual, pansexual, or other sexual orientations. Studies suggest that anywhere from 2 to 10 percent of humans self-identify as homosexual, i.e., gay or lesbian, 1 to 5 percent as bisexual,* and 0.5 to 1.7 percent as trans or nonbinary. There is huge variation in these numbers across geographies and cultures because sexuality and gender identity are deeply personal identities and many individuals do not disclose them on surveys or censuses because of safety concerns, internalized bias, or other reasons.[5]

With that said, when it comes to gender and sexuality, I want to acknowledge that the majority of humans identify as cis men and women and as heterosexual, i.e., exclusively/mostly sexually attracted to the opposite sex. Given that gender is a social identity, these numbers and labels may evolve and shift in the future, but gender's underlying biological identities—sex, gender identity, and sexual orientation—and the temperamental and energetic bases that cultures globally have labeled as masculine and feminine will remain the same.

PATRIARCHY: THE FOUR PHASES
OF GENDER HIERARCHY

For most of human history, as you learned in the earlier chapters, human cultures and societies globally were engaged in numerous social experiments. In every single one of these cultures, the elements that make up gender were and remain the central feature of social organizations. What we understand as gender roles are generally assigned to humans based on their sex. In many animist cultures, trans, gender-diverse, queer, and two-spirit humans as well as cis men and women were and are assigned unique roles that serve a particular function.† To me, these roles were and are acceptable as long as humans serving in these roles are not forced to inhabit them.

---

* The numbers of queer people who are attracted to all genders are not so clear.

† Some examples of this are the Hawaiian *māhū*, who occupy "a place in the middle" between male and female; the Anishinaabe *ikwekaazo*, "men who choose to function as women," or *ininiikaazo*, "women who function as men"; and the South Asian, Oaxacan, and Indonesian third gender of *hijras, muxe*, and *waria,* respectively, i.e., "women who were born in male bodies."

I conceive patriarchy as different from gender roles because the former creates a hierarchy of better-than or worse-than. It is rooted in the false story that cis hetero men are superior to women and queer and gender-diverse humans and that they are entitled to more authority, influence, and power, as well as the right to dominate others, often without consequences.

The gender hierarchy of patriarchy has four basic rules that remain constant across cultures, space, and time:

1. All of humanity is structured in a hierarchy of a binary gender based exclusively on biological sex, i.e., females are women, males are men, and gender-diverse humans are either nonexistent or limited to specific roles generally on the margins of society, such as the *hijras* of South Asia.

2. Men are not only superior to women, they *own* the women of their family or clan, especially women's sexuality and reproductive capacity; girls and women are regarded as sexual objects who are valued more for their perceived physical beauty than for their humanity.

3. While many ancient and medieval patriarchal cultures, such as Hindus, Ottomans, Greeks, Romans, and the Chinese, permitted or glossed over same-sex love and relationships, marriage and/or sacred union officially are limited to people of the opposite sex.

4. Most social structures, property, wealth, and positions of power and influence are unquestioningly held by cis hetero men of the dominant class, descent, and ideological intersectionality, and they are, with few exceptions, passed down exclusively to cis hetero men.

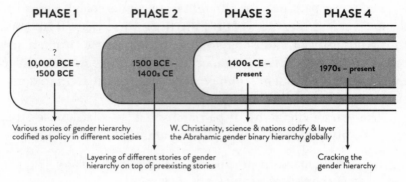

Figure 6.1

Gender transitioned from a marker of who we are as humans into a hierarchical ranking system rooted in the gender binary in four phases: (1) the invention of the gender hierarchy in Neolithic times; (2) the creation of various patriarchal stories of the gender hierarchy in centralized societies in ancient and medieval times; (3) the layering of the Western Christian gender binary story globally; and (4) the cracking of the gender hierarchy in the era of inclusion consciousness (see Figure 6.1 for a visual map of this evolution). Let's walk through deep time to review some of these stories and the corresponding policies that form a social container that trains all humans in gender biases toward ourselves and others.

PRISM EXERCISE

Pause. Take three full breaths and return to your body sensations. Recall our agreements.

As a gendered human in our world today, what did you learn about how males came to dominate all other genders, and where did you learn it? Practice mindfulness of your thoughts and beliefs and document your reflections below or in your journal.

10,000?–1500 B.C.E.: Phase 1, Invention of Stories of the Gender Hierarchy

Recent archaeological research upends the false story proposed by the French philosopher Jean-Jacques Rousseau in the 18th century that prior to the agricultural revolution, men generally did the hunting and women the gathering. In revisiting the ethnographic and archaeological data, scientists found that in about 80 percent of hunting-and-gathering societies, girls and women hunted just as much as boys and men.[6] I sense that future research will demonstrate its complementary proposition, that boys and men gathered as much as girls and women did. So why and how did patriarchy begin?

After spending over a decade reviewing cross-cultural research and mythologies, the answer I have come to is *nobody definitively knows*. Archaeologists, biologists, historians, and philosophers *theorize* that humans lived in gender-egalitarian societies for the vast majority of their existence until about 10,000 years ago, in the Neolithic era. They argue that after the agricultural revolution, patriarchy was seeded in the consciousness of some humans as some tribes learned how to cultivate land and settle in particular areas. These humans created stories of gender for division of labor, patrilineal kinship, male lineage inheritance, and social stratification.[7]

This does not mean that humans uniformly imposed a singular and permanent gender hierarchy globally. Rather, in some centralized societies, a woman's body and reproductive capacity became the signal for family honor and continuing family lines; and human bodies became a signal for specific family and social roles such as child-rearing, warfare, labor, and religious and political leadership. To me, this marks the advent of exclusion consciousness rooted in separation and domination.

Alongside these patriarchal settlements, there existed hundreds of social experiments with matrilineal kinship and gender equality. For example, archaeological evidence suggests that a relatively gender-egalitarian society existed in the Indus Valley society in ancient India, with evidence of goddess worship and female deities.[8]

This was before certain written interpretations of Vedic religious traditions gained prominence. Similarly, scholars suggest egalitarian gender dynamics in the pre–Zhou Dynasty Confucian China.[9]

In these societies, it wasn't that humans didn't formulate ceremonies, rituals, and kinship systems around gender rooted in feminine and masculine temperaments and expressions. They most certainly did. But there was no concept of cis men being superior to cis women and gender-diverse humans and thereby entitled to more authority across all realms of life.

Instead, rooted in the inclusion consciousness of animist belief systems that honored the sanctity of life in each living being, these societies distributed decision-making and leadership across the gender spectrum. Australian indigenous societies prior to European contact are a testament that such gender egalitarianism continuously existed for over 60,000 years, and it is being revived once again through neuro-decolonization efforts in contemporary times.[10]

Scholars in the Western scientific academy, who were largely white cis men, historically claimed that men came to dominate women for reasons such as their muscle power, aggression, and genetics and that women were intrinsically weak, frail, irrational, or *naturally* unequal. You may ask: Based on what evidence did they make these gross generalizations? None whatsoever. Apparently, it's common sense and because—as cis white men—they said so.[11]

None of these pseudoscientific rationalizations stand in the face of actual reality. Take women like my childhood opponent Rosa, or my former employee Monica, who as a strongwoman athlete lifts cars for fun. Monica is certainly physically stronger than most men I know. Similarly, aggression is a human tendency that exists across the gender spectrum, and it is not limited to cis men. There is nothing inherent in human genetics that justifies subordinating entire groups of humans merely because of their body parts.

The rise and spread of patriarchy across our human family goes to the core of the first two root causes of gender: stories and policies. Stories of gender were translated into institutional policies that empowered cis men in entitlement and dominating roles, not unlike my childhood, and subjugated women and gender-diverse humans, like my Amma and my uncle, using terror and violence.

1500 B.C.E.–1400s C.E.: Phase 2, Layering Stories of Gender Hierarchies

The gender hierarchy eventually became a central feature of the social organization of most centralized societies. While the specific stories of gender across these regions varied, they all justified the institutional subordination of women and queer and gender-diverse humans through a particular interpretation of their religion or morality.

For example, starting around 1100 B.C.E. in ancient China, Confucianism interpreted the Taoist concepts of yin and yang to establish social and gender roles rooted in our biological sex. It emphasized the concepts of filial piety and class hierarchies that for the most part placed men in positions of authority within the family and society. Women were expected to be obedient daughters, respectful wives, and nurturing mothers, and they were confined to the private sphere. This story was layered on top of various other stories of gender that existed across the East Asian corridor as Confucianism spread and influenced societies as far away as Japan, Korea, Vietnam, and Inner Mongolia.

As some influential women, like Empress Wu Zetian of the Tang Dynasty, rose up the ladder to challenge the gender hierarchy, cultural norms evolved to establish violent and brutal practices like foot binding to restrict women from holding authority and influence.[12] Such brutality was justified by mental concepts that small feet made young women more beautiful and more eligible to find suitable male spouses; such stories are central to patriarchy, in which a woman's beingness exists to become the wife of a man and produce his heirs to continue the patrilineal line.

Though foot binding was abolished in the early 20th century, and despite transformative changes brought by modernity, the layer of the Confucian story of gender remains alive across China and the Chinese diaspora, as well as in societies influenced by Confucianism.

Though my upbringing was not Confucian, I grew up with different layers of patriarchal stories that made women such as my sisters feel from an early age like they didn't truly belong in their family of origin. In my South Asian birth culture, this tradition likely began in 1500 B.C.E. with the writing down of particular interpretations of religious texts such as Rigveda and the *Manusmriti*, or Laws of Manu, which codified patrilineal gender roles. These interpretations codified the subordination of women and the invisibility of queer and gender-diverse humans. The domination of this story was so deeply entrenched that even written records of illuminated humans like the Buddha and Mahavira display subordinated treatment of women.

For example, the *Vinaya*, the code of conduct for Buddhist monastics, outlines more restrictive and stringent rules for females than for males, including establishing their subordinated status regardless of spiritual attainment; requiring a male monk to grant full ordination for nuns; and making it impermissible for a female to lead and convene a community of monastics without the presence of at least one senior male monk. This religiously mandated story of gender became layered across East, South, and Southeast Asian cultures with the spread of Buddhism. Many Buddhist scholars, including nuns Shih Chao-hwei of Taiwan and Dhammananda Bhikkhuni of Thailand, suggest that an illuminated being like the Buddha could not have enforced such rules, but that these rules were added when the Buddha's story and teachings were written down, several centuries later, to suit the patriarchal norms of centralized societies.

I'll leave the debates about what actually happened to the scholars, but what's important to note is that simultaneous with these stories, there likely existed many other layered stories of gender, including matrilineal and egalitarian ones, that humans practiced within their regional and subregional cultures and communities globally. With that said, there was one story of gender that became the most potent meta-layer of the gender stories globally—the Abrahamic faiths' story of a strict gender binary.

The Abrahamic Faiths' Dominant Story of Gender

The human hierarchy based on the gender binary as natural, irrevocable, and mandated by God likely originated in ancient Mesopotamia and Babylon. This story went on to influence numerous tribes of the modern-day Middle East and Europe and became the dominant aspect of Abrahamic religious dogma that survives to this day. While there are likely many layers of gender stories within the meta-story of binary gender that spread across the diversity of Christian, Jewish, and Islamic societies, two layers are essential: the pre-Christian Greek and Roman stories of gender and the origin story of gender in the Abrahamic religious text of Genesis.

You learned in Chapter 2 about the Greek story that interpreted the universe as a set of eternal laws where everything held a "natural place" in a cosmic hierarchy. Within that hierarchy, cis women held a subordinated role to cis men at each rung, and with few exceptions they were categorically excluded from public life. While same-sex intimate relationships were permitted and socially accepted, marriage existed exclusively between members of the opposite sex to carry on patrilineal lines. Gender-diverse people were relegated to the fringes of society. This story was layered and assimilated with the Abrahamic origin story of humanity; it subsequently became medieval Europe's Great Chain of Being cosmology as well as the Islamic world's *Dhimmi* system.

According to Genesis, the first humans, Eve and Adam, lived happily in Paradise, where they enjoyed eternal life and where their Creator, a masculine and angry God, permitted them to eat from any tree but the tree of good and evil. Tempted by a serpent, Eve ate from that tree and encouraged Adam to do so as well.* This act, known as the "original sin," led them to become aware and ashamed of their naked bodies and want to hide them.

Most importantly, so the story goes, the act led God to expel them from Paradise, with different punishments for each. Adam

---

* Sadly, because of this story, serpents or snakes are perceived as wily in societies influenced by Abrahamic religions. Conversely, the same beings are revered as protectors and nurturers in many indigenous, Hindu, and Buddhist cosmologies.

and all men would be relegated to toil and suffer on Earth, commanded to submit to God's will. For Eve and all womankind, the punishment would be even graver; they'd be relegated to submit to men's will. This story justifies the domination and subordination of all women by men in perpetuity and the policing of both genders in rigid gender roles.

Scholars like Robert Graves, Raphael Patai, and Elaine Pagels dispute this story, drawing from the Talmud and from the Dead Sea Scrolls, ancient Jewish manuscripts discovered in the mid-20th century in Palestine. They claim that before Eve, Adam had another wife named Lilith. In their version, God had created Adam and Lilith equal, but Adam tried to subordinate Lilith, so she left him. Scholars suggest that such interpretations of human equality were rife among ancient Jews and Christians.[13]

In 1945, Muhammad Ali al-Samman, an Egyptian peasant, discovered a large, ancient clay vessel inside a cave near Nag Hammadi in Egypt. Inside was a trove of papyrus manuscripts containing gospels and other writings dating back to a period beginning shortly after Jesus's crucifixion. These scrolls described the creation of male and female in the image and likeness of God as a sign that God is both masculine and feminine, Father and Mother. They further revealed a secret tradition from Mary Magdalene, who according to these scrolls was Jesus's companion and the personification of the Divine Feminine.[14]

These interpretations were outlawed from the official Christian tradition and excluded from its canon of texts, and the records of them were mostly burned as heresies after Christianity became state religion across the Roman Empire in 380 C.E. The first pope, Peter, began the brutal campaign across the empire's territories to Christianize animist and pagan populations, suppress the worship of the Divine Feminine, and perceive God singularly as "masculine," i.e., Father, Son, and Holy Spirit.

Starting with the story of Adam and Eve that I shared above, the Church branded all women as the tainted sex, Mary Magdalene as a whore, and Lilith as a witch, like similar interpretations in the dominant Jewish and Muslim traditions, and established an exclusively male priesthood sworn to celibacy. Hence spread stereotypes that had likely existed in local cultures already, of women as temptresses, created solely for men's desires and to assuage their loneliness.

These stereotypes not only justified women's social, political, and economic subordination and exclusion from public life, but also added the element of shame and hatred for the female form and the acts of sexual intercourse itself. As a result, cultures steeped in this story of gender perceive women as sexual objects that ought to be segregated and covered to prevent cis men from being lured and distracted. This element of shame layered onto the human body and sexual acts is uniquely a feature of the Abrahamic faiths' story of gender in the era of modernity.

For example, prior to modernity, even in patriarchal non-Abrahamic indigenous, African, and Asian cultures like my own, there was an implicit understanding that human sexual organs and female breasts just *were*; the exposure of the human upper body, breasts, nipples, and even genitals did not trigger emotions, feelings, or ideas of shame, guilt, self-consciousness, sexual arousal, or sexual objectification. In many Asian, African, and indigenous cultures, women often did not cover their breasts, arms, or legs before the arrival of the Abrahamic story of gender. Similarly, these cultures didn't view sexual activity as intrinsically shameful and wrong. Such mental associations, concepts, *vedana*, and emotions became a part of the meta-layer of the stories of gender as policies influenced by Christian or Islamic law were institutionalized to demarcate strict gender roles.

The Abrahamic Story of Gender and LGBTQ+ Humans

The absence of queer and gender-diverse humans in the official version of the Abrahamic creation story is used to justify the contention that these humans are anomalies to be fixed, imprisoned, or eliminated. The biblical Sodom and Gomorrah story is used as a further justification for such treatment.

In short, here's how the story goes. God destroys two "cities of the plain," Sodom and Gomorrah, in ancient Babylonia because their residents are committing certain "abominable and sinful acts." The texts do not specify the acts; however, Jewish, Christian, and Islamic scholars claim they were acts of sexual perversion, especially physical intimacy between gay humans.* In addition, recently scholars have demonstrated that the word *homosexuality* entered the Christian Bible as a mistranslation as recently as 1946.[15]

Over time, such interpretations, led by a few people, infected the minds of millions of others, defining queer people with pejorative terms like *perverts* and *sodomites*. These interpretations, translated from the original Aramaic to Greek to various European and global languages, entered the constellation of national and religious policies, including the Haggadah and Sharia, that continue to exclude, marginalize, and even eliminate queer and gender-diverse people.

With the advent of African enslavement and colonialism in the mid-15th century, Christianity's binary gender structure was imposed and layered on top as the meta-story of gender globally. Like the story of race, this meta-story was codified through three vectors: religious law, Western science, and the policies of nation-states.† As you continue to read, I want to gently remind you to avoid succumbing to the dualism of good and bad, right and wrong. What I am sharing with you is what humans did to one another for reasons rooted in *wetiko* or exclusion consciousness.

PRISM EXERCISE

Pause. Take three full breaths and bring your attention to feel your body, remembering our agreements.

As you now know, bias is emotional. I'd like you to practice perspective-taking and imagine being someone you know—perhaps

* A number of contemporary scholars, like John Boswell and Rabbi Jay Michaelson, dispute this interpretation, interpreting the sins instead as arrogance and lack of hospitality.

† *See* the works of philosopher Maria Lugones, who termed this phenomenon *the coloniality of gender*, as it disrupted and consolidated numerous ways gender and sexuality were practiced, particularly in indigenous, animist, and non-Christian cultures.

a family member, colleague, friend, acquaintance, or classmate—who identifies with the Abrahamic religions' story of gender. Try not to use a public figure or someone you don't personally know. Imagine being in this person's body, heart, and mind. Imagine the concepts, associations, and emotions they carry around gender and feel their accompanying *vedana*.

In the space below or in your journal, reflect on how these mental formations influence the way this person views their gender and sexuality. How do they view their own body and the bodies of other humans? Notice and feel the ideas, memories, emotions, and somatic experiences that arise for you in this practice.

Note: This exercise will not lead to an accurate awareness of someone else's views on their gender or sexuality, but rather support building empathy. It can be enhanced by the invaluable experience of nonjudgmentally listening to another's interpretation and articulation of their gender and sexuality.

Take at least five minutes to write your reflections.

1400s–Present: Phase 3, European Christianity Layers the Gender Binary Globally

Recall from Chapter 5 that Europeans justified their colonial and human trafficking enterprises in the name of their imagined Christian God. In the dominant European consciousness, this translated into a paternalistic savior mission of "civilizing" black, brown, indigenous, animist, and non-Christian humans whom they, rooted in their Great Chain of Being cosmology, perceived as animals, heathens, and savages. Central to this savior mission was converting these humans to Christianity, and, more specifically, folding them into the Abrahamic binary story of gender as "civilized" men and women.*

---

* For example, the three *c*'s of Europe's white man's burden were Christianity, commerce, and civilization.

To appreciate how the Abrahamic faiths' binary gender became the dominant gender meta-story globally, I find it helpful to first acknowledge and imagine how gender was socially and emotionally experienced by humans in Christian Europe.

PRISM EXERCISE

Pause. Take three full breaths and return your awareness to your somatic experience.

Imagine being the white Europeans listed below in the year 1700. Then, reflect on how the standard of the dominant Christian binary gender affected your social, political, economic, and cultural rights and liberties, and how you experienced your humanity in your society. Feel free to add intersectional identities without changing the gender category. Last, visit a search engine of your choice and research how you might actually have experienced life in that place at that time.

* I am a Welsh gay soldier in England.

* I am a poor Jewish lesbian in France.

* I am a Sami two-spirit person in Sweden.

* I am a Roma cis woman in Spain.

* I am a wealthy cis nobleman in Italy.

* I am a trans Irish woman in Ireland.

What I hope you'll discern from this exercise is that it was hard to be human in Europe! The dominant story of gender was suffocating for everyone. It forced onto our bodies and psyches roles and ways of being that did not comport with our inner sense of being. Not only that, the thousand-plus years of colonization with the Christian gender binary were so deeply entrenched that often when humans rebelled against the gender norms, not only were they met with terror and violence such as being publicly humiliated or burned at the stake, but they also felt shame, guilt, and self-hatred for transgressing how they "should be."

Even the so-called beneficiaries in this system, the wealthy cis white hetero Christian men, could only benefit from the system if they complied with the rules of gender. In doing so, for generations, they had to suppress their natural human emotions of kindness, compassion, generosity, humility, service, and care, emotions the dominant gender story labeled feminine and undesirable.

Globalizing the Meta-Layer of Binary Gender

In one of my healing circles, I learned the phrase "Hurt people hurt people." For me, this line encapsulates how European Christianity, as well as Islam, layered the story of the gender binary globally. The way this occurred varied based on the span of colonization and the unique way it was structured in each society. However, across societies, and regardless of the colonizing power, the belief in the gender binary was central to the colonial enterprise. It provided the colonizers and enslavers with a sense of pride and purpose in their brutality.

Their public-facing narrative was "We may have wreaked havoc, but at least we are saving their souls by bringing them to God" to hide the self-serving nature of the brutality. Neuro-colonization of this narrative also distracted the subjugated people from revolting against their oppression and succumbing to the intersectional power of the story of race and gender. The result: hundreds of millions of people were trained to pigeonhole their humanity into the gender binary and distrust their body's emotions, desires, and ancestral ways in the name of civilization, progress, and being "good." In *The Wretched of the Earth*, Frantz Fanon writes, "Imperialism leaves behind germs of rot which we must clinically detect and remove from our land but from our minds as well."

A Native Alaskan colleague, Sheila, shared with me that prior to European contact, her indigenous Alaskan cultures were inclusive of queer and gender-diverse humans, whom they called "two-spirit" in their language. The introduction of Christianity about 100 years ago taught her elders to place humans on a gender hierarchy and exclude their two-spirit children out of fear of going to hell. It also forced men and women to be ashamed of their bodies and of sexual intimacy and to adopt Western ways of dress. With that said, the Christian gender binary didn't completely replace their preexisting story of gender, particularly the role women held as healers and decision-makers. Rather, in her words, "the Christian ideas were layered on top."

For numerous societies globally, the process of Christianization and gender indoctrination began several centuries earlier than it did for Sheila's ancestors, as we saw in the previous chapters. In particular, these policies targeted practitioners of animist traditions whom Europeans considered pagans and heathens. Across the Americas, Australia, Asia, and Africa, children were separated from their families, elders, languages, ceremonies, and, most important, their land, and enrolled in boarding schools to assimilate them into the Abrahamic story of gender.

In my country, the United States, this policy was known as "Kill the Indian, Save the Man." Central to this policy was indoctrination in European misogyny, patriarchy, and gender roles. Girls were trained in skills like home economics and taught to cover their bodies, and boys were forced to cut their hair, forget their ancestral ways, and enter the ways of modernity.

Enslaved Africans and their descendants, who also were stripped from their ancestral animist ways, met a similar fate. While Christianity offered some the ability to read and write and a source of inspiration and solace amidst the unspeakable monstrosity of enslavement, it simultaneously indoctrinated them in the gender binary, sexism, homophobia, and transphobia, challenges that persist in many African and African-descent communities globally.

Similarly, I was surprised to learn that in my birth culture, until the 1830s, most humans wore a single garment that they called a *sari* for women and a *dhoti* for men. Despite regional patriarchies, men and women freely exposed their upper and lower bodies. However, learning to cover our bodies, particularly for women, became a central feature of South Asian clothing due to restrictive values imposed by Islamic and European Christian missionaries and colonizers of both genders.

The shame associated with our human bodies has been layered on top of our precolonial gender story, so much so that all contemporary images of Hindu goddesses now show blouses and petticoats, both British imports. In addition, Indians of all genders and religious and political persuasions expend an inordinate amount of their precious mental, emotional, and physical energy protesting women's beauty contests and judging the exposure of women's bodies in the public and private spheres.

The consciousness that transmitted a restrictive binary gender globally remains well and alive today. Sadly, it transcends missionaries, and due to European colonialism, it forms the meta-layer of most stories of gender globally, across religious, ethnic, and ideological lines.

PRISM EXERCISE

Pause. Take three full breaths and return your attention to your somatic experience.

Read the exchange that follows and reflect below or in your journal on the inclusion consciousness behind it. Imagine what's possible in your gendered interactions with yourself and others if we're rooted in its consciousness.

Someone asked a late 19th-century illuminated being, Swami Rama Tirtha, "Why do you call God, Itself [in English]?"

He responded, "Some worship God as *Father in Heaven* and address It as He. Some worship God as Mother Divine and ought to address It as She. Others worship God as beloved sweetheart [Sufis]. So before using any personal pronoun for God we ought to determine whether God is Miss, Mrs., or Mister."

Then what is God?

Neither Miss, nor Mrs., nor Mister, but Mystery.[16]

Western Scientists Codify the Gender Binary as Science

As Europe experienced tremendous economic boons and exchange of ideas from its global colonial and human-trafficking projects, its thinkers began to embrace secular thought and to supplement Christianity with science to explain "natural" phenomena. Within this paradigm, cis male pseudoscientists began to claim a mantle of objectivity in explaining the binary gender hierarchy as being upheld by the laws of nature.

Remember the cast of characters who spewed venom and invented the story of race? Those same guys also theorized and wrote similarly horrifying accounts to "scientifically" demonstrate that women as a whole are a distinct and inferior group of humans, justifying their subordination. They similarly spewed lots of poison about queer, gender-diverse, and other humans who transgressed the rigid Christian gender hierarchy of the time.

The science of gender gained prominence alongside race with Linnaeus's *System of Nature*, which aspired to understand and document all of God's creation. Obsessed with ideal types within each species, like white Europeans when it came to "races" of humans, Linnaeus added another exclusionary ideal set of types to his taxonomy: male and female, each distinct, separate, and unequal and bearing physical and mental traits that are poles apart.[17] The premise of this essential inequality between cis men and cis women, and the nonexistence of everyone else, purportedly rooted in nature, remains in the consciousness of many scientists to this day.*

For example, in 2012, Nobel laureate and English biochemist Tim Hunt said the following at the World Conference of Science Journalists: "Let me tell you about my trouble with girls . . . Three things happen when they are in the lab. . . . You fall in love with them, they fall in love with you, and when you criticise them, they cry."[18] These words repeat the age-old Christian stereotypes that adult women are girls and temptresses who are also hysterical and emotional.

---

* Linnaeus and most European scientists building on his theories also transferred the gender-binary convention and categorization onto all more-than-human beings, like plants, animals, birds, fish, and beyond.

A few years earlier, Harvard president and economist Larry Summers claimed, despite tremendous evidence to the contrary— and counter to the basic decency of our common humanity—that gender inequity on his faculty might be due to "intrinsic aptitude . . . and that those considerations are reinforced by what are in fact lesser factors involving socialization and continuing discrimination."[19] In the context of these comments, these highly educated men are speaking and thinking about women colleagues who, like them, are white.

This is the play of intersectionality in the binary gender story, and it speaks to how Western science codified binary gender differently for white-bodied humans versus humans of color. I'll briefly summarize the establishment's arguments below, sparing you from looking up the details of their racist misogyny elsewhere.

Gendered White-Bodied Humans

Recycling the Christian misogyny of their times, from the 18th to the 20th centuries, scientists, philosophers, and economists used three arguments to codify the superiority of white men and inferiority of white women.

First, they used circular and self-congratulatory logic. Using their Eurocentric lens, they claimed that white men are responsible for all human progress from time immemorial and that because white women were absent among the great thinkers of Europe, they were inferior. These men purposely ignored facts that white women who transgressed strict gender roles met violent retaliation, and they overlooked the policies and culture of their times, which controlled all aspects of a woman's life. Instead, highly respected scientists like Cesare Lombroso would publicly bully and malign women who challenged European gender roles and expectations, like Mary Wollstonecraft, whom Lombroso called "the daughter of a moral idiot and a maniac."[20]

Second, akin to the tactics of bogus racial science, scientists like James W. Redfield conducted ridiculous experiments measuring men's and women's foreheads, ears, and skull size to argue that "animalistic organs" in white women made it impossible for them to exercise powers of thought or circumspection, whereas men's larger brain size made them more suited for civility and reason.[21] These scientists would go on to use these completely unrelated experiments to philosophize on the "natural" temperaments of women: domesticity, caring for children, and a penchant for hysteria, echoes of which we hear in the likes of Tim Hunt to this day.

Third, they would make sweeping claims about "natural disparities" between the binary genders. They restricted all white men to being creatures of reason and therefore suited for civil society, whereas all white women apparently were creatures of charms and wiles suited exclusively for the domestic sphere. They recycled the Abrahamic story of gender under the guise of reason and science. For example, in *Emile* (1762), Rousseau wrote, "Woman is specially made to please man. . . . If woman is made to please and to be subjected, she ought to make herself pleasing to man instead of provoking him." He went on to insist that education for each sex must be different so as not to disturb their dissimilar constitution.[22]

Projecting these three arguments onto the gendered humanity of white bodies restricted them to predesigned social roles. It empowered cis white men with a sense of moral superiority and relegated cis white women to being wards of the state and frail, delicate sexual objects requiring the protection of the state and men, particularly protection against harm from non-Christian and nonwhite men. The scientific justifications for this intersectional gender story continue to show up consciously and unconsciously in white-bodied humans' internal, interpersonal, and institutional experiences of bias.

Gendered Humans of Color

You've already learned how science supported the idea of race and continues to impose it on non-Europeans globally. For example, in drawing his hierarchy of human races, Linnaeus went out of his way to speak about African women's genitalia. That remark had little to do with the incredibly diverse humans of Africa, who exist in many shades of brown, sizes, and body types, and everything to do with the perceptions and consciousness of the creator.

These stereotypes, when justified by science, went on to become the lens through which the gendered bodies of humans were and are viewed. Remember, garbage in, garbage out.

For black women, it became the stereotype of being labeled with hypersexuality alongside many other lies. For humans of other cultures, whether from North Africa, the Americas, Australia, the Pacific Islands, or parts of Asia, gendered stereotypes were fabricated differently depending on the European origin of the anthropologist, ethnographer, or plain old cultural enthusiast "studying" or "observing" them.

This often meant emasculation, criminalization, and dehumanization of men of color because of their long hair, loose clothing, or cultural practices. For example, American craniologist and medical professor Samuel George Morton, after "studying" skulls of murdered Iroquois men, claimed as science that all indigenous Iroquois men are "crafty, sensual, ungrateful, obstinate and unfeeling, and much of their affection for their children may be traced to purely selfish motives."[23] On what basis, you may ask? None whatsoever other than the three root defilements in his mind.

Similarly, for cis women of color, it meant being stereotyped and perceived as exotic, hypersexual, submissive, or an oppressed damsel in distress in need of saving. These pseudoscientists also used the respect some cultures held for their two-spirit and gender-queer members as evidence of those societies' moral inferiority. Policymakers used this research to defend their "Code of Religious Offenses," a moral directive that forbade non-Christian spiritual practices, including indigenous gender-diverse dating and marriage practices as well as the freedom to embody nonbinary gender identities.[24]

Such hateful and bigoted interpretations of human diversity and *beingness* were institutionally sold as objective scientific truths by leading magazines and academic journals to millions of people globally. This pseudoscience was directly used to codify, justify, and sustain a strict gender binary, and to reinforce humanity's gender meta-story policy across modernity.

Nation-States Codify the Gender Binary as Policy

Policies are the second root cause of gender bias because they establish and sustain a cultural container for human interaction and how humans learn bias. In the late 18th century, the French and American revolutions enabled European and the newly legally minted "white people" to legally reform their descent-based monarchic, authoritarian, and hierarchical ways of governance with new social experiments. Democracy was one such experiment, alongside capitalism, socialism, communism, Nazism, fascism, and blends of the above.

The policies of European and American nation-states complemented or wholly replaced Christianity with scientific thought, but used the story of gender from Christianity and "secular science" to justify and strengthen the binary gender hierarchy. The underlying argument? Sex-based human inequality is natural, biological, and irrevocable. As a result, the social, political, economic, and cultural rights and liberties offered by these new forms of governments were contingent upon a human's gender.

Western policies defined gendered humans as follows:

* White cis men, of a particular intersectionality, as naturally dominant, superior, and empowered with all rights and liberties

* Cis women as subordinated, inferior, and, like children, wards of the state; the intersectionality of their other secondary identities such as race, class, and ethnicity further limited their access to rights and resources

* Cisgendered queer humans as perverts, mentally ill, and criminals; to exist, they either had to live in hiding and pretend to conform to heteronormativity or risk imprisonment, death, or exclusion on the fringes of society

* Transgendered and gender-diverse humans, like queer humans, as mentally ill and perverts; to exist, they too had to hide and conform to cisgender roles or risk imprisonment, death, or exclusion

Across modernity, this gendered hierarchy was layered on as the meta-story of gender globally through colonial and imperial institutional policies. Colonized humans who resisted assimilation into European civilization continued, either secretly or overtly, to practice their preexisting gender roles. For example, in Mauritanian society, the colonial French code was layered on top of Islamic gender roles, which were already layered on top of a pre-Islamic matrilineal tradition.[25]

The expression, experience, or embodiment of gender, as a result, was and still is contingent upon the layers of stories of gender within a place and space. For example, in every nation, punishment for adultery or murdering a human is contingent upon the genders of the perpetrator and the harmed party as interpreted through the gendered lens of the arbitrating body. In Mauritania's case, the arbitrating body could be the French code, Islamic law, or their matrilineal customs. With that said, in interfacing with the nation-state, a human's rights and liberties were and are mediated through the meta-story of binary gender, generally rooted in Judeo-Christian colonial policies.

My queer uncle, who was born in the immediate aftermath of an independent India, died by suicide because his very existence was illegal under Section 377 of the Indian Penal Code, a policy imposed by the British across their colonies globally in the 19th century.[*] Many similar policies layered the gender meta-story on preexisting patriarchal, matriarchal, and gender-egalitarian ways globally, affecting all aspects of human life: education, political participation, economic opportunities, the ability to purchase and sell property, divorce, inheritance, and so on.

In 2024, there remain 32 nations, including China, Bangladesh, Malaysia, Egypt, and Singapore, where marital rape is not a criminal offense, and at least 20 nations, including Russia, with marry-your-rapist laws or cultures of female honor killings. These types of policies enable the gender meta-story to come to life among

---

[*] As of 2024, it remains in place in Bangladesh, Malaysia, Myanmar, Pakistan, and Sri Lanka, and has influenced a culture of sexism, homophobia, and transphobia across Africa, Asia, and the Caribbean.

billions of people by policing or immunizing harmful behaviors and speech that stem from many stories of gender.

As a human rights lawyer in training, I had the privilege to spend several years working with women, queer, and gender-diverse humans in nations as far-flung as Myanmar, Laos, Egypt, Japan, Switzerland, Botswana, and Mexico. Through their innovation and advocacy, these people were organizing across their intersectional differences to imagine new policies to alleviate the suffering of gender hierarchies experienced by billions globally.

1970s—Present: Phase 4, Cracking the Gender Hierarchy

For most of modernity, at least in the English language, *sex* conceptualized a permanent binary gender, and *queer* was an expletive that lumped together all LGBTQ+ humans whom the dominant colonial policies considered anomalies, perverts, and "variants" from the norm. In 2024, women continue to face legal barriers to full economic equality in 178 nations; they have only three-quarters of the rights afforded to men globally; and 95 nations do not guarantee equal pay for equal work.[26]

With respect to queer and gender-diverse humans, homosexuality was scientifically considered a "psychiatric disorder" by the American Psychiatric Association (APA) until 1973. These definitions justified the state apparatus across the world that, with impunity, tortured suffragettes, queer, and gender-diverse humans with violence, shock therapies, conversion therapies, and an array of other brutal mechanisms.

Until the late 20th century, *gender, gender identity*, and *sexual orientation* were not commonly understood terms to describe human identities. The word *gender* comes from *genus*, meaning "type, sort, or kind." It was popularized to distinguish it from biological sex and to add nuance of gender identity and sexuality in the late 20th century. Using language, advocates imagined, demanded, and created changes in inequitable and harmful policies that marginalized humans based on hierarchies of sex, gender identity, and sexuality. This work is ongoing and it is rooted in inclusion consciousness, or the explicit desire to alleviate suffering, pain, and inequities on the part of humans who happen to be women, queer, and gender-diverse. Black and brown humans continue to enrich these movements with intersectional analyses of colonialism, systemic racism, and precolonial forms of patriarchy.

When we look at deep time, the convergence of these movements is incredibly recent! As recently as the 1970s, the vast majority of humans in centralized societies didn't even question their gender biases because the consciousness of gender simply wasn't there. Depending on the society, for tens to thousands of generations, humans were socialized to believe that the gender hierarchy was just how things were supposed to be, or how they are. Gender is based on *samaj ke niyam*, as my Amma said—policies justified by religious, scientific, and political stories.

The Convergence Gender-Equality Movements

I believe that the movements of gender equality have been a long time coming, since the very institutionalization of patriarchy itself. They manifested in the micro and macro ways that cis, queer, and gender-diverse humans violated policies in patriarchal societies in opposition to their societies' dominant gender story.*

In the dominant world of white Christians and secularists, Mary Wollstonecraft's *A Vindication of the Rights of Woman* (1792), which applied Europe's Enlightenment ideas to white women, popularized the movement for economic and political equality of the sexes. Within a century, a global women's rights movement, led largely by white women, burgeoned. It demanded equality, suffrage, and freedom for white women, starting with the first American convention on women's rights in Seneca Falls in 1848 and the emergence of women's suffrage committees across Western nations and their colonies.

---

* Some historical figures who broke the rules of gender include Chinese Muslim eunuch and maritime explorer Zheng He; Hindu and Sufi female saints Lalla Led, Mira bai, Rabia al-Adawiyya, and Hazrat Babajan; American nonbinary activist Jennie June; African American entertainer Gladys Bentley; civil rights activists James Baldwin and Bayard Rustin; Crow wisdom keeper Osh-Tisch; and Zuni nonbinary performer We'wha.

These movements were complemented by early writings by queer and nonbinary white Westerners like Englishman Edward Carpenter's *Love's Coming-of-Age* (1896) and American Jennie June's *The Autobiography of an Androgyne* (1918). With the rise of the civil rights and freedom movements and feminism in the post-colonial world, from the 1960s onward, these movements converged to support sexual and gender liberation for all people. As you can imagine, demanding reforms to patriarchy was and remains incredibly dangerous, and we engage in this work because we carry within us a light of inclusion consciousness and live-and-let-live and love-is-love mindsets.

However, a tension emerged early on across these many Western movements for gender liberation: whether to include black, brown, animist, indigenous, and non-Christian humans and humans from the global south. This tension remains to this day, including in the global Me Too movement, and has become a crucible for gender equity and belonging efforts on the basis of sex, gender identity, sexuality, and many other intersectional secondary identities across institutions and nations. I believe that reconciling and healing the fissures caused by the gender hierarchy and legacies of racism and colonialism, among other harmful acts of modernity, with honesty and compassion is the way forward.

MOVING FORWARD

Indigenous elder Angaangaq Angakkorsuaq has a powerful childhood story in which he talks about reading postcards from Western explorers who visited his community in Greenland. One postcard read, "Peace on Earth and Merry Christmas." Upon hearing this, one of his elders asked, "Do these people only want peace on Christmas day?"[27] Tiokasin Ghosthorse, a Lakota elder, reframes this statement from peace *on* Earth to peace *with* Earth.

I was really moved by these statements because they reminded me of another ancestor, Thích Nhât Hânh. He said, "True peace is not an object to obtain externally, but a state of being that is established, maintained, and embodied internally." His community, the Order of Interbeing, epitomized this peace by inducting the first known nonbinary Buddhist nunk, Sister Clear Grace, in his tradition. For the Order of Interbeing, this wasn't a question of right or wrong, the genders of Buddha's times, or the Buddhist canon. Rather, it was about a state of being that stemmed from deep listening, compassion, and a deep desire to alleviate suffering and "expand the spectrum of love."[28]

Patriarchy and the colonial legacy of institutionalizing the gender binary force us away from love. The gender hierarchy has become a war not only between humans but within ourselves. Humans participate in and perpetuate this war for no reason other than our body parts, who our body wants to love, or how we want to express our body. Just take a moment to reflect on these three phrases: *our body parts, who our body wants to love,* and *how we want to express our body.*

Isn't it absolutely ridiculous? As a human animal, we could be doing so much with our time, efforts, energy, and resources, but we expend it policing ourselves and one another, all because we believe in stories about what our bodies *ought to be* instead of what they *actually are.* This, in a nutshell, is gender bias.

Uncle Angaangaq wisely reminds us that the only way we can end any war is by ending the war inside ourselves. This is the way of breaking bias. In Part III, we will explore the three vectors of cultures responsible for our training in gender bias and continue to practice PRISM tools to unlearn bias.

PRISM PRACTICES

Pause. Take three breaths and observe your somatic experience.

✳ American actress and advocate Laverne Cox coined the phrase *possibility models* to take the place of *role models.* Her phrase enables us to imagine what is possible for humans with intersectional marginalized identities rather than pigeonholing them into false stereotypes. In Table 6.1 below, you'll see a few professional identities in the leftmost column. I'd like you to take the first human who arises in your mind after reading the term and write down their name and their gender identities.

Then, I'd like you to go to your favorite search engine and take a few minutes to search for actual humans, current or historical, who fit that professional identity and also have the identities listed in the top columns. (For example, search for a surgeon who is a trans person of color.) From now on, visualize these humans when you come across the professional terms. In this way, you will be building new neural pathways by practicing stereotype replacement.

	Your Association	Trans Person of Color	Nonbinary Person	Cis Man of Color	Indigenous Cis Woman
Influencer					
Spiritual Teacher					
Author					
Celebrity					
Politician					
Musician					
Entrepreneur					
Advocate					
Environmentalist					
Artist					

Table 6.1

* Become mindful of the stereotypes you have learned about different genders from your loved ones, friends, education, the media, and religious or scientific training, if any. Reflect on ways the humans who have the identities listed in the top columns were shaped by the social, economic, cultural, or political policies of their surroundings.

* Investigate with curiosity the different stories of gender that influence your relationship with yourself. In what ways and in which situations do they manifest as entitlement, victimization, undercompensation, overcompensation, self-doubt,

grandiosity, narcissism, or another afflictive emotion associated with the comparing mind? Notice and feel the underlying *vedana* associated with the sensations, stories, memories, and ideas associated with these emotions.

* Recall an instance from your life when gender stereotypes influenced your thoughts, words, or actions toward another human in an interpersonal situation. List the stereotypes you consciously or unconsciously believed in that moment. With mindfulness, breathe, observe, and feel the emotions and sensations that arise as you reflect on this experience. Then, practice loving-kindness toward yourself, practice it toward the harmed human, mentally practice forgiveness for yourself, and mentally seek forgiveness from the harmed human.

* Reflect on a decision you've made in a professional or personal setting that was tinged with gender stereotypes. List the stereotypes you consciously or unconsciously believed in that moment that influenced your decision-making. Imagine the ripple effect of your decision on the lives of humans impacted by this decision. Visualize these humans. With mindfulness, breathe, observe, and feel the emotions and sensations that arise as you reflect on this experience. Investigate what actions you can take today to repair the harm.

* Imagine you are in a world without patriarchy and misogyny. Using words, images, or any other means, visualize and describe what this world looks like. What does it feel like? How do you feel mentally, emotionally, and physically? What do you do with your time? With your energy? With your creativity? What about those you love? How do they spend their time? Let your imagination run wild. There is no right or wrong way to imagine. Just imagine.

PART III

OUR
TRAINING
IN BIAS

Chapter 7

CULTURE

*Everything we consume
acts either to heal us or to poison us.
We tend to think of nourishment only as what we take
in through our mouths, but what we consume with our eyes, our ears,
our noses, our tongues, and our bodies is also food. Are
we consuming and creating the kind of food that
is healthy for us and helps us grow?*

— THÍCH NHẤT HẠNH

By now, you have an understanding of the first two causes and conditions of bias for all secondary identities: story and policies. Together, they build the cultural container that uniquely programs our minds with bias. *Culture* is an amorphous word that evokes different meanings for each one of us. As mentioned in Chapter 3, with the encouragement of my church elder Achebe Betty Powell, I have identified three vectors of culture as the remaining causes of bias: social contact, education, and media.

Over the course of our lives, these three vectors, based on our unique life experiences and surroundings, both actively and subliminally expose us to concepts, emotions, and *vedana* toward different secondary identities. As the famous saying goes, "Where our attention goes, energy flows." Culture builds in our minds neural pathways that become stereotypes, mental habits, and perceptions through which we perceive ourselves and others.

With that said, poet Jane Hirshfield reminds us that:

A tree lives on its roots. If you change the root, you change the tree. Culture lives in human beings. If you change the human heart the culture will follow.[1]

Transforming our hearts holds the doorway for us to shift our culture from *wetiko* toward interbeing. The PRISM tools of prosocial behaviors are the conduit for such a shift because they actively produce in our bodies, hearts, and minds positive mental states like compassion, kindness, joy, gratitude, generosity, and forgiveness. While we can each experience these states as our human inheritance, the shifts they make in your experience will be unique to you given your unique cultural upbringing. This is what we'll be exploring on this last leg of our breaking bias journey.

In this chapter, I will define each vector of culture—social contact, education, and media—that we'll explore in more depth in the following three chapters. I'll also share how because of these three vectors, bias becomes our System 1 thinking and how we can develop System 2 thinking through the PRISM practice. Throughout, I will invite you to pause and use PRISM tools to become mindful of the false stories you ingest from culture and to actively transform and heal them in your thoughts, words, and behavior.

PRISM EXERCISE

Pause. Take three full breaths and return your awareness to your somatic experience. Recall our shared agreements.

Think of a time when you experienced or witnessed receiving the compassion of another human or other living being. In your journal or in the space below, describe this event, mindfully noting your bodily experience. Then, notice and document the emotions, sensations, and *vedana* of compassion in your body. Where is it? What does it feel like? What happens to your thinking mind when you experience it? Notice and document any other observations of your experience.

CULTURE'S FIRST VECTOR: SOCIAL CONTACT

As a child, I grew up in an Indian community where being fuller-bodied with curves was perceived as beautiful and desirable. Throughout my childhood, I observed through my verbal and non-verbal interactions with family members and caretakers that people with such bodies were seen as healthy and beautiful.

Within one generation, that perception has radically transformed. Now those same bodies are seen as unhealthy and less attractive. Today, light-skinned bodies that look like ancient Greek statues are perceived as healthy and beautiful. During this time, human bodies have remained the same. However, due to our minds' exposure to social contact, education, and media, the concepts, emotions, and *vedana* associated with those bodies in the minds of my Hindi-speaking north Indian community have shifted. Unless we become conscious of such human-made stories and associations, these associations become the lens through which we perceive and make decisions toward ourselves and others.

With this in mind, take a moment to define social contact in your own words.

Social contact is:

I adopted the phrase *social contact* after reading social scientist Gordon W. Allport's 1954 classic *The Nature of Prejudice*. In this seminal text of prejudice studies, Allport coins the phrase *social contact theory*, which argues that intergroup contact across secondary identities can support humans in overcoming stereotypes, promote positive attitudes and relations, and decrease biased behavior.

In other words, once cis humans spend quality time with trans humans, and vice versa, and they really get to know one another's dreams, aspirations, struggles, and hardships, an empathy and a connection arise that are rooted in our primary identity. This strengthening of understanding and empathy overpowers the stereotypes stored in our minds.

With that said, Allport added an important caveat to his theory. In order for social contact to be effective, it ought to include five optimal elements:[2]

* Cooperative activities that require mutual interdependence (or interbeing)

* Opportunities for personal interaction

* Common goals

* Equal status between the groups

* Support from authorities

By now, I hope you can sense that because of the first two causes of bias—story and policies—these five optimal conditions are rarely met in social contact. Equal status between groups and support from authorities are often lacking, which is why cross-community trust-building initiatives like Seeds of Peace and intergroup dialogue (IGD), though worthy, have been ineffective in creating durable change, for example, between Israelis and Palestinians or between American law enforcement and communities of color.

These caveats helped me realize that in addition to its potential to reduce bias, social contact actually shapes and reinforces certain mental habits, perceptions, and biases that we hold. These biases are strengthened based on three factors: the physical and virtual spaces that we inhabit; people who are important to us and whose opinions we value; and the choices we make regarding the environments and people we spend time with. The first two are what academics call our "built environment" and "significant humans," respectively.

As a result, I define *social contact* as "the interactions, connections, and communication we have with other humans during our lives due to our *built environment*, *significant humans*, and *our choices*." Here's what I mean by the italicized words:

* **Built environment***: human-made physical and virtual spaces where we live, work, and conduct various activities. It encompasses all physical, tangible spaces like buildings, roads, parks, public spaces, transportation systems, and infrastructure; and all virtual, intangible spaces like apps, websites, online communities, video games, and social media platforms. The design of these spaces shapes many of our experiences, our quality of life, our behavior, our physical and mental health, our well-being, and our social interactions.

* **Significant humans†**: humans who have a meaningful and lasting influence on our perceptions and views of ourselves and others, like our immediate, chosen, and extended families; friends; teachers; and mentors. They can include relationships that were or are helpful and nourishing or harmful and abusive.

* **Our choices**: decisions we make from the available options based on our beliefs, intentions, desires, and goals, including the selection of the people and environments to whom we give our attention.

As social animals, we are wired for social contact. It plays a crucial role in how we form relationships, establish connections, maintain social bonds, and learn conscious and unconscious biases. In modern times, social contact includes our verbal, nonverbal, written, or digital in-person or virtual conversations, interactions, communications, and any other form of engagement that allows us to exchange stories, information, ideas, emotions, and experiences. We'll explore this cause and condition of bias further in Chapter 8.

---

* This term was popularized by the urban planning, architecture, and environmental psychology disciplines, and I have adapted it to include virtual environments.

† I have adapted this phrase from *significant adults* used in developmental psychology and education to refer to humans beyond immediate family members who play a crucial role in a child's growth, learning, and socialization.

CULTURE'S SECOND VECTOR: EDUCATION

When I say *education*, I refer to what we understand as educational systems that you've been a part of, not your independent penchant for learning or skills acquisition, for personal, professional, or spiritual growth. Education is an incredibly emotional issue because it reminds us of our childhoods and the children in our lives. When it comes to children, most humans, regardless of whether they are parents or not, get emotional. Our species is biologically wired to honor the sanctity and innocence of young humans. For me, this is precisely why, when it comes to education being a root cause of bias, we need to look at the reality of education rather than pontificating on what we think it ought to be. With that in mind, take a moment to define *education* in your own words.

Education is:

I define *education* as "*schooling* and *curricula* established with the intention to assimilate humans into hierarchies through *disinformation*, *misinformation*, and *knowledge gaps*." Here's what I mean by the five italicized words in this definition:

* **Schooling:** formal instruction provided in primary, secondary, tertiary, professional, vocational, and religious educational institutions, i.e., knowledge, values, and methods of discipline through defined curricula, teaching methodologies, classroom-based learning, assessments, and interactions with instructors, peers, administrators, staff, law enforcement, aid workers, and/or volunteers

* **Curricula:** courses of study in an educational institution, i.e., content presented as "right" knowledge in learning materials like textbooks, videos, audio tracks, images, worksheets, and lesson plans

* **Disinformation:** false or misleading educational content intentionally placed to sow hierarchies, hatred, separation, and division in human minds and to entrench power for a dominant ruling group of people

* **Misinformation:** unintentionally placed false or inaccurate educational content, likely due to disinformation or human error, that may still have the effect of sowing separation, division, and hierarchies in human minds

* **Knowledge gap:** the absence of information and content on particular topics and subjects

Unlike social contact, education as a cause and condition of bias is a trillion-dollar industry that was standardized and globalized in the 20th century. We'll delve deeper into this cause and condition of bias in Chapter 9.

CULTURE'S THIRD VECTOR: MEDIA

I have been lucky to have been exposed to more than a dozen languages in my life.* I am not proficient in most of them, but I can appreciate how language communicates a people's cosmology and understanding of their humanity, whether it is gender neutrality or referring to nature, plants, and animals as living kin versus objects.

Most of my language study and learning took place in relationality with other humans, from haggling in Kuala Lumpur or Hyderabad's street markets to homestays in Mexico and Korea to spending time with Indian, Chinese, and Burmese Buddhist teachers. My polyglot elders, whether they are Surinamese, Nigerian, Malaysian, or Bulgarian, confirm that social contact was how they learned to speak multiple languages, and along with that, to appreciate the stories, fears, and biases of different humans.

Until modernity, social contact and local ways of knowledge transfer, teaching, and learning were the ways humans learned stories and biases that were institutionalized by the policies of their centralized societies. This shifted in modernity with the advent of media. Before proceeding, define *media* in your own words.

---

* They include: Hindi, Punjabi, Urdu, Pahari, Bengali, Malayalam, Sanskrit, Pali, Persian, English, Spanish, French, Russian, Korean, Japanese, Mandarin Chinese, Burmese, and Malay.

Media is:

I define *media* as "print, broadcast, and digital systems of mass communication, information sharing, and consumption of stories to influence mass perceptions." After the invention of the printing press in Europe, in the last 500 years, three media systems grew, evolved, and spread globally: print, broadcast, and digital.

While media scholars debate the number of media types, for simplicity I bundle them into these three enterprise systems based on their chronological invention. Each system comprises many institutions that serve as platforms and channels for communication and consumption of many types of stories. See Table 7.1 for a summary of the media systems, various platforms and channels within each system, and what is required for humans to interact with media. We'll review this final cause and condition of bias in Chapter 10.

Media System	Advent	Platforms and Channels	Use Requirement
Print	1400s	Books, newspapers, magazines, posters, billboards, signs, pictures, etc.	Six senses, knowledge of language, literacy, money
Broadcast	1900s	Radio, film, TV, records, tapes, cassettes, CDs, DVDs, cartridges, etc.	+ Equipment (TV, radio, CD player etc.), money
Digital	1990s	Websites, e-mails, blogs, mp3s, apps, podcasts, social media, audiobooks, e-books, streaming services, AI services like ChatGPT, etc.	+ Internet, equipment (computers, phones, tablets, etc.), money

Table 7.1

CULTURES BEFORE MODERNITY

As you know from Parts I and II, before the advent of capitalist modernity, the human world was made up of thousands of decentralized, nomadic, or centralized bands, tribes, and societies that were held together by unique stories of origin, social structures, and morality, including, for some, ideas of "us" and "them." Humans were born into certain societies with certain bodies and socialized into their societies' stories primarily through the cultural conditioning of social contact. Education as an industry didn't exist. Most humans couldn't read or write. Rather, they learned and trained in various knowledge and wisdom systems through apprenticeships and other methods of instruction. Similarly, modern-day media systems didn't exist. This was true whether humans lived in territories now known as Canada, Hawaii, Australia, Mongolia, Sudan, or Ecuador.

Thousands of cosmologies coexisted to make meaning of our human existence and our relations with one another. From a nondual perspective, none were right or wrong, better-than or worse-than, but they all stemmed from a certain consciousness—exclusion or inclusion—driven by a mix of intentions. From a deep-time lens, the most enduring stories were and are always rooted in inclusion consciousness. This is why at the core of all wisdom traditions lie the same truths: interbeing, relationality, sanctity, and love.

In most societies, these stories were passed down intergenerationally through various technologies of oral tradition. For example, for hundreds of years after the historical Buddha, his life story and teachings persisted solely through oral traditions. Similarly, when the colonizing British took an interest in Hindu philosophy and mysticism in the 19th century, they were shocked to learn that the wisdom-keepers of the Vedas across the Indian subcontinent— whether they were in Kashmir, Kerela, or Bengal—although they looked different, spoke different languages, observed radically different ways of being, and were sometimes illiterate, spoke identical sacred mantras in Sanskrit. I have learned similar stories from wisdom-keepers globally; for example, my Muslim elders remind me that the Prophet Muhammad, a beloved teacher of billions, couldn't read.

In societies with writing systems, some stories were written down so humans wouldn't forget them. However, since most humans couldn't read, these stories spread from person to person around a circle, or through art, symbols, dance, song, sculpture, and so on. In such settings, stories were owned by everyone. People chose to either share them as they were, modify and then share them, or let them die.

Until modernity, only the most compelling stories survived the test of time because they were rooted in inclusion consciousness at their core, even if they were corrupted by the exclusion consciousness of political or religious leaders. And as these stories spread, they were adapted to the needs of communities and societies. When it comes to the major world religions, we bear witness to such a phenomenon when we observe how different communities adapted stories of great prophets and beings like Rama, Buddha, Jesus, or Muhammad before modernity.

MODERNITY: A CULTURE OF DOMINATION AND DISEMBODIMENT

On June 12, 2016, 49 people were targeted and killed, and another 53 wounded, for being queer and gender-diverse at Pulse, a gay nightclub in Orlando, Florida. This was one of the worst mass shootings in American history. As a queer person, the incident triggered something deep inside of me. But I could not feel or put words to what I was experiencing. For weeks, my somatic therapist, Kim, kept asking me to describe how I felt, and I was confounded because I could not feel. I felt numb. I was trying to understand with my mind what was happening to my body. I knew there were feelings and sensations beneath the numbness, but I could not access them.

As I continued to work with Kim, I began to peel away the layers of repressed emotions, memories, and psychic harms that were hidden in my body. Over time, I started noticing, acknowledging, and feeling the diversity of emotions like regret, despair, sorrow, grief, shame, and disappointment. Kim continued to remind me that my condition wasn't unique. Herself a descendant of Holocaust survivors, and of a long line of "men who couldn't feel," she mentioned that "young people these days call your condition *toxic masculinity.*" She said she preferred the term *unhumanness*, though, because it wasn't limited to men.

According to quantum physicist and ecologist Vandana Shiva, this condition spread in the human consciousness with the reductionist and mechanistic scientific story of European Enlightenment thinkers like Descartes, Newton, Locke, and Bacon.[3] Those disembodied men put forth a story of our humanity that valorized the human mind over all other aspects of our humanness: our bodies, emotions, hearts, imagination, and connection with more-than-humans.

Invested in the dualisms of good and bad, right and wrong, and civilized and savage, their ontology severed our connection from nature, one another, and most important, our own bodies. It privileged the rational and logical mind over our emotions and somatic experiences and conditioned us to distrust our intuition and inner knowing so that instead of feeling empowered in our own being, we abdicated our power to external authorities. Recall Descartes's foolish aphorism "I think, therefore I am." All wisdom traditions remind us that thinking is merely *one* aspect of who "I am."

Claiming separation, individualism, domination, and extraction as right and all other ways of being as wrong, European domination globalized this way of being and perceiving the world. We weren't born with such perceptions; rather, we learned them. I remember sitting through economics courses in high school, college, and law school wondering if there was something wrong with me because to me extraction, domination, exploitation, and harming the living Earth were neither rational nor reasonable.

This story about our humanity—with specific concepts, emotions, and *vedana*—arose in the minds of certain humans who then *forcefully* and *violently* infected others with it through policies and culture. The policies curated human social contact by erecting certain built environments; policing human families, interactions, connections, and communication; and training human minds in such ideologies across societies through education and media.

For the past 500 years, anyone who spoke up against or breached the policies or norms they established was ridiculed, intimidated, imprisoned, assassinated, or eliminated. Imagine the millions of humans forcibly removed or killed for their knowledge of and kinship with animals and plants; those consigned as untouchable and humiliated or killed for even looking at another human in the wrong way; the enslaved pursued by slave hunters; the freedom fighters and abolitionists filling the prisons of Western powers from Mexico and Algeria to India and Indonesia; and the humans tortured because they fell in love with another human of the wrong intersectional identities. The apparatus to keep us separate and hating one another—and ourselves—requires *a lot* of effort and an inordinate amount of cruelty and terror to keep in place.

Have you ever wondered why some humans go out of their way to make such an effort? Can't they just spend that same amount of time advancing policies and building systems that bring people together or remind us of our shared humanity and interdependence with more-than-humans?

Imagine being someone you know who operates from a dominating worldview. Reflect below or in your journal on what motivates them. What are their intentions? Motivations?

I have asked hundreds of people this seemingly rhetorical question, including the Amazon executive I mentioned in Chapter 2. Regardless of their education, class, color, language, or gender, they, like you, intuited and identified the intention as *power*. For me, this widespread acknowledgment demonstrates a deep intuitive awareness and wisdom that resides within us across our secondary identities.

PRISM EXERCISE

Pause. Take three full breaths and bring your attention to feel your body.

Let the word *power* rest in your body. Where does it land in your body? Who and what associations arise for you when you reflect on this word? Where do you have power?

Take a few more breaths, close your eyes, and reflect on the meaning of this word and the instruments you have been trained to associate with power.

Power:

Instruments of power:

Neoliberalism and Money: Modernity's Theology and Currency of Power

In 2010, my mentor Susan Davis invited me to attend a sermon at Middle Collegiate Church, one of the longest-running Christian congregations in what is now the United States. That morning, my now pastor, the Rev. Jacqui Lewis, preached on the following verse:

> For the love of money is a root of all kinds of evil. Some people, eager for money, have wandered from the faith and pierced themselves with many griefs. (1 Timothy 6:10)

Jacqui started preaching with the line that precedes this well-known passage: "Those who want to get rich fall into temptation and a trap and into many foolish and harmful desires that plunge people into ruin and destruction." I heard in these words the wisdom of my own ancestral Hindu, Buddhist, and Sikh teachings—that it isn't desire, abundance, money, or the goddess Lakshmi that is the cause for separation, but rather the attachment to or exclusive love of money. My Muslim and Sufi teachers call this attachment the worship of false idols.

Until that moment, I knew very little about the Bible or its wisdom. I had discarded it completely because of monstrous deeds humans justified using this text. After hearing these words, tears streamed down my cheeks as I realized how I had succumbed to *wetiko* by believing what I had learned from my surroundings instead of investigating the source myself.

As I reflected on these lines' deep wisdom, I witnessed what I had learned about capitalist modernity come alive in my mind: patriarchy, misogyny, enslavement, genocides, ecocides, ethnocides, theriocides—all rooted in a consciousness of the *love* of money over everything else. Even after the abolition of slavery, instead of repairing the harms done to generations of humans and cultures, Western nations, including the United States and the United Kingdom, went out of their way to compensate former slave owners for their loss of capital. I recalled what I had learned at Cambridge, about how Western nations colluded to make Haiti pay reparations of $21 billion to France to compensate French plantation owners for their loss of "property," i.e., enslaved humans.[4] This was the price of freedom Haitians willingly paid from 1825 to 1947.

As you learned in Chapter 2, entranced by the love of *money*, in the post-colonial era where they couldn't directly dominate, extract, and exploit black and brown humans or the Earth, Western powers established a global economic and political system known as neoliberal capitalism that reduces all aspects of life—the living Earth, humans, and nonhuman life—exclusively using the currency of money. The exclusion paradigm of neoliberal capitalism became the dominant global ideology and force in shaping economic policies starting in the 1970s. In this paradigm, there is no room for other forms of currency like kinship, generosity, compassion, relationality, community, or sentience because these parts of our beingness cannot be monetized.

Most scholars perceive neoliberalism as a theology because it provides its believers and advocates a comprehensive worldview like institutionalized religions. However, unlike most spiritual traditions, the neoliberal theology is built upon three major flawed beliefs.

First, the belief that all humans are rational. After getting through this much of the book, I hope you can appreciate that we aren't! Second, the belief that all humans are selfish and only care about themselves. Clearly, we aren't or you wouldn't be reading this book, not to mention that this flawed belief is contrary to our biological instincts and every human society that has ever existed. And third, the flawed belief in a cosmic force or "the invisible hand of the market" that apparently guides the order of the economic universe with efficiency and ultimately benefits society as a whole.[5] No such force exists. What exist are national and international policies that regulate all economic affairs. In law school, I remember sitting in Corporations, Corporate Finance, and other business law courses reading through thousands of dense administrative regulations written by humans working for various governments to prop up the belief in a fictional invisible hand.

At a personal level, the impact of these systems is most apparent in the temperaments of humans who subscribe to this theology as die-hard capitalists, regardless of whether they are American, Chinese, Indian, Russian, or Nigerian. I see it in my friends who are economists, venture capitalists, and finance professionals. They have "made it" by all external measures of success, i.e., all the things money can buy, but they deeply struggle with being human and fear feeling human emotions like grief, sadness, or despair because they are wedded to concepts of being rational and logical. They are identified with the Cartesian lie that they are because they think.

At a human level, the desire to dominate externally actually begins within, by dominating and suppressing the emotional and feeling parts of our beings. This consciousness has been reared into our nervous systems through social contact, education, and the media, most rapidly since the rise of neoliberal capitalism. The results have been nothing short of catastrophic: extreme inequality in every society that adopted this ideology; concentration of money—and thereby power, given that money is the only currency of power in this paradigm—in the hands of the very few; astronomical mental health challenges; and the devastating loss of ecosystems, more-than-humans, ancient languages, cultures, and wisdom.

Anthropologist Wade Davis reminds us that though we universally condemn genocide, which is the extinction of a people, "we have not condemned ethnocide—which is the end of people's way of life and is frequently legitimized in public policy in many quarters of the development community."[6] I know a thing or two about the development community because I received my master's degree in development studies, which teaches the ways Western nations can "develop" people in the global south into Western consumer and material ways of being by any means necessary, including the destruction of their cultures, languages, and ways of relating with one another and the Earth.

In the West, and in societies across the Americas, Asia, and Africa emulating the West, the accumulation of money has become the singular obsession of many humans. They are unaware of, and frankly don't want to know, what is done in its pursuit: fracking, razing of forests, destruction of ecosystems, species extinction, reducing ancient cultures to sex work and manual labor, and unspeakable injustice and exploitation.

I grew up in India before its leaders adopted the theology of neoliberal capitalism. During that time, we rarely saw plastic packaging—all things were made of organic materials like banana leaves, mud, glass, or metals. We carried our own cloth bags for shopping. We reused and recycled *everything*. We spent time outside, even in congested cities like Delhi. And our lives overall followed the rhythms of the seasons and the Earth. Since the 1990s, the theology of neoliberalism has supplanted numerous nonmonetary forms of currencies around the world, including in India, in the service of more extraction, inequality, domination, and disembodiment.

The indigenous people of the Amazon, who have survived 500 years of Spanish, Portuguese, British, Dutch, and French genocide and ethnocide, warn that in pursuit of money, people who have adopted Western ways of being have forgotten who they are—one member of the larger family of living beings and systems—and where they come from—the Earth.[7] Despite the continuous harms they've experienced for more than 500 years, their inclusion consciousness still perceives our materialistic capitalist cultures, and our suffering, through the eyes of compassion: as the youngest siblings in the human family who are suffering from *wetiko* and disembodiment. In an exchange with Tiokasin Ghosthorse, Brazilian scholar Vanessa Andreotti describes it as follows:

> We need to parent this toddler [Western culture] with a machine gun in their hands and allow this culture to come to its maturity rather than replace it with other things. It's like we're the uncles, aunties, and grandparents who need to be around . . . to orient and guide their pathway away from the harm it is doing and more harm that it can do.[8]

Rooted in this cosmology of *ubuntu*, Amazonian indigenous communities continue their advocacy and organizing efforts not only to protect their ancestral lands and cultures, but also to wake us up from the delusion of our separation from them and the living Earth.

PRISM EXERCISE

Pause. Take a break and get embodied: stretch, jump, tap, or dance. Remember that you have a body! Bring mindfulness to your body and its sensations, emotions, and feelings.

Reminding yourself of our shared agreements, reflect on ways you enact the narrative of "the love of money." What aspects of social contact programmed you into this narrative? How does this narrative influence how you experience your dominant and subordinated identities, like class, race, religion, or gender? How does it affect your personal or professional decisions that impact other people?

Modernity's Disembodied Culture and Injustice

In June 2010, as a legal intern in New Orleans, I once sat in on sentencing hearings. I was in a sparsely furnished courtroom with a judge, a prosecutor, a defense attorney, clerks, security guards, a box full of defendants who were exclusively poor black boys and men between the ages of 15 and 40, and people who were likely their relatives. Unemotionally, the judge declared prison sentences of two years, three years, four years for what I perceived to be petty offenses—trespass to property, breaking cell phones, or low-level possession of marijuana. By that time, I'd been at many elite educational and professional institutions where my colleagues possessed, consumed, and transacted marijuana and many other "controlled substances" without any legal consequences.

After every sentence was announced, my body unconsciously breathed louder and louder to contain my disgust at what I experienced as a travesty of justice. Within minutes, the court's security officer escorted me out because my heavy breathing disturbed the "peace in the court." Every day in the United States and across the globe, humans of a particular intersectionality are thrown away and disposed of in prisons because in the minds of certain decision-makers, the actions of humans of a particular intersectional humanity appear "criminal" and "worthy of punishment." Those same actions committed by others, like my wealthy, highly educated white classmates, are rarely even charged, forget being prosecuted.

Prior to this experience, I'd worked in authoritarian Burma/Myanmar, and yet the injustice I felt in my gut in that New Orleans courtroom was far more visceral. Unlike the United States, the Burmese *junta* didn't flaunt a façade of equality, justice, and liberty. What shocked me even more about what I had witnessed was the cruelty with which the legal system branded black humans as savage, nonhuman, and criminal. I sensed in the body language of these humans a familiar helpless despair. A despair of many ancestors who were mercilessly kidnapped, enslaved, and treated as three-fifths human. At that moment, I was reminded of what my professor Bryan Stevenson often shared: in most poor communities of color across Western societies, boys and men of color expect to be incarcerated as a rite of passage.

Tears flooded down my cheeks and I was devastated with grief. Yet, when I shared how I felt with my legal colleagues, I was accused of being "emotional and irrational." I wasn't seeking any solutions from them, only solace in the form of a hug or comforting words. Instead, I received lots of heady language to explain away, ignore, and repress the pain my colleagues too likely felt in their bodies, hearts, and minds—what my therapist Kim termed *unhumanness*.

Mehrsa Baradaran, an Iranian American legal scholar, calls *injustice* "a feeling that we feel in our gut and spirit."[9] As a refugee, she acknowledged and felt this feeling early in her life as she witnessed the horrors of the Islamic Republic of Iran. She credits the revolutionary act of *feeling injustice* as her guiding light in becoming an advocate and scholar of the law.

Prior to working in New Orleans, I had known and acknowledged injustice, but I hadn't felt its fullness in my body. When I began to feel it, I had to acknowledge that what I witnessed was systemic bias; in other words, there wasn't a single person I could blame for it. Institutional actors with varying levels of influence and authority—the drafters of the sentencing code, the legislators who adopted it, the lobbyists for the prison industry who advocated for it, the attorneys, the judges, and many other operatives—shared certain perceptions about a group of humans. Therefore, despite beautifully crafted civil rights and antidiscrimination policies on the books, injustice remained because the humans designing and enforcing such policies held certain shared perceptions about certain humans, in this case humans who are monetarily poor, black or brown, and cis men.

PRISM EXERCISE

Pause. Take three full breaths and return to your body's experience.

Take a few minutes to recall an incident of injustice that you've witnessed or experienced. Place one or both hands on your heart. Then, acknowledge and feel this injustice in your body. If thoughts, memories, or concepts arise, notice them, but bring your attention to the sensations in your body. Feel these sensations and notice the *vedana* that accompanies them.

Breathe with these sensations and offer comfort to your body through gentle touching, rubbing, tapping, humming, singing, or another form of sincere care. If grief, sadness, anger, or another emotion arises, notice it and offer it your loving presence and witnessing.

Stay with your body, not needing to change it or run away; watch the sensations and emotions pass through your body for a few minutes.

Take a few more deep breaths. In the space below or in your journal, reflect on this experience of tracking your somatic experience.

HEALING THE DISEMBODIMENT WITH PRISM

In Chapter 1, you learned about our two thinking systems: the fast and automatic System 1 thinking, and the slow and deliberate System 2 thinking. I think of System 1 and System 2 thinking as our hardware, and the various forms of biases we learn as software programs that get installed on our hardware based on our individualized experiences with culture, i.e., social contact, education, and media. Ultimately, any biases we experience, witness, or enact—however small or large—stem from the software programs we are running in our minds or other humans are running in theirs.

Our breaking bias aspiration is to shift our thinking from System 1 to System 2 by practicing PRISM tools, which support us in making the unconscious conscious, interrupting mental reactivity, and correcting misinformation and imagined fears we've learned about "others." To appreciate the neurological and behavioral process of this transformation, let's first dig deeper into System 1 thinking.

Within System 1 thinking are a host of our bodily reactions that are commonly known as the survival instinct. These reactions are in fact shortcuts and habits we've developed over time. They are our body's physiological and psychological reactions to *perceived* threats, actual or imagined. As you can sense, when it comes to bias, perception is key to whether we react (System 1 thinking) or respond (System 2 thinking) to threat.

The survival instinct is a beautiful thing because it reveals that we are biologically wired with a deep desire to live *and* to fear death and pain. Physiologically, when this instinct kicks in, our brain secretes stress hormones like adrenaline to prepare the body to react quickly. Within our body, this manifests as an increased heart rate, increased blood flow to the muscles, sharpening of our five senses, and shutting down of nonessential functions like digestion. Depending on our individualized temperament and habits, our body reacts in one of six ways:

* **Fight:** Under this reaction, we confront the threat directly, choosing to stand our ground and defend ourselves or our loved ones. This can involve physical or verbal confrontation or intimidation.

* **Flight:** Under this reaction, we prioritize our safety by attempting to escape or move away from the threat. This can involve running, seeking shelter, or finding a safe place to hide.

* **Freeze**: Under this reaction, we minimize any movement and stay completely still because we perceive that the threat may harm us if we move but may not notice us if we don't, or because our bodies go into a state of shock or disorientation.

* **Fawn, Feign, or Faint**: Under this reaction, we either accommodate the threatening party to feel safe, or pretend to be unconscious or dead, or actually lose consciousness or even die from cardiac arrest or a spontaneous stroke due to the fear and shock of the threat.

Like any habit, our minds get programmed with these reactions through practice, and we have the capacity to override them by using PRISM tools and developing System 2 thinking. How can you do this? By becoming aware of your unique reactivities in the form of body sensations, emotions, thoughts, stories, and their accompanying *vedana* through the PRISM tools that begin with mindfulness. By noticing, acknowledging, observing, and feeling your experience, you'll strengthen the muscle of awareness that over time will support you in pausing before reacting and, ultimately, in responding differently. In addition, this process will support you in shifting from disembodiment to embodiment; from feeling separate from to feeling one with your body, heart, and mind; and from exclusion to inclusion consciousness.

This awareness is what advocates of peace, equity, and justice around the globe continue to practice. I imagine millions of Indians, South Africans, and African Americans of many intersectionalities who, with practice, overcame fear in exchange for loving-kindness, achieved interbeing by cultivating love of their oppressor, and used their indomitable courage to keep their eyes on the prize. They trained their nervous systems to walk, march, stand, sit, and withstand the verbal, psychological, emotional, and physical violence of their oppressors. One example of this were the training camps held by the Student Nonviolent Coordinating Committee to protest Jim Crow segregation in the American South. These acts of revolutionary strength were powered by their awareness and acknowledgment of how things were and the moral audacity to imagine and demand a different reality.

CHOOSING SKILLFULLY WITH PRISM

In the book *Influence*, psychology professor Robert Cialdini speaks to the false mental concept with which many humans delude themselves: that we are not easily influenced by our cultural environment. In experiments, when people are asked to rank the influences on their lives, they rank their environment at the bottom, but when tested, the environment is on top. Where our mind goes, attention flows, and this is how our brain begins to be programmed by the narratives of our surroundings.

In 2014, I wanted to invite my friend Bayeté Ross Smith to participate in my organization's Vision 2040 media campaign. Bayeté is a multimedia artist who, at the time, was working on a mixed-media multigenerational conversation between black men of various intersectionalities, from senior corporate executives and civil rights elders to artists, teachers, and the incarcerated. We met for coffee, and at one point in our conversation, Bayeté asked me to participate in his project.

As a non-black person, I realized that in our engrossing two-hour conversation that spanned post-traumatic slave syndrome to abolitionism, I hadn't shared why and how I came to this work, an information gap that may have led him to perceive me through his expansive understanding of blackness—one that spans global cultures, phenotypes, and traditions, but shares a vocabulary of lived somatic experience of subordination, enslavement, and coloniality. Realizing this, I transparently shared my life journey and we laughed off the misunderstanding. The experience, however, piqued my curiosity.

I am acutely aware of the dangers of pretending to be someone I am not, so in confidence I discussed the matter with my coach, Rha Goddess. With investigation and empathy, we realized that unless people know my story, black and brown people project that I am one of them. This insight forced me to own my story and appreciate the effect PRISM was having on my interpersonal relationships: people across difference felt seen, heard, and safe around me. This ability to offer safety isn't something special that I possess, but a skill I have been cultivating since the day I witnessed systemic racism in the New Orleans sentencing court. Isabel Wilkerson calls this skill *radical empathy*, which is something we feel, enact, and experience as a result of practicing three PRISM tools: individuation, prosocial behavior, and perspective-taking.

The injustice I felt in that courtroom triggered my survival brain, which presented me with choices: angrily oppose it (fight), deny it (flight), ignore and repress it (freeze), be immobilized by it (feign), or accommodate it (fawn). Many of my lawyer colleagues succumb to these choices because they are compatible with the conditioning of our System 1 thinking. The causes and conditions of my life, however, had other plans for me.

A few days after completing my internship, I left the built environment of New Orleans's criminal justice system, established on stories of hatred, retribution, and torture, for a Buddhist monastery in Taiwan where I temporarily ordained as a monk. In this built environment, I was surrounded by humans from various walks of life who had dedicated their lives to alleviating suffering through ancient healing technologies that cultivated positive states of mind like loving-kindness and compassion. Through daily practice of PRISM tools for four weeks, System 2 thinking kicked in, and new ways of being became possible for me.

Upon my return, I delved deep into the academic study of racism, sexism, and identity, and complemented it with stories of my many elders, activist colleagues, and humans across difference. I moved to East Harlem to bear witness to the policy implications of systemic biases on racially subordinated humans. I befriended humans across the color line and danced, sang, prayed, and cried with them; and most important, I let myself feel their heartbreak, their fears, and their despair in my own body.

For me, there was no separation. I had to consciously make myself aware of the capital-T truth of our oneness and watch when *wetiko* trickled in to create hierarchies of better- or worse-than. These feelings of mutual interdependence and connection with humans across intersectionality were and continue to be important parts of my healing. Like you, I too am a social animal.

When I stood on my 18th-story window ledge about to jump off, I felt cut off from my social beingness. In that moment of grace when I fell backward into my apartment instead onto the traffic below, I immediately called someone I had met only a few days before; a queer Asian American woman who made me feel seen, heard, and safe. She happened to be walking in my neighborhood, and within minutes, she was in my apartment. The next morning, I met with a psychiatrist and a psychologist, initiating my healing journey. To me, the events of that night are nothing short of a miracle. Whenever I've had dark moments since, with mindfulness and stereotype replacement I remind myself that it was the compassionate and loving presence of another human that opened the possibility of another way.

INCLUSION CONSCIOUSNESS, EMBODIMENT, AND HEALING

In 1970, blinded by their political and economic theologies, American leaders overthrew the Cambodian government and installed a military regime. In response, a communist insurgency known as the Khmer Rouge grew across that nation that, attached to its own *wetiko consciousness*, carried out a genocidal plan to remake Cambodia. They mercilessly tortured and butchered 20 percent of the Cambodian population over the next nine years, including scholars, teachers, doctors, Buddhist monks, and anyone they perceived as elites. These policies caused a massive refugee crisis that continues to reverberate in the bodies, hearts, minds, and memories of millions globally.

In response, in 1978, Maha Ghosananda, one of the few Cambodian wisdom-keepers to survive the butchery because he happened to have been in Thailand when it began, cashed in a plane ticket he'd been given to travel to France and instead used the money to print 40,000 leaflets of the *metta sutta*, the loving-kindness practice we've been using throughout this book.[10] He shared these leaflets in Cambodian refugee camps to empower the people to counteract and transform their fear and pain and to build their courage to start fresh—that is, to shift their hearts and minds from System 1 to System 2 thinking.

Fifteen years later, as some semblance of political stability was established in Cambodia, he began leading annual peace walks across Cambodia's killing fields with thousands of people in his retinue. They walked on the Earth blighted by napalm, land mines, and advanced military technology, planting trees and honoring the millions of humans and more-than-humans lost.

Through the physical act of walking the Earth in the tradition of freedom seekers around the globe, Ghosananda empowered survivors to face, acknowledge, and feel the horrors of the past in their bodies, hearts, and minds with mindfulness and loving-kindness. This radical act of walking planted in the consciousness of participants and witnesses the seeds of reconciliation, healing, and moving forward.

To me, Ghosananda's actions exemplify that culture isn't a permanent external fixture that happens to us. Rather, it's something that we choose to sustain or transform in our hearts through our thoughts, words, and deeds. Per Hirshfield's potent words, culture lives in humans like you and me; if we change our hearts, culture will follow. Ghosananda was just one person who shared and spread his inclusion consciousness and shifted the hearts of millions. His example is just one of thousands of beings walking for peace, justice, reconciliation, and healing. They are the reason why I am confident that as more people like you break bias and shift the inclination of your heart toward compassion, generosity, and inter-being, our cultures will follow.

In the following three chapters, you will explore and, with PRISM tools, transform the ways the three vectors of culture have programmed your mind with bias.

PRISM PRACTICE: COMPASSION

Pause. Find a quiet, comfortable, and safe place where you can be free of distractions for at least 10 minutes.

Cultivating compassion is an ancient practice that supports us in responding in ways to alleviate our pain or the pain of others.

TIP: Read the instructions before starting so you can complete the exercise without needing to open your eyes during the practice.

To begin, find a position for your body that is upright. Place your hands comfortably on your lap or knees, and bring your eyes to a gentle close while guiding your attention to your breath.

Take 5 to 10 deep and soothing breaths, keeping your attention on the full length of each inhale and exhale.

First, direct compassion toward a secondary identity that causes you pain. Imagine this part of your being, and repeat the following four phrases silently in your mind toward this identity at a comfortable pace 5 to 10 times. Feel free to adapt the phrases so they feel natural to you.

Compassion for Self:
May I be free from pain and sorrow.
May I be free from hatred and oppression.
May I be free from suffering.
May I take care of myself and be happy.

Second, direct compassion toward a loved one, e.g., a family member or a friend, who shares your secondary identity and may experience pain due to that social identity. Visualize this being in your mind, feel their pain, and repeat these phrases to them at a comfortable pace 5 to 10 times.

Compassion for a Loved One:
May you be free from pain and sorrow.
May you be free from hatred and oppression.
May you be free from suffering.
May you take care of yourself and be happy.

Next, direct compassion toward all beings who share this secondary identity and may experience pain due to that social identity. Visualize these beings in your mind, feel their pain, and repeat these phrases to them at a comfortable pace 5 to 10 times.

Compassion for Many Beings:
> May we be free from pain and sorrow.
> May we be free from hatred and oppression.
> May we be free from suffering.
> May we take care of ourselves and be happy.

Lastly, extend compassion to all beings everywhere. Imagine and feel compassion radiating outward toward all people, all living beings, and the living Earth.

Compassion for All Beings:
> May we be free from pain and sorrow.
> May we be free from hatred and oppression.
> May we be free from suffering.
> May we take care of ourselves and be happy.

After completing the above, open your eyes and stretch.

Take a few minutes after this practice to reflect and journal on your somatic experience. Remember, repetition of this practice regularly supports building the habit of compassion.

It is a powerful way to strengthen courage and to offer comfort to yourself and others.

Chapter 8

SOCIAL CONTACT

A lie is a lie is a lie, no matter how big the power that tells a lie.

— DR. VANDANA SHIVA

One summer evening, I was in a car with my older sister's Indian American friends. I was a high school freshman, and my sister, Arusha, was driving us to her favorite bubble tea spot. We were all laughing about something when I heard myself, referring to some non-Indian people, mindlessly blurt out, "They are Christians." At that moment, my mind had unconsciously associated being Indian, a nationality, with being Hindu, a spiritual or religious identity. The car suddenly got quiet and my eyes met Reena's, who is Indian and Christian.

As we drove on, I felt imprisoned in the car. I remember an all-encompassing heaviness flooding my face, jaw, chest, gut, and hands. What I was feeling was overwhelming shame, guilt, and remorse. These emotional states were triggered after my mind became aware of the impact of my unskillful words: I had not only excluded Reena from the truth of who we are as people of Indian origin, but also her family and millions of Indians who are non-Hindus. I might have engaged in similar ways before, but this instance is the clearest memory I carry of when I became aware of enacting bias.

Within moments, my teenage mind remembered dozens of instances with my Indian family members, teachers, friends, and even non-Indian classmates when they too used the national identity of Indian interchangeably with the religious identity of Hindu.

Not only that, I sensed that the places and spaces I inhabited, like student clubs, Hindu temples, cultural centers, and even grocery stores, reinforced that association. I didn't know it at the time, but I was actually practicing the PRISM tool of individuation. Instead of beating myself up with shame stories, I started to investigate with curiosity the causes for how I came to hold such inaccurate views. I realized that it was due to social contact, i.e., my interactions with significant humans and the built environment.

Upon having these insights, I had a choice: forget the incident or own my actions and transform this association. The guilt I felt wouldn't let me choose the former. So I owned my mistake, apologized to Reena, and committed to decoupling the association between nationality and religious identity in my mind. Choosing to strengthen this habit in the years since has permitted me to build intimacy with many communities beyond Indians who have felt excluded from their national or religious identity due to a dominant association between those identities, e.g., Christian Palestinians, Baha'i Iranians, Burmese Muslims, animist Hawaiians, and Hindu Pakistanis. In this chapter, we'll dig deep into the cultural vector of social contact, the third root cause of bias.

PRISM EXERCISE

Pause. Take three full breaths and return your attention to your somatic experience.

Take a moment to recall an incident where you enacted bias in an interpersonal setting because of false perceptions you held about another's secondary identities. Recall the moment when you became aware of your *mea culpa.* Bring mindfulness to your somatic experience as you recall the incident. With compassion, stay with your body sensations, not needing to change them. Watch them pass through your body for a few minutes.

Take a few more deep breaths. In the space below or in your journal, reflect on the significant humans and the built environment that may have taught you such views. What actions have you taken in response since then? What actions are you inspired to take moving forward?

SOCIAL CONTACT AND OUR TRAINING IN BIAS

Over the course of our lives, despite what we say, feel, and even consciously believe, we receive certain inputs through our six sense doors to understand our physical and virtual surroundings. With repetition, and without alternatives, what we see, hear, feel, touch, and experience becomes our reality, programmed as our System 1 thinking. Social contact is how our training in bias first begins. Recall that I define *social contact* as "the interactions, connections, and communication we have with other humans during our lives due to our built environment, significant humans, and our choices."

From an early age, we receive cues from our surroundings and our loved ones about various human secondary identities. These cues consist of concepts, emotions, and *vedana*. With repetition and reinforcement, they get stored in our consciousness and become the perception through which we attach meaning to various forms of human bodies, including stories about us versus them.

In law school, I watched many documentaries on various freedom movements to get a visual, auditory, and visceral feel for what our ancestors went through in their efforts. In the documentary *Let Freedom Sing: How Music Inspired the Civil Rights Movement*, I was struck by a comment from a black civil rights leader who had been one of the students to integrate her segregated elementary school. She recounted the painful sight of white women standing in front of the school holding their babies while they yelled the N-word at her. After hearing dozens of similar testimonies from Afro Brazilians, Algerians, South Africans, Indians, and Indonesians, I would wonder what motivated adults to take the radical action of leaving their homes, putting their daily tasks on hold, and spending their precious time being cruel to a six-year-old.

This is exclusion consciousness in action, powered by lies. From a young age, through their built environments and significant humans, these humans were trained in false stories about the humanity of black, brown, and non-Christian people. In their daily lives, they had no social interaction across difference in their built environment where there was equal status; all public and private facilities—from parks, pools, and theaters to cemeteries, churches, and restaurant entrances—were separate. Similarly, most humans they loved and trusted, including spouses, parents, friends, pastors, and employers, shared their dominant identity and views.

I am not justifying their actions, but merely attempting to illustrate how a false story and policies built a cultural container that policed all aspects of human social contact based on secondary identities. Your mind may want to discredit these examples as remnants of a bygone past. Don't feel shame if this is the case. I have been there too. And in such moments, instead of bypassing, I have to consciously become mindful of what's happening in the present moment: the enactment and enforcement of policies banning books and knowledge, the building of walls, the widespread hate speech and the intimidation of subordinated identities, the prohibition of certain humans from entering bathrooms, and banning the mere existence of queer and gender-diverse humans.

The same exclusion consciousness that powered colonization, apartheid, and Jim Crow laws powers these contemporary actions. The human forms may be different, but the mechanism, impact, and scale of it is much greater today than it was in the past due to globalization and the widespread reach of Western capitalism. Rooted in people's daily thoughts, words, and actions are stories of self and other, of right and wrong ways of *being* a human, that get programmed in our minds through social contact.

At this point, I invite you to return to your body. Feel any sensations in your body as you take a few deep breaths. Now the good news is that every built environment you encounter, from public monuments and parks to apps and websites, is a product of the perceptions of humans like you and me.

And just as we have significant humans in our lives, humans like you and me are significant humans for others. By cultivating PRISM practices and developing System 2 thinking, you can make different choices in thoughts, words, and actions in your own built environment and with your own significant humans. In addition, you can choose to use your power of authority and influence to encourage breaking bias in your spheres of influence. Let's dive deeper into how you can break bias in each one of social contact's three elements.

BREAKING BIAS IN OUR BUILT ENVIRONMENT

After my sophomore year in college, I returned to India to study Urdu and volunteer with communities legally labeled as "scheduled castes," "scheduled tribes," and "other backward castes," legal phrases based on the flawed racist science we reviewed in Chapter 5 and coined by the British to rule South Asia; it was retained by India's leaders after gaining independence in 1947. In between, I spent weekends with my aunt. My aunt was an officer in the elite Indian Administrative Services and received benefits such as access to housing as a part of her compensation package. One day I got lost in her housing complex and instead of the "officers' quarters," I ended up in an area with a sign that read "servants' quarters."

Like my aunt's complex, this too was a housing complex for government employees, except in terrible condition, without functioning toilets or kitchens. The humans who lived here, labeled "servants," were no different from me in appearance, but most were members of scheduled castes, tribes, and other backward castes. They performed the essential work of cooking, cleaning, washing, and driving people like my aunt and her family. Without them, my aunt's family couldn't function, and without my aunt, the government couldn't function.

Later that evening, I mentioned to my uncle my sadness at witnessing such a disparity. He tried to comfort me by saying that "the government is actually doing them a favor because otherwise they'd be begging on the streets." He went on to speak about the *inherent* and *natural* inferiority of poor people and I felt like I was speaking to a classist British or French aristocrat. Notice the story of "us" and "them" he was running in his mind.

My uncle's views are similar to views I've heard about Arabs in France, the Roma in Hungary, black people in America, or non-Muslims in Pakistan from humans with dominant identities, as well as from subordinated humans who "pass" or have become assimilated in the dominant paradigm. In all these societies, because of institutional policies, everyone is surrounded by the sheer physical and virtual reality of hierarchies that separate and segregate humans based on class, caste, religion, ethnicity, race, and/or gender, even in sacred spaces like temples, mosques, and churches.*

Listening to my uncle, it became clear to me that the humans who designed the built environment for officers like my aunt and for those designated as servants shared his views. From the era of British colonialism, these humans were and are the policymakers who finance, administer, and make decisions for physical and virtual spaces that decide the intricacies of our built environment. They share particular perceptions of various secondary identities, specifically intersectionality of class and caste, and ideas of how humans ought to interact across differences in such spaces.

American sociologist Douglas Massey calls what I witnessed in India "hypersegregation." It is an extreme form of physical segregation where subordinated groups are concentrated in certain areas as a direct result of historical and ongoing policies. Hypersegregation isn't just physical isolation, but also social and economic confinement away from people with dominant identities like my uncle, with limited access to high-quality education, health care, jobs, food, and other resources, perpetuating cycles of harm, trauma, and inequity.[1]

---

* For example, my female Muslim students from Canada, France, Malaysia, and Iran have shared with me inequities they experience in their sacred spaces. The male section of their mosques is more comfortable, spacious, and inviting, whereas females are relegated to the back or the basement closest to the kitchen, all cues that program the humans in those built environments with a particular gender hierarchy. With awareness, curiosity, empathy, and imagination, they have partnered with their male counterparts to reform these spaces or create new spaces that do not consciously or unconsciously reinforce a gender hierarchy.

Becoming mindful of the false perceptions behind this built environment prevented me from succumbing to the story of hierarchy it overtly and implicitly upheld. This is the magic of mindfulness. And with mindfulness, we can remember that our built environments are a manifestation of the consciousness, shared perceptions, and intentions of their human creators. Without such awareness, our minds start to believe lies about ourselves and others—that we are better- or worse-than because of our secondary identities. Such fixed views block curiosity, empathy, and the imagination of alternative realities.

For subordinated identities, our built environment can create a prison of self-loathing where our minds succumb to the false stories our environments reinforce. For example, when I lived in India, the word *servant* was considered a normal description of a person's profession. This was true both for the ones assigning the term and the ones to whom it was assigned. Twenty years on, millions of Indians, including my uncle and aunt, have abandoned this word because they have become conscious of the false hierarchies it sustains, and more important, its social, emotional, and mental harms.

With such shifts in perceptions, hearts, and minds, many entrepreneurial humans globally are imagining and innovating physical and virtual spaces that dignify humans across intersectionalities. My architect friend Deanna Van Buren is one shining example. As someone who has spent decades imagining and designing built environments for some of the biggest firms in the world, she understands the impact of physical spaces, buildings, and architecture on augmenting the mental, emotional, and physical suffering of subordinated humans in America.

As a result, leaning into her power and expertise, she founded an architecture and real estate development firm, Designing Justice + Designing Spaces, with the vision to use architecture "to address the racism, poverty, and unequal access to resources caused by the criminal legal system."[2] Deanna's firm has designed many spaces for marginalized humans returning home after being caught in the web of stories and policies that sustains America's system of mass incarceration.

While you as an individual may not have Deanna's expertise or passion, you do have choices. You can become conscious of the shared perceptions of humans who designed the built environments that surround you. With PRISM tools, you can become mindful of the false hierarchies they uphold, imagine different possibilities, and make different choices. With this awareness, you will be able to use your positionality to inform and influence others, and make decisions that incline toward equity, repairing historical harms, and healing.

PRISM EXERCISE

Pause. Take three full breaths and bring your attention to feel your body.

In the table below or in your journal, list one aspect of your built environment, physical or virtual, where you spent a significant amount of time as a child, in your adult life so far, and in your life now. Reflect on the consciousness, perceptions, and intentions of the humans who created this environment. What identity-based hierarchy and separation programs were/are they running?

In what ways do their perceptions influence your perceptions about your dominant and subordinated identities, about others, and about decision-making in your professional or personal life?

In completing this exercise, remember, our goal isn't to call anyone as right or wrong. Rather, per the guidance of our elder Ruby Sales, it is to support you in applying hindsight, foresight, and insight to have clearer sight into how you've learned bias via your built environment.

Life Phase and Your Built Environment		The Consciousness, Shared Perceptions, and Intentions of the Creators	Ways This Environment Influences Your Consciousness, Perceptions, and Intentions
As a Child	An example of your physical environment, e.g., *neighborhood, school*		
	An example of your virtual environment, e.g., *video games, e-learning*		
As an Adult	An example of your physical environment		
	An example of your virtual environment		
Now	An example of your physical environment		
	An example of your virtual environment		

Table 8.1

BREAKING BIAS WITH OUR SIGNIFICANT HUMANS

Significant humans are people who provide us with guidance, support, and emotional connections that shape our identity, values, and skills, and contribute to our understanding of the world. When we are young, these humans include members of our family, schools, and physical and virtual environments. As we grow older, they extend to include our spouses and those we interact with in our professional environments. With e-mail and social media technologies, they have also extended to include those we've never physically met but have come to trust because of ongoing interaction and communication.

Our attachment and emotional ties to these humans build the trust, loyalty, and safety we feel toward them. We often unquestionably believe what they say, defend their actions, and even abdicate our own intuition, reason, and values in their favor. This is why we experience emotional and psychological harm, betrayal, and even trauma when the words or actions of these humans breach our trust, loyalty, and safety.

For most of my life, I had a challenging relationship with my father. He is one of my significant humans and I am so grateful for all that he has done for me. However, ever since I was a child, he has blamed the exclusion and marginalization certain people experience in society on their genetics. He's been running a simplistic Mendelian program in his mind that there are two kinds of people in the world: those with good genes, who are rich, successful, and attractive, and those with bad genes, who are poor, unsuccessful, and unattractive. Growing up, it troubled me to my core and I'd spend hours arguing with him, trying to convince him that he was wrong—to no avail, of course.

In 2016, my mother and I were discussing poverty in India. I was sharing with her the segregation and inequalities based in caste, religion, and class that I'd witnessed there while doing field research for my graduate thesis. Overhearing our conversation, my father interjected to tell me that I was wrong, that that was an India of the past, and ultimately, that nothing can be done for poor people because they are genetically defective. Recoiling at his unwelcome interruption, I sensed my jaw, shoulders, and hands tensing up. However, instead of reacting defensively as I habitually would, I took three deep breaths and responded with three words I'd never said to him before: "Tell me more."

Staying mindful of my breath and body, I found myself curious about where he was going with his argument. As I listened to him, I realized that my father lived in a completely made-up reality, a reality that felt true in his mind but did not fit the actual facts on the ground. As he went on, my body began to relax and my mind began to piece together his upbringing. He grew up in an extremely sheltered built environment where my grandparents shuttled him between home and school and later between home and work. In his reality, there was very little poverty and no caste system in India because he did not experience or witness it firsthand.

As someone wedded to his identity as a doctor, he served all patients with exceptional care, but not because of who they were; rather, because of his self-concept of what it means to be a good doctor: someone who can diagnose and offer treatment for illness. As I continued to ask him questions, he shared a story of one of *his* significant humans, his grade-school science teacher, "Masterji." I could sense my father's respect for this teacher because Masterji had empowered him to become a doctor. Then my father shared that Masterji used to always say that all the problems in the world are due to "bad genetics" of "bad people."

I suddenly realized that my father had taken in this false story through his significant human—a story likely rooted in false and racist theories of eugenics that the British exported globally through colonization. And he had been running this program ever since. This is the power of social contact. In that moment, what had been unconscious and beneath the surface for decades became conscious and rose above the surface.

For my father, choosing to trust the false ideas of his significant human imprisoned him in a false concept; for me, the discovery freed me from the hierarchies I was creating of "good" and "bad" ways of being a father. Now, through regular perspective-taking, I've come to see my father for who he is—a vulnerable human who, after his brother died by suicide, wasn't permitted to feel his emotions because of gender roles, and who was kept from seeking help because of cultural taboos.

I share this story not to defend or justify my father's views, but rather to illustrate how PRISM helped me reach a place of understanding and forgiveness, a place that has enabled me to invite in many more possibilities for myself and for him. In the years since we had this conversation, I have noted a dramatic shift in my father's views and attitudes. The more I practice mindfulness, curiosity, and empathy in my interactions with him, the more he's been able to open up and loosen his own fixed views.

PRISM EXERCISE

Pause. Take three full breaths and return your awareness to your somatic experience, recalling our agreements. In your journal or in the space below, list three significant humans in your life as a child, in your adult life so far, and in your life now.

Child:

Adult:

Now:

With curiosity and empathy, notice your significant humans' perceptions of one or more subordinated identities in your society, e.g., religion, race, ethnicity, sexuality, or gender. Upon what stories of hierarchy are their perceptions founded? And who were some possible significant humans who shaped and reinforced their perceptions?

Reflect on ways their views influenced your own perceptions (at least before you read this book) toward these subordinated identities.

BREAKING BIAS WITH OUR CHOICES

By now, I hope you're able to appreciate that though your built environments and significant humans have shaped your perceptions about others, moving forward you have (1) the power of choice over what and how you think in your environments, (2) where and in which environments you place your attention, (3) with whom you spend your time, and (4) how you show up in your interactions with your significant humans. This is where the third element of social contact, our choices, empowers us to overcome social contact's training in bias.

Let me demonstrate with a personal example. In law school, one of my favorite professors once shared with me that if poor black women would stop getting pregnant and cashing welfare checks, "their race" would make more economic progress. Pause here for a moment and let this statement land in your body. Notice your somatic experience—sensations, emotions, and *vedana*—and how your experience may be connected to your secondary identities, particularly race, gender, and class. Take a moment to document your experience below or in your journal.

Now, with perspective-taking, list some of the stories, concepts, and *vedana* that may have shaped my professor's perceptions. What emotions accompany them?

I'd heard these stereotypes before, but I was incredibly disappointed that they were coming from her. This same human had mentored and coached me from a deep sense of genuine care. While she must have felt safe with me to share her views, as she did so I felt unsafe, hurt, and judged. A part of me wanted to confront her and call her out for her views. Instead, I imagined how I would feel in my body if someone called me out in that way. I felt a rising defensiveness and shame. From my Buddhist training, I knew that these emotional states are unwholesome and sever connection. This is where PRISM came in handy.

First, I practiced stereotype replacement by becoming mindful of what Bryan Stevenson often says—all of us are more than the worst things we have said or done. I curiously brought to awareness what I knew about who my professor actually was as opposed to who she *should* or *ought to* be. I investigated how this human, who has many subordinated identities herself, like being Jewish, a descendant of Holocaust survivors, and a woman in the legal academy, came to hold such views. I reflected on the factors that blocked her ability to see, feel, and empathize and to instead fall prey to blanket stereotypes of entire groups of humans, without even being conscious of them.

Curiosity helped me *see* that she is a highly educated wealthy white cis hetero female who downplayed her gender and religious identity (she went out of her way to mention that she wasn't observant and her husband wasn't Jewish) to consciously or unconsciously fit into the dominant paradigm of the legal profession. In addition, unlike me, she had no intimate relationships with poor black women. Yes, she had black maids, assistants, and students, but no relationship where there was equal status, as with friends or family members.

In her hypersegregated built environment, she exclusively interacted with humans who shared her racial, class, and educational background and generally reinforced her views. In other words, she physically and virtually lived and worked in environments where she rarely formed intimate friendships and relationships with humans across difference. Research shows that 91 percent of white Americans have *zero* friends of color; 83 percent of black Americans have *zero* white friends; and 64 percent of Latine Americans have *zero* white or black friends.[3] In non-Western societies like Egypt, Iraq, India, or Singapore, a similar reality holds true with respect to race as well as other secondary identities, such as religion, caste, and class.

Such segregation obstructs natural opportunities for social contact; it impedes us from forming intimate connections across our relative differences, and keeps our minds from counteracting the stereotypes we are fed about one another through the three vectors of culture. Humans with different secondary identities thus exist as monolithic ideas in our minds, not as the actual humans we each are. In such an environment, for people like my professor whose views of race and class remain unquestioned at the unconscious level, the hypersegregation influences their speech, interactions, and decisions.

As I began to understand my professor's experience, I began to feel compassion for her. I no longer operated in shoulds, rights, and wrongs. Rather, I felt that I could be honest with her in a nonjudgmental and shame-free way about the impact of her statement on me. So I prepared my body, heart, and mind for the conversation, using the five shared agreements in this book. I shared with her my story of exclusion and marginalization; how I have been impacted by similar stereotypical tropes; and most important, that I was bolstering the courage to have this conversation with her because I deeply respected her. After I finished, I felt what Brené Brown calls a "vulnerability hangover" in my body: racing heart, clammy hands, and a sense of hollowness in my head.

After a pause, my professor sincerely apologized to me. Not only that, she reflected out loud how she had felt ashamed for uttering those words. She admitted that despite her experiences with sexism and antisemitism, she had adopted some despicable views concerning race that required further examination. Lastly, she thanked me for giving her this opportunity to grow. Ever since that day, she has undergone an earnest transformation. She has become a committed student, advocate, and patron of antipoverty and racial equity efforts in her professional life.

UNLEARNING BIAS BY CHOOSING PRISM

I share this incident to demonstrate the power of inclusion consciousness. With the support of awareness, curiosity, kindness, and compassion, you have the capacity to overpower and transform the habits of exclusion consciousness. Like *wetiko*, inclusion consciousness is also infectious. However, staying with it requires conscious practice and purification of our minds from the lies we've come to believe about ourselves and others. This is the process of neuro-decolonization, or cleansing from our minds, bodies, and nervous systems the mental habits of modernity's narratives of separation, hatred, greed, and selfishness. This is the work of consciousness shift. According to Malcolm Gladwell's research, we don't need everyone to make such shifts, but just enough of us, what he calls a "critical mass," to tip the scale toward breaking bias, healing, and repair.[4]

This is what all our wise elders and ancestors, regardless of their intersectional identities, practiced in the face of hatred, vitriol, and violence, from those who resisted Mao's and Stalin's cultural revolutions to the Indian *satyagrahis* and American civil rights leaders. With practice, this consciousness can become System 1 thinking that is rooted in the wisdom of our interbeingness and relationality. There is a famous Christian hymn that goes, "This little light of mine, I'm gonna let it shine." This is our light of inclusion consciousness, and when practiced by millions, it will evolve into new currencies of power—ones that value love, repair, and healing.

PRISM PRACTICES

Pause. Take three breaths and observe your somatic experience.

* Become mindful of stereotypes you've learned about your gender, race, ethnicity, appearance, or another visible secondary identity. Reflect on ways your physical and virtual built environments and significant humans reinforce such views. Investigate with curiosity the built environments and significant humans who support you (or can support you) in actively replacing such views with counterexamples.

* List five attributes of your secondary identities that your mind often judges or finds painful. Feel the somatic experience and the *vedana* of these aspects of yourself. Reflect on aspects of social contact that strengthen such thoughts and associations. Consider ways you can limit such social contact or, using PRISM tools, how you can choose to show up differently in such spaces, places, or contexts.

* List five attributes of your secondary identities that bring you ease and you admire about yourself. Feel the somatic experience and the *vedana* of these aspects of yourself. Reflect on aspects of social contact that can strengthen such thoughts and associations. Consider ways you can strengthen such social contact or, using PRISM tools, how you can choose spaces, places, or contexts that help you cultivate such self-appreciation.

* Reflect on ways social contact has programmed you in stereotypes with respect to some of your secondary identities.

Become mindful of situations where such stereotypes block your ability to connect with humans across difference. Feel the underlying emotions and sensations, and notice the concepts and stories your mind repeats in such instances. Imagine ways you can show up differently; visualize your body, speech, and emotions in those instances.

✳ Take an inventory of 5 to 10 significant humans in your life. Notice their visible secondary identities. Notice any patterns of sameness you see among these humans. With curiosity, reflect on ways you can build meaningful relationships with humans across difference, especially through choosing different virtual or physical environments and spending high-quality time with humans who are visibly different from you.

✳ Imagine and bring to awareness the mental formations and *vedana* of the following humans. What separation programs are they running? Reflect on their relationship with the Carl Sagan and bell hooks quotes in Chapter 2 (page 69) and Chapter 6 (page 175).

  ✳ Humans who believe in the narrative of white Christian manifest destiny

  ✳ Humans who believe in a fixed interpretation of Islam's prohibition of "idol worship"

  ✳ Humans who believe in a singular religious identity for a nation

  ✳ Humans who believe in supreme leaders to create a future utopia

Chapter 9

EDUCATION

*The only thing that interferes
with my learning is my education.*

— ALBERT EINSTEIN

In the past decade, I've delivered hundreds of lectures, key-notes, and presentations on mental health, unconscious bias, social entrepreneurship, and inequity at universities, bar associations, tech companies, health systems, and nonprofits. As an educator, I generally consider my audience in preparing my remarks, partic-ularly their intersectional secondary identities, what they likely know, and how far they may be willing to stretch.

In one such presentation, I decided to take a little risk. I stood on the red dot at the TED headquarters in New York and presented to their entire staff about unconscious racial bias and its first root cause, the story of race. After sharing a condensed version of what you learned in Chapter 5, particularly how European skull collec-tors created the rank hierarchy of race, I encountered a theater full of emotions that I was used to by now. "Every person in Congress and every human needs to know this!" "What do we do about the impact of this story?" And most commonly, "Why did I not learn this in grade school?"

Just then, I heard a pensive and doubting voice from the rear of the amphitheater. I could sense this person's disbelief as they ques-tioned my premise—that there is no gene for race. They said, "Of course race is genetic." They went on to reference scientific research on the different levels of competence and abilities between human "races," such as sports, music, and math. They then referenced having attended some of the best schools in the world and being friends with leading scientists of all races and said that the fact that no one ever questioned the biological nature of race was evidence that what we call *race* must have a biological basis.

Nazi propaganda chief Joseph Goebbels described this person's experience as follows: "If you tell a lie big enough and keep repeating it, people will eventually come to believe it."[1] This is how the Nazis seduced entire countries into accepting the murder of millions of Jews, Roma, queer, and other subordinated humans.

I responded to this person's comment with anthropologist Alan Goodman's words that I shared in Chapter 5, that to grasp the myth of race requires an absolute paradigm shift in perspective. This is because our six sense doors repeatedly receive the input of this mythology and white superiority, subtly and overtly, through the three vectors of culture. In this chapter, we will unravel the cultural vector of education, the fourth cause and condition responsible for our training in bias.

EDUCATION AND OUR TRAINING IN BIAS

Recall that *education* is "*schooling* and *curricula* established with the intention to assimilate humans into hierarchies through *disinformation, misinformation,* and *knowledge gaps*." If social contact is where our training in bias begins, education is how bias gets fortified in our consciousness as we learn certain concepts, emotions, and their accompanying *vedana* through our schooling and curricula, that over time become our perceptions toward different forms of bodies.

As we begin, I want to note that by *education*, I mean educational systems, not independent learning, skills acquisition, and personal growth. I also want to invite you to be present to how education is actually structured in your society, not to the lofty ideals it stands for. This reality check is extremely important for this root cause because for you, as it was for me, education may have been a way out of poverty, exclusion, and marginalization. Thus, you may carry, and rightly so, many positive associations and emotions toward this topic.

The discussion ahead isn't designed to invalidate these emotions. Rather, I have structured this chapter to help you see the big picture of (1) what education is today, (2) how it came to be what it is, (3) its purpose, outcomes, and role in our bias training, and most important, (4) ways you can unlearn the biases you may have learned through your education. With this in mind, let's begin with an exercise.

PRISM EXERCISE

Pause. Take a few breaths, feel grounded in your body, and recall our agreements.

Imagine being a white human who protested integration efforts in a Western nation like the United States, Australia, or Canada. In the space below or in your journal, take a few minutes to investigate what they likely learned—which might include nothing at all—about black, brown, and indigenous humans in their K–12 science, history, or literature classes. What about in college or graduate school, if they pursued those credentials?

Now let's step into the present and imagine being a human who protests teaching about the existence of queer and gender-diverse humans, or the history of colonialism, enslavement, and segregation. In the space below or in your journal, reflect upon what they learned about queer and gender-diverse humans, or the histories mentioned above in their K–12 science, history, or literature classes. What about college or graduate school, if they pursued those credentials?

Lastly, step into your own experience. Reflect on what you learned in your K–12 science, history, or literature classes about race, gender, class, colonialism, enslavement, and what has been done to our living Earth in the last 500 years in the pursuit of money. What about college or graduate school, if that's relevant in your case?

Who was portrayed as beautiful? Ugly? Civilized? Monstrous? A winner? A loser? A hero? A villain? Did such portrayals affect how you view yourself or others as better-than or worse-than? In what ways? Remember to feel your somatic experience and breathe as you move through this exercise.

I start with these exercises to help you appreciate the concepts, emotions, and *vedana* wired into our minds and nervous systems through schooling. Today, the vast majority of humanity spends at least 6 to 12 hours a day in schools from as young as age 3 to at least 16 years old. Have you ever wondered why and how, regardless of culture or geography, most "schools" are dramatically similar globally? For example:

* Children are legally required to attend.

* They run from kindergarten to grade 12.

* They have a standardized curriculum rooted in mental learning, not real-life experiences or skills training.

* The curricula are approved by political bodies in set subjects like math, science, literature, history, and the arts; history curricula focus on wars, war heroes of the dominant identities, and nationalist pride.

* All curricula are taught at a fixed rate based on age and grade level, even if that doesn't work for students. There is little to no opportunity to explore a subject in depth, to develop a passion, or to hone a skill. There's a fixed amount of time for each subject per day.

* Children are divided by age, not by what they need or want to learn. Whether childhood, or adulthood for that matter, is joyful is irrelevant.

* The teacher is the authority, and whether they can teach well or whether they hate children is irrelevant. Teachers are considered qualified only if they have the required credentials. The children provide empty heads that the teacher is paid to fill. There is little to no recognition of teachers who inspire and empower children.

* Students and teachers alike believe that the main purpose of schooling is to prepare students to learn the right answers to pass exams and be better than others through competition.[2]

This structure of schooling plants disinformation, misinformation, and gaps in knowledge about various human identities in the minds of students. With repetition and reinforcement, these mental formations become the perceptions through which we come to view ourselves and others.

PRISM EXERCISE

Pause. Take three full breaths and bring your attention to feel the sensations in your body.

Depending on your knowledge of the subject, what I have shared so far may feel harsh or not harsh enough. I invite you to notice how my assessment *feels* in your mind, heart, and body. In the space below or in your journal, document any emotions, ideas, and even criticisms that arise and feel their accompanying sensations.

Now, with curiosity, using what you've learned in Parts I and II so far, think, investigate, and write below or in your journal how the K–12 education system outlined above may have come to be.

MY ENTRY INTO EDUCATION

My family moved from Delhi to Queens, New York, after I finished the fifth grade. In India, I attended an English-medium private school, meaning that all subjects except Hindi were taught in English. In my new home, however, I had to attend my zoned inner-city public school based on our zip code because my parents couldn't afford to send me to "better" schools. For the remainder of my middle and high school education, I found myself in schools with overcrowded classrooms, insufficient resources, significant interpersonal conflict, and a constant police presence. As an immigrant, succeeding at school became my only way out.

Thankfully, my Indian education provided me with a strong foundation in math, science, geography, and other subjects, which allowed me to excel with sufficient support from my teachers and with hard work. In college, after working as a recruiter for Teach for America (TFA), an American education equity nonprofit, I realized that my educational experience was the norm for children like me—those of color, immigrant, poor and/or working class—which I, like many others, found deeply unfair. Working for TFA taught me that our current educational system is an evolution of the segregated, unequal system of the Jim Crow era despite many efforts to reform it.

The most prominent of these efforts was argued at the U.S. Supreme Court level in 1973 in *San Antonio Independent School District v. Rodriguez* less than 20 years after the same court declared segregation in schools unconstitutional in *Brown v. Board of Education* (1954). In *San Antonio v. Rodriguez*, parents argued that the school finance system, which relied on the local property tax for school funding, was unfair because it prevented poorer children, who were largely black or brown, from obtaining a high-quality education. The majority of the court—with dominant secondary identities and likey shared perceptions about the humanity of black, brown, and poor people—did not think so. As a result, for generations afterward, access to high-quality education and opportunities has been guaranteed only to those children whose families can afford it.

Sensing the unfairness of these views, I gave hundreds of impassioned presentations on the ways our education system sustained class- and race-based disparities to inspire my fellow students to become a part of TFA. With that said, while I supported TFA's work, I knew it was a Band-Aid solution, like hundreds of nonprofits working on this issue globally. After college, I worked as an educator and education advocate in South Korea and Myanmar, confronting the same identity-based inequities I grew up with in India and the United States. And I began to see patterns of marginalization across these systems, which led me to write my graduate thesis on comparative education.* One afternoon while researching at the Cambridge University Library, I *literally* slipped off my chair (I know, nerd move!) when I discovered the origins of the modern education system and their identical purpose in simple and clear terms: the assimilation of children into human hierarchies.[3]

THE ORIGINS OF THE MODERN EDUCATIONAL SYSTEM

Prior to our current educational system, every society had unique ways to teach and train its young in cosmologies, life skills, and values. For example, in animist cultures with inclusion consciousness, humans did not use written language; rather, they used oral traditions, song, ritual, dance, and other technologies to train the young in reciprocity, interbeingness, generosity, and compassion. They taught them the ways they had developed to read the stars, winds, seasons, land, and clouds; to cultivate land; to make their own clothes; to harvest and prepare foods; to domesticate animals; and so much more. These training systems prepared young people for different stages of life as they took on more responsibility;

---

* You can access it here: anuguptany.com

it prepared them to become good elders and ancestors so they could pass this knowledge down to future generations.

In hierarchical centralized societies, until the 19th century, education and intellectual pursuits, particularly literacy and numeracy, were luxuries restricted to privileged humans of a particular intersectionality, including cis men, the wealthy, dominant castes, religious leaders, and scholars. Beyond these institutions, humans still learned and acquired knowledge in skills in formal and informal ways, including apprenticeships, guilds, and instruction from significant humans such as family. The purpose of education was to be able to administer the institutions of control within centralized societies. Given the widespread practice of exclusion based on various secondary identities like religion, class, descent, and gender, the masses didn't need an education.

This began to shift in modernity, particularly after European industrialization. Recall from our earlier chapters that the favorite pastime of most rulers in centralized societies was invading one another to win more territory. In the late 18th century, around the time of the American and French revolutions, the Prussians (modern-day Germans) encountered a problem. Most of their soldiers were farmers, and when an adversary shot at them, they'd run back to their farms and families. This annoying tendency prevented the Prussians from gaining more land. They needed soldiers who would blindly obey, even if ordered to go on a suicide mission.

To create such humans, Prussia used policies to mandate a system of schools exclusively for peasant boys that had four structural elements:[4]

1. Obedience to an authority figure, the teacher.

2. The inculcation of nationalism* over oneself, one's family, one's land, and God. Nationalism is a vital part of all modern educational systems.

---

* I define *nationalism* as "identification with an idea of one's own nation and support for its interests."

3. Concepts of being separate from and superior to the Earth, to more-than-humans, and to humans who didn't share the nation's dominant identities.

4. Training in hierarchical identity formation based on age, seniority, gender, ability, class, etc., through separation and segregation of children based on secondary identities. As this system spread globally, race, ethnicity, religion, gender, *jati*, and other hierarchical arrangements were (and still are) used to justify *de jure* or de facto separation, segregation, and treatment of students.

The Prussian authorities needed better marketing than "send us your children so we can make them our cannon fodder." As a result, schools taught children to be literate and numerate, but not how to think independently or critically, as is still the case in modern-day authoritarian regimes like Myanmar. Children were presumed to be *tabula rasa*, or blank slates, that the teacher imprinted with the "right answers," identical to what you may have experienced in your schooling. With this system, Prussia became a military powerhouse and successfully expanded its territory to much of modern Germany.*

With the advent of the Industrial Revolution, as urban factories sprang up, Europe's farmers needed to be trained to become reliable factory workers—to show up on time, follow orders, and by extension accept boredom as their fate in life. Prussia's educational model was adopted across Europe to churn these workers out.

This system evolved to gain support from missionaries and reformers like the American Horace Mann, who thought school systems could improve the lives of poor Christians as well as save non-Christians from their "savage" ways. He lobbied Massachusetts to adopt a similar system, and other American states soon followed.[5] As European empires spread their tentacles, this top-down educational system was instituted globally, overtaking and

---

* Within 100 years, the German state was using textbooks, curricula, board games, segregation in the school environment, etc., to strengthen a made-up Aryan racial identity, fueling entitlement, victimization, hatred, and separation. Decades of misinformation, disinformation, and knowledge gaps in German schooling and curricula trained Germans to perceive human minorities as less than them, ultimately enabling the Holocaust.

supplanting numerous mechanisms of learning, training, and intellectual cultivation.

British colonial operative Thomas B. Macaulay summarized this system's intention best: "to do our best to form a class who may be interpreters between us and the millions whom we govern."[6] Or to colonize the minds of people via neuro-colonization as I've mentioned before, to dominate and subjugate more humans, non-humans, and the Earth. In the United States, Carlisle Indian Industrial School's slogan of "Kill the Indian, Save the Man" captured this intention well. The effect: the creation of a docile workforce that maintains hierarchies and domination so those in authority can continue to accumulate money.

Educational systems of this kind remain intact today and they are growing globally. Censorship, selective histories, and nationalism—rooted in exclusion consciousness—are being taught to millions of children from the Philippines and India to Colombia, Mexico, and Japan in efforts to sustain the supposed superiority of certain dominant identities while also feeding intergroup divisions, inequality, and conflict.

In *Empireland*, journalist Sathnam Sanghera provides detailed documentation of how British curricula up to the modern day systematically exclude any mention of the monstrosity of their colonial empire, forming a huge knowledge gap.[7] Instead, from a young age, humans are taught a sense of narcissistic pride toward their nation, in their civilizing victories, and in who is rightfully British (and who is not).

Similarly, while working in Malaysia in 2009, I was surprised to find little to no mention of that country's pre-Islamic animist, Buddhist, and Hindu past in its museums and cultural sites. My Malay colleagues informed me that the Malaysian state considers its pre-Islamic history the age of ignorance, or *jahiliyya* in Arabic. Thus, it is omitted from public spaces and from education. Malaysia isn't unique in making such an omission. Systems in all countries, including the United States, omit history that countervails education's nationalist purposes.

PRISM EXERCISE

Pause. Take three full breaths and return your attention to your body, recalling our shared agreements.

I'd like you to investigate your experience in education with a bias known as *nationalism*.

In the space below or in your journal, reflect on what your K–12 education taught you about your nation. Which one of your secondary identities was visibly included in your national identity? Which ones were excluded? Which human identities were portrayed as *other*? Explore some of the visual, auditory, or conceptual cues you received from your schooling and curricula about self and other.

BREAKING BIAS BY FILLING THE KNOWLEDGE GAPS

Gabriela Ilieva was my favorite professor in college. Ethnically Bulgarian, she came of age behind the Iron Curtain. She taught me subjects few would guess to be her expertise: Hindi and the South Asian political economy. To me, she symbolized the best of the human spirit when it's rooted in inclusion consciousness. Clad in pleather pants and sporting a mohawk, to some she was the antithesis of what a Hindi professor is "supposed to look like," but here she was teaching me how to write essays in Hindi and feel comfortable conversing about advanced Hindi literature like *Godaan* and "Toba Tek Singh."

Throughout my college years, I spent hours visiting her office, where in conversation she was teaching me about my ancestral history for free, outside the bounds of the required reading for her classes. She taught me how colonial British policies systematically blighted the regions of modern-day Bihar, Uttar Pradesh, and

Bengal to avert rebellions; how they first partitioned Bengal based on religious differences and went on to create similar demarcations in India, Sri Lanka, Burma, Palestine, the Levant, Cyprus, and many other places; and, in particular, how their scorched-earth policies led to the 1943 Bengali famine, also known as the Bengali holocaust, in which three million humans starved to death.*

As someone who had served as a tour guide at the Museum of Jewish Heritage in New York, I rarely used the word *holocaust* casually. I felt so cheated that I had never been taught in my 12 years of education how a nation fighting the Nazis could engage in the same type of horror. It was then that Gabriela shared with me how Winston Churchill, the celebrated prime minister of Britain, responded to the famine: "Why hasn't Gandhi died yet?" Churchill later went on to say, "I hate Indians. They are a beastly people with a beastly religion. The famine was their own fault for breeding like rabbits."[8]

Some strong words from a widely respected human who had authority and influence over the entirety of the British Empire. These words, a playbook for the story of race, justified objectification of anyone who didn't fit his intersectional vision of humanity, i.e., wealthy white European Judeo-Christian Western-educated people. Such words aren't a relic of a bygone past; they reverberate among political leaders pursuing their own ambitions for more land, power, and fame.†

Pause here for a moment and notice the mental concepts and *vedana* that accompany the word *beast*. His use of *beastly*, connected to the cosmology of the Great Chain of Being, not only diminishes hundreds of millions of Indians of many intersectionalities, but also relegates nonhuman/more-than-human beings to the status of "things," justifying their elimination without any feelings of remorse, guilt, shame, or emotional pain. When ideas such as these

---

* If you have doubts, read Elkins's *Legacy of Violence* or Tharoor's *Inglorious Empire*.

† For example, on October 16, 2023, in justifying the policy of declaring war on Gazan Palestinians, Israeli prime minister Benjamin Netanyahu's office said that this conflict is "a struggle between the children of light and the children of darkness, between humanity and the law of the jungle," once again using speciesist imagery to justify Israel's genocidal policies and actions.

are left unquestioned, our human minds become infected with the underlying exclusion consciousness of the racist and speciesist mental concepts and their associated *vedana*.

Psychology scholars like Erich Fromm, Viktor Frankl, and Gabor Maté call the use of words such as these "psychopathic." Yet our educational systems continue to valorize such humans and to tolerate, expect, and even defend such words under the guise of free speech.

With that in mind, I am going to be honest: when Gabriela first shared this piece of history with me, a part of me that had internalized the racism I'd learned from the three vectors of culture believed Churchill—believed that Indians like me were a beastly people. This was why I had distanced myself from yoga and meditation, refrained from speaking Hindi in public, and looked down upon immigrants who spoke English with accents that weren't American or British. I had believed this false story of being a beast who needed to be civilized through Western modes of consumption and materialism. I wasn't born with these attitudes, but I had acquired them through programming since I was a child, even in India. With repeated exposure, such concepts become a part of our survival brain and System 1 thinking, and before we know it, they become our reality.

PRISM EXERCISE

Pause. Read Churchill's statements again and notice the impact of those words in your body. If your mind wants to distract you with justifications, notice those thoughts, and then bring yourself back to your body. Feel what it was like to be the humans at whom such statements were directed. Continue to breathe with these sensations.

In the space below or in your journal, reflect on where you see similar rhetoric in your society. Toward whom? Try to be specific about the targeted secondary identities, e.g., ethnic or religious groups, LGBTQ+ people, the poor.

Now, return to Chapter 1's loving-kindness practice and perform it for your body, for the humans Churchill is talking about, for the more-than-humans he refers to as *beasts*. Then, if you're capable, extend loving-kindness toward the consciousness that prompts the likes of Churchill to make such remarks.

HEALING THE DISEMBODIMENT OF EDUCATION

As a child, I was very talkative and social. But my Indian teachers thought my inability to stay quiet was a problem. This got me into lots of trouble because I always wanted to talk to my classmates despite my teachers' warnings. So then came the name-calling, angry outbursts, slaps, punches, pinches, ear-pulling, beatings with sticks, fingernails dug into my hands, and orders to stand in the corner for up to 30 minutes with my head between my legs and my hands over my ears.

The days I didn't get hit in my elementary school were some of my happiest ones because my cheeks, ears, arms, legs, back, or some other body part weren't hurting from physical beatings, not to mention recovering from the public humiliation and psychological taunts. My experience wasn't unusual, particularly for boys. At the systems level, these behaviors were passed down to my teachers through their own experiences in schools, which in India had originated only five generations prior under the British Raj. However, at the personal level, these experiences instilled in my body and mind fear, submission to authority, and numbness to pain. This was my training in becoming disembodied and ignoring, suppressing, and not feeling the physical, emotional, and mental pain I experienced.

When I was teaching in Korea, I daily witnessed similar violence perpetrated on the bodies, minds, and hearts of my students. I also witnessed similar incidents firsthand in Morocco, Mexico, and Taiwan, as well as secondhand while doing research on schooling systems as far apart as Brazil, Mozambique, Indonesia, and Fiji. In the West, due to legal bans on corporal punishment, many public schools have adopted a different punitive approach that criminalizes children's and young people's misbehavior, trauma, and addiction. And due to bias, generally young people with subordinated identities are the ones who get criminalized.

In law school, I was part of a student group called the Suspension Representation Project. This initiative trained law students to represent children in court-like settings to keep them from being suspended or expelled from school. Through this program, I represented children as young as six years old. Every one of these children came from a black or brown, poor, traumatized, non-English speaking, or immigrant background, and they were about to be legally labeled *delinquent*. This program brought alive what many scholars call the "school-to-prison pipeline."[9] At an individual level, the impact of this phenomenon is to cut marginalized humans from their bodies, hearts, and minds and force them to assimilate into *the right way* of being human or else perish in state-operated facilities or prisons.

PRISM EXERCISE

Pause. Take three full breaths. Notice and feel your somatic experience, recalling our agreements.

The information I've shared in this section may be upsetting. I invite you to return to Chapter 7's compassion practice. If afflictive emotions like anger, shame, blame, and grief come up, extend compassion to those emotions. You can also seek support to explore these emotions.

In the space below or in your journal, imagine ways of teaching and learning that would feel joyful and fulfilling for you.

Mental, emotional, psychological, and physical violence was (and is) an essential ingredient of education worldwide. It is no wonder that most young people have experienced some form of bullying and mental health challenges in educational environments.[10] With that said, a different way is possible.

Mohandas Gandhi remarked that "true education is that which draws out and stimulates the spiritual, intellectual, and physical faculties of children." In the 20th century, as European powers were introducing their educational system to entrench domination over human minds globally, Gandhi, and other social reformers such as Paramahansa Yogananda, E. F. Schumacher, and Rabindranath Tagore, outlined and executed detailed plans and ideas for how education can support children and adults in developing their full potential as humans.*

In the last century, political leaders from around the world, trained in Western superiority and entrenched in *wetiko*, deemed these plans foolhardy and regressive. In privileging the mind and hierarchies, they adopted policies and established educational systems that beat inclusion consciousness out of many societies globally. But inclusion consciousness still persisted, even in some of the most unlikely places, like Myanmar.

I witnessed it firsthand while teaching at Phaung Daw Oo, a free school run by Buddhist monastics for over 10,000 impoverished and orphaned children of all religious and ethnic backgrounds in Mandalay. Despite the surrounding violence of the military *junta*, in this school, hundreds of children were trained in the heart and mind qualities of mindfulness, loving-kindness, and common humanity. Desmond Tutu, the Dalai Lama, and Thích Nhât Hânh are products of such learning and training systems.

As at Phaung Daw Oo, our ancestors had so many ways of knowing through human faculties beyond the mind. In one of my favorite ancient stories, a Buddhist nun was having trouble understanding the meaning of a sutra despite years of effort. So she went to the enlightened Zen master Huineng for guidance. The master

---

* Paramahansa Yogananda created "How-to-Live Schools," and Rabindranath Tagore established Shantiniketan.

responded, "I am illiterate. Would you please read out the passage for me first? Then perhaps I may unveil its meaning for you."

Astonished, the nun arrogantly said, "If you can't even read, how are you able to understand its meaning?" He then famously responded: "Truth has nothing to do with words. Truth is like the bright moon in the night sky. Words are like this finger which points at the moon. Though the finger can point out where the moon is, it is not the moon itself. To see the moon, one does not necessarily need the finger, right?"

It is said that with Huineng's guidance, the nun soon became enlightened.

Western science too has demonstrated the numerous benefits of training in skills like loving-kindness, compassion, resilience, and joy to combat trauma, fear, and bullying. At this stage of our human evolution, we have enough of the knowledge and wisdom we can possibly need to address the challenges of our time. The task for us is to bring our attention to that wisdom and put it into practice.

We need people like you to imagine, with ongoing practice of the PRISM tools, what many artists and activists call "ancient emergent possibilities": *ancient* because they've been known to us since ancient times, *emergent* because they are emerging and will emerge in novel forms, and *possibilities* that can shift education's structure away from domination, competition, and separation to truly draw out each child's and each adult's spiritual, intellectual, and physical faculties.

PRISM EXERCISE

Pause. Take three full breaths, feel your somatic experience, and recall our agreements.

In the space below or in your journal, take a few minutes to list the ways your education trained you to perceive aspects of your *beingness*—your biological, social, or experiential identities—as wrong, bad, sinful, and something to be ashamed of, or valuable, desirable, and something to be grateful for.

Then, knowing what you know now, reflect on whether these instances were a result of disinformation, misinformation, and/or knowledge gaps.

As you read through your reflections, notice that a single person wasn't responsible for your educational programming to hate/appreciate aspects of yourself or others. It was a result of the efforts and actions of many people with shared perceptions of aspects of our humanity. Imagine how this consciousness traveled through the three cultural vectors and infected many groups of humans through education.

LEARNING EMBODIMENT WITH PRISM

As a senior in high school, I studied the Japanese language at Baruch College. Until that point, I had known very little about Japan, but learning Japanese helped me appreciate this region's culture, cosmology, and unique systems of being. During every lesson, Professor Takeda advised us to dispel our attachments to how this language ought to be and to instead appreciate it for what it is. In this way, what seemed "different" and "other" to our minds—Japanese—would become familiar over time.

In essence, she encouraged us to practice PRISM. She helped us enter a world beyond rights and wrongs, oughts and shoulds; instead, she invited us to be mindful of and to engage with what is—the Japanese language that uses three different lettering systems, *hiragana, katakana,* and *kanji,* to communicate ideas. Becoming familiar with the structure of the Japanese language, she used her teaching cues to help us practice stereotype replacement, i.e., replacing our own mental models around how language *ought to be,* a "right way," with ideas about what language *can be.* This very subtle shift in our perception was the momentum we needed to approach this unfamiliar terrain with individuation, i.e., interest and investigation, instead of a comparing mind that places experiences into hierarchies.

Professor Takeda reminded us of these instructions at the beginning of every class because she knew we were all conditioned with certain mental habits. In this way, through practice, she softened our minds, hearts, and bodies (prosocial behaviors) to overcome what we'd thought would be impossible and help us imagine new ways of being (perspective-taking). Within four months, her classroom full of non-Japanese students could fluently read and write two of three Japanese lettering systems and have functional conversations in Japanese.

Her teachings apply not only to language learning but to all aspects of human differences. These are techniques we each need to unlearn the disinformation and misinformation we've learned, retained, and taught about one another through our education. I have personally used this framework to incorporate nonbinary gender pronouns such as they/them in my thoughts, words, and imagination in English, Hindi, and Urdu.

Indigenous scholar Robin Wall Kimmerer imagines a more innovative thought experiment. She imagines what would happen if those of who speak and think in English referred to all animate beings, such as plants, animals, and natural elements, with a pronoun other than *it*. As you can sense, *it* relegates nonhuman living beings to the status of objects. Kimmerer suggests we establish a gender-neutral pronoun *ki* to refer to such beings in the third person. To her, *ki* would signify our kinship with these beings while acknowledging that they, like humans, are also infused with life, energy, and consciousness.[11] I am not suggesting that we make such a transition, but just asking you to use perspective-taking and imagine what such a transition in our language would feel like in how we relate to ourselves and the living world around us.

The beauty and power of breaking bias is that our human minds are malleable and we've all been endowed with the same five attributes of our primary identity. PRISM is our gateway to unlearning old habits, learning new habits, and enacting new possibilities of learning and growing together beyond the limitation of education.

PRISM PRACTICES

Pause. Take three breaths and observe your somatic experience.

∗ Return to the definition of education and then scan through the human cultures below. Notice the concepts, emotions, and *vedana* that arise in your mind for each culture.

  ∗ Haitian Vodou culture:

  ∗ Tibetan culture:

  ∗ Guarani culture:

  ∗ Polynesian culture:

Reflect on what concepts, emotions and *vedana* you learned, if any, about these cultures in your schooling and curricula. What ideas do you hold about such humans? What role did your education play in teaching you these ideas? How do these ideas somatically manifest in your body?

∗ Watch/listen to one or more of the following TED Talks:

  ∗ Chimamanda Ngozi Adichie, "The Danger of a Single Story" (2009)

  ∗ Elizabeth Lindsey, "Curating Humanity's Heritage" (2010)

  ∗ Wade Davis, "Dreams from Endangered Cultures" (2003)

Using what you've learned, apply one of the PRISM tools to support you in breaking any biases (e.g., race, ethnicity, religion, gender, class, nationality, language) that you hold toward humans who are Haitian, Tibetan, Guarani, and/or Polynesian.

∗ Reflect on ways education has programmed you with stereotypes with respect to some of your secondary identities. Become mindful of any stories you cling to about "others" because of something you were taught. Investigate feelings, emotions, and stories that keep you from transforming such stories in your mind. Become mindful of these emotional states and reflect on their relationship with the three root defilements of *wetiko*.

* As inclusion consciousness spreads, movements of "unschooling," "deschooling," and alternative modes of education have arisen globally.[12] Research these movements and reflect on ways they can strengthen your breaking bias journey. Notice any fears, doubts, and resistance that may arise, *feeling* the somatic experience and consciously *observing* their narratives.

Chapter 10

MEDIA

The media is the most powerful entity. They have the power to make the innocent guilty and to make the guilty innocent, and that's power because they control the minds of the masses.

— EL HAJJ MALIK EL-SHABAZZ

In the mid-'90s, my American classmates were shocked to learn that I was a vegetarian. This was decades before vegetarianism and veganism became widely accepted in the West. Their shock was just as surprising for me because vegetarianism was mainstream where I came from. It is estimated that 40 percent of Indians are vegetarian and another 30 percent are predominantly vegetarian, eating eggs, fish, or poultry occasionally. Until immigrating to America, vegetarianism was all I knew.

One day, I asked my classmate Jimmie what he thought people in India ate. In all seriousness, he answered, "Monkey brains." I was aghast! Most Indians couldn't imagine hurting a monkey, given their association with the deity Hanuman, forget eating their brains! "Calm down, calm down," he said. "I thought that's what you guys ate because that's what I saw in *Indiana Jones.*" He was referring to the global Hollywood blockbuster *Indiana Jones and the Temple of Doom*, which depicts the fictional adventures of a white explorer who saves native Indians from their own savagery during the British colonial era.

This film was the only reference Jimmie had of India in his imagination. He hadn't talked about India or Indians with any of his significant humans. He hadn't learned anything about India in seven grades of schooling. He didn't read any books about India, Indian history, or Indian people. He didn't see any Indian-looking people in movies, TV shows, cartoons, advertisements, or video games. All he knew about India was from one film, and what he remembered from that one film was a scary, bad guy with brown skin and an Indian appearance like mine who ate monkey brains.

Similarly, the three vectors of culture exposed him to visual, auditory, and written associations in which only humans with Harrison Ford's intersectional identities were heroes and good guys. This is the power of media. In this chapter, we'll uncover how culture's vector of media, the final cause and condition of bias, trains our minds with biases.

MEDIA AND OUR TRAINING IN BIAS

Our training in bias begins with social contact and is fortified through education. Media reinforces, magnifies, and fills in any gaps because media exposes all our senses to various human identities. This is particularly dangerous when we have not personally met or known a person of the identity being portrayed, as was the case for my classmate Jimmie. Recall that *media* is "print, broadcast, and digital systems of mass communication, information sharing, and story consumption to influence mass perceptions."

One day while I was teaching my eighth-grade students in Korea, some of them started teasing me, calling me "scary Xerxes." They had recently watched a Hollywood blockbuster, *Sam Baek* in Korean, or *300*. In this film, the entire cast of heroes and freedom-loving, good, and beautiful humans is played by Anglo-Saxon white actors, not the spectrum of olive-hued people that most Greeks actually are; and most Persian characters are portrayed as ugly, savage, and evil and played by black and brown actors—including my apparent lookalike, the ancient Persian monarch Xerxes as played by Brazilian actor Rodrigo Santoro.

Underneath *300*'s reductive story of good and bad "civilizations," a loaded word rooted in the comparing mind, the film portrays ancient Greek and Persian societies not as they probably were, but as what the humans financing, directing, and casting the film perceived and imagined them to be—the result of disinformation, misinformation, and knowledge gaps. These humans' shared perceptions determined their decisions on the design of the final product that is the film, from casting and costuming to dialogue, cinematography, and other elements of storytelling. This is institutional bias in action.

In this way, the media makers propagate exclusion consciousness by dehumanizing or tokenizing subordinated identities, or making them invisible, and valorizing certain dominant identities. Here's what I mean by these terms:

* **Dehumanize**: a negative portrayal of subordinated identities, e.g., as a villain, an antihero, evil, ugly, scary, a sexual object, backward, savage, primitive, lacking humanity, etc.

* **Tokenize**: restricting subordinated identities to a singular portrayal, e.g., sidekick, comic relief, sexual object, noble savage, love interest, or a superhuman philanthropist, etc.

* **Invisibilize**: the background presence or nonexistence of subordinated identities

* **Valorize**: a positive portrayal of dominant identities, e.g., a hero, a savior, trustworthy, beautiful, desirable, fun, divinelike, the right way to be human, etc.

In the case of the film *300*, the first three applied for humans who are black and brown, white women, men with emotions, and the disabled, and the last applied for cis, straight, rational, muscular, and virile white Anglo-Saxon men. Regardless of whether these decisions are made deliberately or inadvertently, they ultimately train millions of humans globally to tie our secondary identities to certain mental concepts, emotions, and *vedana*. These stereotypes become stored in our consciousness, and when such associations are the only depictions we see, hear, imagine, and feel through media outlets for the news, films, or social media, they become our reality.

PRISM EXERCISE

Pause. Take three full breaths, feel your body, and recall our shared agreements.

In the space below or in your journal, list the top three sources of media you consume. Reflect on the humans who fund and create this media. What are their secondary identities? What identities of humans do these media valorize? What do they dehumanize, tokenize, or invisibilize?

MEDIA AND HABITS OF THOUGHTS

In my rural Korean town near Naju, most of my students had no reference point for brown humans like me other than what they saw in *300*. This became their mental model for humans who looked like me, as well as reinforcing their preexisting mental models for white humans. The media they consumed also impacted their perceptions of themselves and others.

My students consumed just as much translated American media, such as *Friends* and *Seinfeld*, as they did Korean shows. And often, they annoyingly took photos with my white friends, because to them my friends looked like the characters they saw in those shows. They'd share these photos on Cyworld, a Korean analogue to MySpace, as a way to increase their own social value.

These seemingly harmless decisions reinforced Cyworld-wide shared perceptions of white skin and European appearance as Jesus/God-like and aspirational, and of dark skin and non-European appearance as undesirable and invisible. I have experienced this manifesting as entrenched colorism and widespread self-loathing within myself and across people of color in Western and non-Western societies.

My Korean students as young as 13 applied skin-lightening creams and opted to get eyelid, nose, and calf reduction surgeries so they could look white, which in their minds was more beautiful and worthy of love and respect. Across South Asia, cosmetics companies use various media platforms and channels to advertise skin-lightening creams promoted by beloved Indian celebrities like Shah Rukh Khan.[1] Even my physician mother, who has dark skin, applied skin-lightening cream for years and gifted it to me until I was in my 20s.

Notice if your mind resorts to judging these humans for not knowing better. No shame if it does; that's how I was trained to view this too. But such a judgment prevents us from having empathy for these humans with subordinated identities and acknowledging the cultural containers—and the creators of these containers—who infect the minds of these humans with such self-loathing.

Media's visual, auditory, and experiential cues subtly train the minds, hearts, and bodies of humans of all intersectionalities in the most desirable way to be human. Since India opened its economy and media in the mid-1990s, humans with brown, and especially dark brown, skin color are rare in mainstream films and on television.

PRISM EXERCISE

Pause. Take three full breaths and become aware of your somatic experience.

In the table below, you'll find the three media systems that I explained in Chapter 7: print, broadcast, and digital. For each media system, select a platform and channel that you consume and a particular story you've consumed on that platform and channel in the last week.

Then, with interest, investigate the *consciousness* of the story you consumed. What qualities of inclusion or exclusion consciousness was it rooted in? What effects does this form of media have on your thoughts, perceptions, and feelings toward yourself and other humans, and on your decision-making?

Media System	Platforms and Channels	Story/Content	Your Thoughts, Feelings, and Perceptions Toward Yourself and Others
Print	e.g., book/*The Book of Joy*		
Broadcast	e.g., TV/NBC, Radio/Hot98		
Digital	e.g., Instagram/@jayshetty, Netflix/*Queer Eye*, Podcast/*Unlocking Us* with Brené Brown		

Table 10.1

ORIGINS OF MEDIA

Over the course of history, new social experiments, whether they were animist bands or large empires, came and went, and with them their stories too flourished and then died. This shifted in modernity with the invention of the printing press, which officially brought into existence what we understand and interact with as the media.* This technology enabled humans to mass produce, reproduce, share, and consume stories with one another beyond social contact and geographical boundaries.

---

* The Chinese, Koreans, and other societies with written languages had invented ways to duplicate writings but they required wooden or metal blocks or the intensive manual labor of copying. The printing press allowed for the mass production of written materials using the very portable medium of paper.

PRISM EXERCISE

Pause. Take three full breaths. Now imagine you're in Europe in the 16th century.

The printing press was invented around 1440 and took off across Europe in the following decades. Around the same time, the Vatican empowered the Portuguese and the Spanish to begin their brutal enterprises of enslavement and empire building to dominate and subjugate non-Christians.

Imagine being one of the humans running these institutions in the early 1500s. In the space below or in your journal, take a few minutes to imagine their intentions and the consciousness beneath those intentions. If this exercise gets you emotional, practice observing those emotions and body sensations, then return to being in the minds, hearts, and bodies of these humans.

Prior to print media, in societies with written languages such as Arabic, Chinese, Tamil, or Latin, the written word was considered sacred. Most humans could not read or write, but they knew that certain humans who could were custodians of spiritual or religious wisdom that was passed down. With the advent of print media, that belief carried over so that, without critical or analytical thinking, consumers of print media assumed what they read was truth. At the same time, humans who controlled print media planted their own consciousness and intentions in the minds of their audiences. Over time, print media transformed humans from active participants in shaping stories into passive consumers of them. Reflect on that for a moment—even in our language, media is something we *consume*.

In addition, for the first time in human history, print media began to expose human minds to storytellers, and their states of consciousness, outside of direct social contact. With repeated exposure to such stories, certain humans took actions that caused horrific harms on billions globally. Every modern conflict was fabricated in the minds of a select few and transmitted to the consciousness of millions via media.

For almost 400 years, print media was the *only* means of mass communication and consumption of stories. During this time, most humans outside of Europe still had some autonomy over their minds as long as they couldn't read, or couldn't read a particular language, or chose to limit their consumption of stories and ideas. No single story dominated human consciousness across cultures. But this changed in the last century with the advent of broadcast and digital media systems.

PRISM EXERCISE

Pause. Take three full breaths, return your awareness to your body, and remind yourself of our agreements.

Choose two secondary identities, one dominant and one subordinated, that you have. Reflect on how the print, broadcast, and digital media you consume shapes your self-perceptions about these identities.

Now, take three breaths and imagine being a media maker or content creator in your society under the spell of the following ideologies:

* White supremacy and Nazism

* Religious fundamentalism, e.g., Christian, Jewish, Hindu, Buddhist, or Muslim

* Political fundamentalism, e.g., communist, capitalist, ethnic, or democratic ideologies

> In the space below or in your journal, take some time to inves-
> tigate the stories media makers and content creators fuel when
> influenced by these ideologies. What is their consciousness? Their
> intention? Their motivation? How does their media affect your lived
> experiences, based on your two secondary identities, in your society?

THE FULL SENSORY EXPERIENCE
OF BROADCAST AND DIGITAL MEDIA

The greatest advantage science and technology has offered
some humans is free time. Until very recently, most humans used
the vast majority of their time and energy just to make a living.
Only a few with dominant intersectional identities had time for
pursuits like philosophy, the arts, or religion. Today, at least in the
global north, a majority of humans have some free time. And how
do most of us use that free time? On media. A funny social media
meme describes it as "Dear God, please give me another life. This
one was used up by Facebook and WhatsApp."

In 1980, an average American, across age, gender, and class,
watched 44 hours of television a week; in 2021, they spent more
than that on digital media and another 3 to 4 hours on television.[2]
With broadband reaching the far corners of the world, humans
across societies are following suit. Imagine what they could do,
what *we* could do, with that time.

Brother Anandamoy, a 20th-century Swiss American illuminated being, helped me understand the impact of broadcast
and digital media on human consciousness. He said that prior to
broadcast, "Our homes used to be a fortress. Humans went out
to work, go to school, or do any other activity, and then returned
to their fortress, healed their wounds, and recharged in their fortress. Broadcast destroyed the fortress. How can we possibly have

peace in the home, if we are bringing the world into the home? It was bad enough with radio, but not as bad as TV, where you see it visually and feel it internally. And what they are sending, this is sensationalism. They are not sending peace-creating things because they are not exciting enough. They send out the ugliness, the violence, the gross vibrations."[3]

I saw this happen firsthand in my own lifetime. As a child, I spent most of my free time outside, playing with my friends, or cooking with my Amma. In the 1990s, as cable TV was introduced in India, my Amma and I spent less time being with each other and more time with TV. Since immigrating to the United States 30 years ago, my parents have spent more non-working hours with TV, and now with Facebook and WhatsApp, than with my sisters and me or with their grandchildren. In addition, within the time we have spent together without a TV, we have spent more of it talking about the news, advertising, shows, or movies we've watched on TV than sharing and discussing our inner lives.

In the 21st century, digital media has further penetrated our lives with "smart" devices like laptops, mobile phones, tablets, watches, and glasses. Now the world has entered not only our homes, but also our moment-to-moment attention: before we sleep, after we wake up, and while we eat, cook, shower, defecate, have sex, and/or be with other humans, whether they are friends or family, work colleagues, or strangers.

In addition, broadcast and digital media have shifted the lifetime of a story's survival from *survival of the fittest* (humans deciding which stories to share with one another via social contact) to *survival of the richest* (humans who control media platforms and channels deciding which stories ought to survive).[4] Our media exposure builds within us the mental habits of abdicating our critical thinking and analytical powers and no longer trusting what we see, hear, feel, and imagine.

Unless we become mindful of the intentions and consciousness of the decision-makers behind the media we are consuming, we succumb to their stories. This is not a personal failing on our part, but a function of our biology. The media we consume is designed to shape our perceptions by training us to *think*, *feel*, and *imagine* in a certain way. With repeated exposure, certain biases in the forms of thoughts, associations, emotions, and *vedana* arise in our inner experience, and we begin to trust them as true. Recall what Tsoknyi Rinpoche called this process of transference: *real but not true.*

It is no surprise, as a result, that many police officers in the global north perceive black and brown teenagers like Nahel Merzouk or Michael Brown as monsters and criminals. As shown by Jennifer Eberhardt's research, contact with these boys' bodies triggers in these officers' minds and nervous systems a feeling of fear or hatred that leads them to act in a certain way: to shoot and kill them.[5] Similarly, most humans in those nations' justice systems acquit these officers of charges because they too share their perceptions and nervous system responses. What happens in the minds and nervous systems of these police officers, juries, and judges is real, but it isn't true.

Such actions and social trends are a consequence of the five root causes and conditions of bias. Today, our handy digital devices, the unregulated ubiquity of media, and our habitual consumption of it make it the most powerful root cause in programming us with false stories and bias.

PRISM EXERCISE

Pause. Take three full breaths and bring your attention to your body.

In the space below or in your journal, take a few minutes to list the stories you consume on your top three media platforms and some reasons *why you consume them.*

Your answers likely spanned three categories: to be informed, entertained, or info-tained. Take a moment to reflect on why. Investigate why your mind needs or wants to be informed, entertained, or info-tained.

MEDIA AND SYSTEM 1 TRAINING

For almost a decade, I've been actively practicing mindfulness and stereotype replacement to counteract learning bias from media. For example, if I read, hear, or watch news stories that dehumanize humans like Meghan Markle or Simu Liu because of their gender and descent, I notice the storytellers' exclusion consciousness and lack of empathy and actively visualize the positive qualities of the stereotyped humans with counterexamples.

A few years ago, I noticed that every time my attention was placed on negative stories, even with the use of PRISM tools, my mind was still being passively programmed to view myself and others through the lens of the storytellers. While PRISM helped me counteract the stories' false messages, I noticed that sometimes my mind and body unconsciously returned to emotions of victimization and memories of my own bullying because of a subordinated identity I shared with the human who was being dehumanized. And these associations triggered in my own being emotions of anger, hatred, and disgust, kicking in the fight-or-flight reaction.

When I am not mindful of my survival brain being activated, I get hooked into reactivity. While I can generally manage it in individual instances, the accumulation of these triggers eventually leads me to react. Historically, this has taken the form of arguing with my friends or family members, writing long treatises on social media threads, drinking alcohol, and even masturbating with porn to get rid of the unpleasant *vedana* and the afflictive emotions of grief, overwhelm, and depression.

I've spent hundreds of hours investigating how and why I succumb to such behaviors when my heart, mind, and body know that this activity causes me or my loved ones harm and that I always feel remorse, guilt, or shame after engaging in them. Through strengthening awareness with the PRISM tools, I realize that my reactions are not personal and unique to me. This is what media has been designed to do. Even the wisest and most compassionate of us get caught in this behavior, as I have learned from many of my elders and teachers.

Media Consumption and Disembodiment

Media is designed to take our attention away from the present moment. Realizing this led me to another point that I asked you to investigate in the last PRISM exercise: Why do I seek out media? Why do I willingly give my attention away to it? Why do I feel like I need to be entertained or informed?

After deep introspection, I discovered two reasons for my engagement with media. The first came easily—social contact; it's an activity I engage in to connect with my loved ones, as I learned to watch Indian television with my Amma after cable TV arrived in India, or to connect with other humans as we socialize and talk about the latest movies, video games, or celebrity gossip.

To understand the second reason, I imagined being an alien who arrived on Earth and observed modern humans. I saw humans giving their attention away to plastic boxes that produced sound and projected various particles and vibrations of light on screens. I then observed humans socializing with one another about the light particles, waves, and vibrations they consumed instead of sharing with one another what they carried inside them: their dreams, aspirations, desires, and pain.

I witnessed the deep vulnerability and innocence in each and every one of the humans. I witnessed their pain, shame, hurt, dreams deferred, innocence lost, betrayals, and disconnection, and their inability to acknowledge and feel these experiences. Hence, they—we—get habituated to seek out media to escape our feelings, emotions, body sensations, and the present moment.

More specifically, I noticed that I sought out media to avoid acknowledging thoughts or feeling emotions with unpleasant *vedana*, and/or I sought media to delve into thoughts or emotions with pleasant *vedana*. My Buddhist teacher and therapist DaRa Williams helped me see that this looping behavior is what most of us have learned to label as *boredom*.

There is nothing wrong or right with this behavior, but our actions have consequences. I noticed that the stories I exposed my mind to fueled in me wholesome or unwholesome thoughts and emotions that impacted how I perceived, reasoned, remembered, and made decisions.

Since the 1970s, even for humans who are going about our business and don't seek out media, the built environment takes our attention away from the present moment—like a billboard selling something while we're on a nature walk, breaking news notifications on our phones, or Google ads on a screen while we're doing homework. These subtle cues take us away from our bodies, emotions, and minds and turn us toward the external—and, if we are unaware, subtly program us with particular perceptions and consciousness.

For us humans, the repeated practice of escaping the present moment, whether it is conscious or unconscious, becomes a habit, which can become a dependency and an addiction. Over time, what we expose our senses and consciousness to starts to become what our minds imagine to be our reality and what we perceive as truth.

In the last decade, this is how humans have been programmed to believe some of the most ludicrous fantasies and conspiracy theories, with catastrophic impacts on democratic institutions, social cohesion, and mental health. And through the lens of deep time, what we have experienced and are experiencing is *not new.* In the 20th century, the Nazis, communist regimes, white supremacists, and religious fundamentalists used print and broadcast media to program humans in their ideologies to justify exclusion and mass slaughter, and in the four centuries before that, church, European, and other centralized societies used various types of print and visual media to justify the torture of women, genocide, exclusion, and enslavement.

Throughout this time, the human *being* that we are has not changed. Today, we still have the same six sense doors and sense abilities. However, with advances in technology, the platforms and channels for programming us with bias and exclusion consciousness have multiplied manifold.

PRISM EXERCISE

Pause. Take three full breaths and return your attention to your body.

Recalling our shared agreements, let's take a field trip into deep time. Imagine being one of your ancestors in their respective place and space in the time listed below.

* 1920s

* 1720s

* 1420s

As this ancestor, bring to awareness and list your prominent secondary identities. What media, if any, did you consume in your day-to-day? With whom did you consume this media? What did this form of media teach you about yourself and others?
Feel free to do this exercise for more than one ancestor.

Media and Exploitation of Our Biology

Stories are designed to take their audiences on an emotional journey. Biologically, when stories activate emotions with a strong pleasant or unpleasant *vedana*,* our brain's reward-based system is triggered.[6] If the feeling is pleasant, we want more of it. For me, this has meant getting stuck watching videos of cute animals or synchronized dances on TikTok or Instagram. Or if it is an unpleasant feeling, we want to get rid of it through one of the survival brain responses. For me, this has looked like yelling at the television,

---

* Like excitement, lust, pleasure, anger, or hatred—scholars call these emotions highly charged positively or negatively valenced emotions. Brother Anandamoy called them "sensational" or "exciting."

resharing the content on my Instagram, or engaging in long philosophical debates on Facebook or LinkedIn threads.

The stronger the emotion and the *vedana* triggered in our nervous system, the stronger is our reaction to that feeling. But there is a
catch. Recall that we are biologically wired for negativity. Our minds
are Velcro for negative experiences and Teflon for positive ones. This
means that even if there are 99 wonderful things in our lives, our
minds will focus on the 1 thing that is challenging or troubling.
This is our survival brain and System 1 thinking in action.

Unless we become mindful that we are operating from this faulty
evolutionary hardware, we continue to scroll, read, or flip channels,
riding on that underlying *vedana*. Our ongoing interaction with
and exposure to media biologically trains us in reward-based learning. Over time, we develop habits like watching the evening news
or scrolling on social media that can even become addictions, and
depending on what stories our minds get exposed to, the consciousness of the storytellers can become our reality and truth.

With the advent of media, media creators and funders, motivated by exclusion consciousness, have distributed stories of human
hierarchies to exploit our biology and influence our behavior—to
rig elections, topple governments, encourage genocides, destroy
ecosystems, or declare war. Whether they are marketers, designers
of tech algorithms, or producers of news shows, they exploit this
aspect of human psychology and physiology to fulfill their intention and accumulate their chosen currency of power: money, political power, fame, influence, or all of the above.

Filipina journalist and Nobel Peace Prize laureate Maria Ressa
notes that in our current media paradigm, "lies laced with anger
and hatred are rewarded and spread faster than facts and truth."
And "the distribution and spread of a lie is so much greater than
the fact-checking that follows that by the time the lie is debunked,
those who believe it often refuse to change their views."[7] In other
words, the damage is done because humans who engaged with the
media are already in survival brain and System 1 thinking. This is
how propaganda networks rewrite history.

Today, regardless of geography, the formula in media remains the
same: make slight adjustments to the depiction that valorizes a certain "kind of human" while tokenizing, dehumanizing, and/or invis-
ibilizing all others, as *300* or *Indiana Jones and the Temple of Doom*

do. Sadly, this formula is also used in media that we enjoy, like the *Pitch Perfect* series, Bollywood's *Dhoom* films, Spanish telenovelas, or Korean soap operas. Over time, succumbing to these different forms of media, we subtly get trained in meaning-making by associating human identities with certain mental concepts and *vedana*, like my classmate Jimmie who thought I ate monkey brains.

As media come to dominate all corners of the world, stories that aren't written down or portrayed on video or audio will be lost to our collective consciousness. AI technologies like Midjourney and ChatGPT only reinforce these challenges, because the underlying datasets they use are filled with stories written, imagined, and shared by certain humans in certain languages of particular intersectional identities with certain perceptions, e.g., white, European, Judeo-Christian, and Western-educated. With the powerful reach of media, the thoughts of the media creators can become our destiny.

PRISM EXERCISE

Pause. Take three full breaths and return your attention to your somatic experience.

Toward the end of her life, anthropologist Margaret Mead said, "I fear that one day we [will] see the entire range of the human imagination reduced to a more narrow modality of thought . . . and we would wake from a dream one day having forgotten there were even other possibilities."

Notice how these words land in your body. In the space below or in your journal, reflect on ways they resonate with your experience. Investigate which PRISM tools can support you in using your power as a media consumer and a media creator to interrupt your programming in bias toward different human identities.

INCLUSION CONSCIOUSNESS AND MEDIA

As a child, I loved watching *Ek, Anek aur Ekta (One, Many, and Unity in Diversity)*, an animated film that was a part of the weekly children's programming from the Indian public television channel, Doordarshan. With a catchy Hindi melody, the film highlighted the strengths of human diversity and collaboration across religious, linguistic, and gender differences through simple metaphors of nature.[8] This film reached everyone who tuned in to watch television at the designated hour because there was only *one channel* on television; cable TV didn't arrive in India until the 1990s.

This film was conceived by Vijaya Mulay, an Indian bureaucrat of a certain intersectionality, who wanted to remind Indian viewers that "diversity is our greatest strength, and unity in diversity is something that we have managed to follow . . . and it has to be cherished."[9] She used her own funds to communicate this intention with lyrics, music, and animation and applied her authority and influence to broadcast and spread it to tens of millions of Indian viewers weekly for more than a decade.

Mulay isn't an exception. Shortly after immigrating to America, I was introduced to *Mister Rogers' Neighborhood*. In this show, Mr. Rogers used music and playful storytelling to teach millions of humans everywhere how to cope with the different modulations of life by encouraging them to *feel* the joys of kindness, love, diversity, and many other prosocial behaviors. He reminded his audiences of the timeless truth that "what is essential is invisible to the eye."[10] This is inclusion consciousness in action. Like Mulay, Rogers's primary intention with his show was to foster love, unity, compassion, and understanding, not fame, acclaim, likes, or profit for himself or his organization.

PRISM EXERCISE

Pause. Take three full breaths and bring your attention to your body.

In the space below or in your journal, identify three stories you've consumed in the last week that feel rooted in inclusion consciousness. Which media systems and platforms did they belong to? Who are the storytellers? What are their intentions? Most important, was this media readily available to you or did you have to seek it out?

MEDIA, PRISM, AND DEVELOPING SYSTEM 2 THINKING

The good news is that with regular PRISM practice, we can gain or regain control over who and what we invite into our consciousness. I experienced this firsthand after working with Rha Goddess, my executive coach. I met Rha a few months after I graduated from law school and I began working with her to bring my passion for breaking bias to life.

Early in our biweekly coaching sessions, she asked me, "If your attention is constantly going toward coverage of war, shame, and blame, how will you bring to life your vision for equity, beauty, and unity?" She then demanded that I go on a media fast for at least two months. No news, no tabloids, no gossip, and no social media.

I did as she asked. Instead of my regular media consumption, I went on walks in nature, spent time with friends and family, practiced yoga, ran around Central Park, listened to Tara Brach and the Rev. Jacqui Lewis's talks and sermons, and read books I'd been putting off reading for years. Within weeks, I felt more energized, more centered, and surer of myself. Rha was proud, and she advised that if I were to resume consuming media, I should limit it to media that shared my vision for the world. My immediate thought was that that doesn't exist! Sensing my cynicism, she invited me to attend and download the conversations from a virtual summit where she was speaking: "The Spring of Sustainability 2012."[11]

I listened to every conversation and felt deeply inspired by dozens of humans who shared my longing to feel connected with myself, other humans, and the living Earth, and who were actively healing the disconnection and discord in our world.* I have since discovered and subscribed to many wonderful channels of media like *The Sun* magazine, *Yes!* magazine, the *On Being* podcast, the *Soul Pancake* YouTube Channel, and *Super Soul Sundays* that continue to fill my consciousness with possibilities beyond division, hatred, and hurt and help me break my own learned biases toward people my mind viewed as "others."

This gentle shift in habits helped me embody the ancient wisdom Brother Anandamoy taught me, that our minds are our temples. We must consciously guard the stories and ideas we let into this temple and consciously cultivate what we want to grow in it. If our attention remains on hatred and separation, that's what will grow. If our attention is placed on compassion and love, that too shall grow. If you don't believe me, try it! I'm taking this suggestion straight from the Buddhist path. In encouraging the practice of mindfulness, the Buddha extolled the principle of *ehipassiko*, or "don't just take my word for it, come experience it for yourself."

Releasing the Stories and Taking Control of Where Our Attention Goes

Media refers to the institutionalized systems for certain humans with dominant identities to communicate and infect the masses with their state of consciousness, and for the rest of us to passively consume it. I began to seriously investigate media's role in my mental health on a silent meditation retreat in my late 20s. The retreat was designed for young activists, and it required us to be open to investigating the challenges that had brought us there: burnout,

---

* Like Jane Goodall, Vandana Shiva, Van Jones, and many more.

depression, anxiety, and loneliness. Early in the experience, it became clear to us that our engagement with the media fueled these afflictive states. It also became clear that these emotions stemmed not only from our subordinated identities, but from our dominant ones, such as being citizens of countries in the global north.

For me, this meant noticing, acknowledging, and feeling the truth that my daily existence, from my food, clothes, and housing to the devices I depended on, stemmed from a supply-chain economy that was rooted in active harm to fellow humans, animals, plants, and the living Earth. Yet all the media I consumed—the news, films, TV shows, music, and video games—actively denied these realities. Instead, they reflected back at me invisibility or fear of marginalized humans and more-than-humans, along with ideas of what I needed to own, what I needed to look like, and what I needed to do to have a good and happy life: make money so I could consume more things, services, places, experiences, and ideas.

As I became mindful of where media grabbed my attention, an inner voice tried to console me by sharing with me ways I resisted media's narrative: I shopped responsibly, recycled, and composted. Though my ego congratulated itself, my awareness drifted deeper to acknowledge painful truths: that despite my efforts, sweatshops persisted, forests were razed, rivers were polluted, ecosystems were destroyed, at least nine human languages were lost every year and with them libraries of ancient wisdom. Then I saw an image of a poster for the movie *Avatar* with the phrase "weapons of mass distraction" scribbled across it in bright red letters. I had seen that poster at my local Brooklyn subway station the prior week.

In that instant, I realized media's role in our life: to keep us distracted from *how things actually are* and instead program us with self-loathing and fear of the other so we continue to consume and help someone make money. I sensed that I couldn't recycle my way out of this system. I and we all are completely entangled in it. Suddenly, I felt all alone, and familiar thoughts that made me feel small and insignificant started arising: *Am I crazy? Why can't I be more like my doctor friends or my family members who are blissfully ignorant about these things? There are people much smarter than I am who know these things. Who am I, a poor, lowly immigrant with an illiterate grand-mother, to even think I can do anything about it?* With such thoughts arose a deep self-hatred.

By that time, I'd done enough healing to intuitively recognize that I couldn't be alone or stay silent. I went to speak to our teachers. They lovingly invited me to tend and befriend the pain instead of repressing it. "Where is it in the body?" they asked. "Can you *feel* its sensations? And can you be with it and watch it pass with loving-kindness and compassion?"

Then they shared something that brought forth tears of healing: that I was not alone, that the Buddha, the Dharma, the Sangha, and all the Great Ones across time and space were protecting me. Their words were the medicine my spirit needed to go within. I felt safety in my body and with my emotions. And with a deep wisdom I knew that I had the tools and the time I needed—seven days of the retreat—to tend and befriend the despair that lay beneath the self-hatred. So, in my seated meditation posture, covered with my favorite blanket and holding my favorite stone, I practiced PRISM with three sincere phrases: *I love you* (affection), *I am sorry* (remorse), *please forgive me* (forgiveness). And out came the stories and images stored in my consciousness.

* Ecosystems ravaged from Indonesia to Brazil: I love you, I am sorry, please forgive me.

* Chinese and Bangladeshi sweatshop workers: I love you, I am sorry, please forgive me.

* Queer and trans bodies beaten and mutilated: I love you, I am sorry, please forgive me.

* Humans of all hues and genders locked in prisons: I love you, I am sorry, please forgive me.

* Villages of Burmese, Congolese, and Palestinian families burned to the ground: I love you, I am sorry, please forgive me.

* Women, men, and children being sexually abused: I love you, I am sorry, please forgive me.

* Generations of Africans perishing in mines: I love you, I am sorry, please forgive me.

* Beautiful nonhuman beings hunted and fished to extinction: I love you, I am sorry, please forgive me.

* Ancient languages and cosmologies obliterated by misguided missionaries in every corner of the Earth: I love you, I am sorry, please forgive me.

And the list continued. It went back in time, it stayed in the present, and it jumped into the future. My body throbbed, shook, and scintillated with many sensations and I offered them the same three phrases: *I love you, I am sorry, please forgive me.* I had completely surrendered to all the Great Ones. At a certain point, the list felt complete, and sensations of deep relaxation, openness, and love pervaded my body. After a few hours, I returned to awareness and found my clothes drenched in my tears, snot, and sweat, indicating the physical release of the concepts and emotions I had been carrying in my body and mind.

Later that evening, our teacher, JoAnna Hardy, read the following words from Thích Nhât Hânh's poem "Please Call Me by My True Names":

> I am the child in Uganda, all skin and bones,
> my legs as thin as bamboo sticks.
> And I am the arms merchant,
> selling deadly weapons to Uganda.
> I am the twelve-year-old girl,
> refugee on a small boat,
> who throws herself into the ocean
> after being raped by a sea pirate,
> and I am the pirate,
> my heart not yet capable
> of seeing and loving
>
> . . . .
>
> My joy is like Spring, so warm
> it makes flowers bloom all over the Earth.
> My pain is like a river of tears,
> so vast it fills the four oceans.[12]

After releasing more tears, I felt tremendous gratitude for myself, my teachers, the Earth, and other retreatants. I sensed that the "I" and "me" I created were actually the moment-to-moment manifestation of how steeped my consciousness was in *wetiko* and the mind's three defilements. And I saw a direct link between my habits of media consumption and how I felt toward myself and others.

Today, media is far more powerful than social contact and education because it is ongoing. It can radicalize teenagers in Tennessee, Paris, or Jakarta to do the unthinkable. It can shame humans—regardless of how much money or status they have—into ending their own lives. And most important, it can train us in abdicating our power and believing the biggest lie of all: that we can't do anything about it.

Our media system and institutions are reflections of who we are. If we are to transform our systems, institutions, and communities toward being more compassionate and understanding, we must begin with transforming ourselves, including shifting what we take into our consciousness and what we put out through media platforms.

As Thích Nhât Hânh reminded us, "In our consciousness, there are many negative seeds and also many positive seeds. The practice is to avoid watering the negative seeds, and to identify and water the positive seeds every day." Through this practice, as our inner transformations ripple out one person at a time, we will *be* the transformative change we seek and reflect the ultimate truth of our interdependence, oneness, and *ubuntu*.

PRISM PRACTICES

Pause. Take three breaths and bring your attention to feel your body.

✳ Reflect on ways the media you consume trigger your survival brain. Be specific about particular platforms, channels, and/or stories. Notice how the contacting of such media with your various senses triggers in you different concepts, emotions, and *vedana* and investigate the ways they affect your: self-concept and feelings toward your secondary identities; your concept of others and your feelings toward others; your decisions at home or work that impact other humans; and your outlook on life and your connection with plants, nonhumans, and the living Earth.

＊ Become mindful of stereotypes—specifically demonization, invisibility, tokenization, or valorization—that you notice in your mind about your gender, race, ethnicity, appearance, or another visible secondary identity. Reflect on ways your consumption of print, broadcast, and digital media reinforces these views.

＊ Investigate with curiosity how you might think, feel, and behave if you didn't consume media for one week. Imagine and visualize yourself not consuming media for this time. Challenge yourself to go on a weeklong media fast. Notice your thoughts, emotions, and consciousness during this time. Notice boredom and the desire to be distracted with pleasant *vedana* or to avoid unpleasant *vedana*. Observe in your experience what needs to be healed. Where does it hurt? Practice loving-kindness and/or forgiveness toward what arises, feeling your somatic experience.

＊ Notice the media/stories you create or share through social media or social contact. Observe the underlying consciousness of such stories. What stereotypes or separation consciousness, if any, do they promote? Observe your pattern of sharing stories and their mental, emotional, and physical effects on humans consuming your stories.

＊ Reflect on the positive emotions and outlook you'd like to feel and experience in your day-to-day. List the media you consume that help promote your intentions. List the media you consume that contravene your intentions. Investigate the emotional patterns and internal reward systems that keep you hooked to media that violate your intentions for yourself. Cultivate a mindfulness practice of noticing and observing the sensations and sharing loving-kindness phrases for yourself when you notice the urge to escape.

THE PROMISE
OF BREAKING BIAS

*People thought of revolutions chiefly in terms of taking state power.
But we've had revolutions, and we've seen how the states which they
have created have turned out to be like replicas of the states which they
opposed. You have to bring those two words together and recognize that
we are responsible for the evolution of the human species. It's a question
of two-sided transformation and not just the oppressed versus the
oppressor. We have to change ourselves in order to change the world.*

— GRACE LEE BOGGS

On the night of his illumination, the historical Buddha had a showdown with Mara, the Buddhist name for *wetiko*. Mara sent the Buddha every imaginable weapon of distraction—beautiful maidens, doomsday scenarios, cynicism, self-loathing, threats of harm to his body and his loved ones—to arouse in him anger, lust, disgust, fear, shame, hopelessness, anxiety, and other derivative states of the three defilements. With a heart full of compassion, the Buddha practiced mindfulness, keeping his attention focused on his goal: liberation. In this gentle and patient way of noticing, acknowledging, observing, and feeling, he overcame every one of the afflictive emotions, concepts, and body sensations thrown his way.

At last, Mara, exhausted by its own antics, aroused in the Buddha the mental state of doubt: doubt of self, doubt of his intentions, and doubt of his practice. In attempting to make the Buddha feel insignificant, Mara demanded to know *who* would bear witness to his liberation. Equipped with the boundless loving-kindness and wisdom he had accumulated through six years of practice, the human who was not yet the Buddha took his hand from his lap and touched the Earth as his living witness. At that moment, it is said, the Earth shuddered, and he became the Buddha; his heart-mind was liberated from *wetiko*, from separation, greed, hatred, and ignorance.

I have read and heard this story hundreds of times and yet it never gets old because it highlights three relatable truths about our humanity.

First, this story speaks to our capacity to *be* more than the worst things that we've thought, said, felt, or done. For over 2,600 years, billions of humans globally, including yours truly, have experienced the boons of this truth in our own bodies, hearts, minds, and souls through simple PRISM practices that begin with mindfulness. Different wisdom traditions use different words and techniques to describe these practices, but ultimately, in the words of Muslim mystic Rumi,

> The differences are just illusion and vanity.
> Sunlight looks a little different on this wall than it does on
> that wall and a lot different on this other one, but it is still one light.

Some of the most hardened and hateful humans known to history have been transformed by PRISM practices—practices that are simple, but not easy at first because they are directly against our System 1 thinking and cultural conditioning. This is the micro-work of breaking bias that begins in our bodies and consciousness.

Second, this story acknowledges the essential prerequisite for transforming stereotyping and weakening our identification with exclusion consciousness: kindness and compassion. As I've shared throughout this book, compassion patiently supports us in being with, feeling, and transmuting afflictive emotions, concepts, and sensations so we can overcome doubt and imagine new possibilities.

This brings me to the final reason this story continues to hold power for me. Empowered by his compassionate heart-mind, the Buddha triumphed over Mara through the radical act of touching the Earth. In this simple act, he embodied the wisdom of interbeing and vanquished the mind virus of *wetiko*. This action declared to Mara, *You are not real. What's real is the Earth, right here, below me. It is from the Earth that my body has come and it is to the Earth that it will return.*

In the words of poet W. S. Merwin, this simple act demonstrated to generations of wisdom-seekers that:

> The Earth is what we're talking about. Accepting the Earth, not owning the Earth, not possessing the Earth, but the Earth just as it is, abused and exploited and despised and rejected and plowed and mined and shat on and everything else, you know. It's still the Earth, and it is, we owe everything to it.[1]

In the last 500 years, particular members of our human family whom our indigenous relatives call their younger siblings have forgotten this truth in their quest for more power, fame, and, ultimately, the human-made fiction of money. They've designed and forced all of humanity into a global political system that breeds hatred, competition, and separation; an economic system that requires at least 3 percent annual growth to avoid stagnation and recession; and a culture that severs our connection with our bodies, one another, more-than-humans, and the living Earth. Scholars point out that for our current global system to remain stable, it requires a doubling of the global economy every 23 years.[2]

Where does such growth come from? Deforestation of rainforests, polluting the oceans and air, mining, fracking, extraction, and the destruction of living ecosystems and ancient human cultures. At this point in our history, we have crossed six of the nine planetary boundaries and are in the midst of the sixth mass extinction. The doubling of our global economy every 23 years is a material impossibility.

We feel the impacts of this separation in the polycrisis of ecological collapse, wildfires, atmospheric rivers, tornadoes, hurricanes, pandemics, mass shootings, rising authoritarianism, meaningless wars, extreme inequality, mental health crises, and entrenched poverty and suffering among our human and nonhuman relatives. The roots of every single one of the crises are seeded in the minds of humans like you and me. Albert Einstein, one of the most famous humanists of the 20th century, is supposed to have said, "No problem can be solved from the same level of consciousness that created it."

In the years that have passed since I got off the ledge, I have come to realize that despite the upward movement of our collective consciousness, we remain entrenched in the operating system of Kali Yuga, the Age of Darkness. This system, rooted in exclusion consciousness, offers sanitized simplistic solutions like electric cars, solar panels, recycling, carbon offsets, and social media activism. These solutions are insufficient to meet the existential crises we face because they obscure the core of the challenge: our hearts, minds, and unregulated bodies.

In moments when I feel despair, overwhelm, and fear, I use the PRISM tools to get out of my head and feel my heart and body. I bring awareness to the stories attached to the emotions I feel, holding them with loving-kindness. I then gently shift my attention to the wisdom of my ancestors that assures us that in the grand scheme of things, the worst of the Kali Yuga is behind us and we have now entered the Dwapara Yuga, the Age of Morality, as evident from the rise in inclusion consciousness.*

Toward the end of his autobiography, Paramahansa Yogananda wrote:[3]

> World siblinghood is a large term, but humans must enlarge their sympathies, considering themselves in the light of a world citizen. They who truly understand that it is my America, my India, my Philippines, my Europe, my Africa and so on, will never lack scope for a useful and hopeful life.†

---

* Reiterated by Eckhart Tolle in *A New Earth*.

† I have adapted his language with gender-neutral words.

There is no better time than now to step up, grow up, and show up for ourselves, one another, and our Earth. Many elders remind us that we don't inherit the Earth from our ancestors, we merely borrow it from our children. At this time, we have no choice but to face the challenges of our times. To do so, we must make qualitative and quantitative changes in our souls and lives in the footsteps of all ancient and modern wisdom-keepers. For me, breaking bias is our starting point to create new realities toward a world where all beings belong, just as we are, in the fullness of our diversity.

In this book, I have shared with you the fundamentals you need to know and the tools you can apply to embody, envision, and imagine new realities. Now it is up to you to *be* the change.

May you be happy. May you be healthy. May you be safe. May you live with ease.

And may we create a compassionate and equitable world by breaking bias together.

GLOSSARY OF TERMS

antisemitism: false beliefs or habits of thoughts that lead one to think, speak, or act in ways that directly or indirectly harm humans of Jewish descent

biological identity: a type of secondary identity that describes the various aspects of a human's body form based on their biology and genetics

caste: an artificial, arbitrary hierarchy of graded ranking of human value in a society

conscious bias: learned false beliefs about a secondary identity, accepted as true, that distort how humans perceive, reason, remember, and make decisions toward themselves and others

consciousness: One of the five attributes of the human primary identity that refers to the human ability to have and be aware of our mind consciousness, sense consciousness, store consciousness, and *manas*, i.e., the belief in a separate self

diversity: the authentic representations and expressions of humanity

education: the fourth root cause of bias, it encompasses schooling and curricula established with the intention to assimilate humans into hierarchies through the use of disinformation, misinformation, and knowledge gaps

exclusion: restricting humans from access to activities, opportunities, protections, resources, or rights because of their secondary identities

experiential identity: a type of secondary identity that a human acquires over the course of their life based on their actions and efforts, the roles and functions they assume, and what happens to them

form: one of the five attributes of the human primary identity that refers to its corporeal body, up to six functioning sense organs, and accompanying six sense experiences, i.e., eyes for sight, ears for sounds, tongue for taste, skin for touch, nose for smell, and the sixth sense, the mind, for thoughts and emotions

gender: a layering of stories that assign and expect humans to perform specific social roles based on the intersection of sex, gender identity, sexuality, and other secondary identities within families, institutions, and societies

inclusion: ensuring that humans who've been historically excluded because of their secondary identities have equal, equitable, and fair access to activities, opportunities, protections, resources, and rights

individuation: the practice of investigating and decoupling group-based associations from individuals and experiences with curiosity; it is the *I* in the PRISM Toolkit

interbeing: Buddhist concept that describes the interconnectedness and interdependence of all things in the universe; used interchangeably with *ubuntu* and inclusion consciousness

internalized bias: a form of conscious and unconscious bias where harmful mental formations influence a human's thoughts, words, and actions toward themselves, i.e., how they perceive themselves and how they perceive others are perceiving them

interpersonal bias: a form of conscious and unconscious bias where harmful mental formations influence a human's thoughts, words, and actions toward others

intersectionality: the particularity of one's humanity based on their secondary identities

institutional bias: a form of conscious and unconscious bias where shared biases of humans who have decision-making authority or influence over an institution impacts many people via human relationships, service delivery, and product development

Islamophobia: false beliefs or habits of thoughts that lead one to think, speak, or act in ways that directly or indirectly harm humans who are or are perceived as Muslims

marginalization: the unreasonable restrictions (resources, rights, opportunities, and experiences) humans have and the pain they feel in a society for no reason other than their being, i.e., their intersectional secondary identities

media: the fifth root cause of bias, it includes print, broadcast, and digital systems of mass communication, information sharing, and story consumption to influence mass perceptions

mental formations: one of the five attributes of the human primary identity that refers to the three primary ways the human mind engages thoughts: mental concepts, emotions, and mental habits

mindfulness: the practice of noticing and becoming aware or conscious of what is happening in one's experience—body, heart, and mind—in the present moment; it is the *M* in the PRISM Toolkit

misogyny: a deep-seated hatred, contempt, sexual objectification, and distrust of women and feminine energies

neoliberalism: also known as neoliberal capitalism, an economic philosophy from the mid-20th century that commodifies all aspects of life with a monetary value; it has since become the dominant rationale for economic policies globally

neuro-decolonization: the process of cleansing the mind, body, and nervous system of mental formations that are unwholesome and unskillful and training them to cultivate the wholesome and skillful

perception: one of the five attributes of the human primary identity that refers to the human ability to recognize, interpret, and label sensory inputs and experiences

perspective-taking: the practice of imagining possibilities of being beyond one's lived experiences; it is the *P* in the PRISM Toolkit

policies: the second root cause of bias; they are the formal and informal principles of action adopted by an institution or groups of institutions, i.e., systems

privilege: the unearned advantages (resources, rights, opportunities, and experiences) humans have and the ease they feel in a society for no reason other than their being, i.e., their intersectional secondary identities

pRosocial behavior: the practice of cultivating positive mental states and emotions that intend to alleviate suffering or benefit others; it is the *R* in the PRISM Toolkit

race: a story that ranks humans on a hierarchy based on descent and appearance

social contact: the third root cause of bias, it encompasses the interactions, connections, and communications that we have with other humans during our lives due to our built environment, significant humans, and choices

social identity: a type of secondary identity that a society assigns to a human, often based on their biological and experiential identities

stereotype: false mental formations attached to subordinated identities

stereotype replacement: the practice of becoming mindful of group-based associations, stereotypes, and unwholesome habits and actively replacing them with real, positive counterexamples or wholesome habits; it is the *S* in the PRISM Toolkit

systemic bias: the outcome of institutional biases within particular industries, sectors, localities, nations, and beyond

trauma: experiences that are life-threatening and/or emotionally, cognitively, and physically overwhelming

unconscious bias: learned habits of thoughts about a secondary identity that distort how humans perceive, reason, remember, and make decisions toward themselves and others

ubuntu: Zulu concept that describes the interconnectedness and interdependence of all things in the universe; used interchangeably with interbeing and inclusion consciousness

vedana: one of the five attributes of the human primary identity that refers to the bare affect or feeling tone beneath every sensory experience, on the spectrum of pleasant, neutral, and unpleasant

wetiko: Algonquin word for a mindset that is driven by selfishness, greed, hatred, and ignorance; used interchangeably with exclusion consciousness

ENDNOTES

Introduction

1. Martin Luther King, Jr., "The Birth of a New Nation, Sermon Delivered at Dexter Avenue Baptist Church," April 7, 1957, King Papers Project, https://kinginstitute.stanford.edu/king-papers/documents/birth-new-nation-sermon-delivered-dexter-avenue-baptist-church.

2. Brian B. Drwecki et al., "Reducing Racial Disparities in Pain Treatment: The Role of Empathy and Perspective-Taking," *Pain* 152 (2011): 1001–1006; Yoona Kang, Jeremy R. Gray, and John F. Dovidio, "The Nondiscriminating Heart: Lovingkindness Meditation Training Decreases Implicit Intergroup Bias," *Journal of Experimental Psychology* 143 (2014): 1306–1313; Nilanjana Dasgupta and Anthony G. Greenwald, "On the Malleability of Automatic Attitudes: Combating Automatic Prejudice with Images of Admired and Disliked Individuals," *Journal of Personality and Social Psychology* 81 (2001): 800–814; *see also* BE MORE with Anu, PRISM Tools to Break Bias, https://www.bemorewithanu.com/our-research#keysources.

3. Daniel Goleman and Richard J. Davidson, *Altered Traits: Science Reveals How Meditation Changes Your Mind, Brain, and Body* (New York: Avery, 2017); Sarah Bowen et al., *Mindfulness-Based Relapse Prevention for Addictive Behaviors: A Clinician's Guide* (New York: Guilford Press, 2011); Jon Kabat-Zinn, *Full Catastrophe Living: Using the Wisdom of Your Body and Mind to Face Stress, Pain, and Illness* (New York: Delta, 1990).

4. Ocean Vuong, *On Earth We're Briefly Gorgeous: A Novel* (New York: Random House, 2019).

5. Eckhart Tolle, *A New Earth: Awakening to Your Life's Purpose* (New York: Dutton/Penguin, 2005).

6. Swami S. Yukteswar Giri, *The Holy Science* (Los Angeles: Self-Realization Fellowship, 2020).

7. Dhruv Khullar, "How Prejudice Can Harm Your Health," *New York Times*, June 8, 2017. https://www.nytimes.com/2017/06/08/upshot/how-prejudice-can-harm-your-health.html.

8. Richard Sima, "Racism Takes a Toll on the Brain, Research Shows," *Washington Post*, February 16, 2023. https://www.washingtonpost.com/wellness/2023/02/16/racism-brain-mental-health-impact/; Jonathan M. Metzl, *Dying of Whiteness: How the Politics of Racial Resentment Is Killing America's Heartland* (New York: Basic Books, 2019).

9. Tobias Baer, Sven Heiligtag, and Hamid Samandari, "The Business Logic in Debiasing," McKinsey and Company, May 23, 2017, https://www.mckinsey.com/capabilities/risk-and-resilience/our-insights/the-business-logic-in-debiasing.

10. Ani Turner et al., *The Business Case for Racial Equity*, Altarum Institute and W. K. Kellogg Foundation, 2018, https://altarum.org/sites/default/files/uploaded-publication-files/WKKF%20Business%20Case%20for%20Racial%20Equity.pdf.

11. Yuval Noah Harari, *21 Lessons for the 21st Century* (London: Vintage, 2019).

Chapter 1

1. Nelson Cowan, "The Magical Mystery Four: How Is Working Memory Capacity Limited, and Why?" *Current Directions in Psychological Science* 19 (2010): 51–57, https://www.ncbi.nlm.nih.gov/pmc/articles/PMC2864034.

2. Thích Nhât Hânh, *Being Peace*, 2nd ed. (Berkeley, CA: Parallax Press, 2008).

3. Anurag Gupta, "*Vedana* of Bias: Latent Likes and Dislikes Fueling Barriers to Human Connection," *Contemporary Buddhism* 19 (2018): 145–159, https://doi.org/10.1080/14639947.2018.1453238.

4. David Levesley and David Taylor, "Powerlifting for Your Brain: The Many Benefits of Meditation, According to the Experts," *GQ*, October 19, 2022, https://www.gq-magazine.co.uk/article/benefits-of-meditation.

5. Donald O. Hebb, *The Organization of Behavior* (New York: Wiley, 1949).

6. Daniel Kahneman, *Thinking, Fast and Slow* (New York: Farrar, Straus and Giroux, 2013).

7. Amrisha Vaish, Tobias Grossmann, and Amanda Woodward, "Not All Emotions Are Created Equal: The Negativity Bias in Social-Emotional Development," *Psychological Bulletin* 134 (2008): 383–403.

8. Daniel Goleman and Richard J. Davidson, *Altered Traits: Science Reveals How Meditation Changes Your Mind, Brain, and Body* (New York: Avery, 2017).

9. john a. powell, *Racing to Justice: Transforming Our Conceptions of Self and Other to Build an Inclusive Society* (Bloomington: Indiana University Press, 2012); Poverty and Race Research Action Council, *Structural Racism*, 15, Issue 6 (2006), http://www.prrac.org/newsletters/novdec2006.pdf; Poverty and Race Research Action Council, *Implicit Bias: A Forum*, 20, Issue 5 (2011), http://prrac.org/newsletters/sepoct2011.pdf.

10. Yoona Kang, Jeremy R. Gray, and John F. Dovidio, "The Nondiscriminating Heart: Lovingkindness Meditation Training Decreases Implicit Intergroup Bias," *Journal of Experimental Psychology* 143 (2014): 1306–1313.

11. Jamil Zaki, *The War for Kindness: Building Empathy in a Fractured World* (New York: Crown, 2019).

Chapter 2

1. Ewen Callaway, "Oldest *Homo sapiens* Fossil Claim Rewrites Our Species' History," *Nature* (2017), https://doi.org/10.1038/nature.2017.22114.

2. David Graeber and David Wengrow, *The Dawn of Everything* (New York: Farrar, Straus and Giroux, 2021).

3. Alnoor Ladha and Martin Kirk, "Seeing Wetiko: On Capitalism, Mind Viruses, and Antidotes for a World in Transition," *Kosmos Journal* (January 2022), https://www.kosmosjournal.org/article/seeing-wetiko-on-capitalism-mind-viruses-and-antidotes-for-a-world-in-transition; *See also,* Jack D. Forbes, *Columbus and Other Cannibals: The Wétiko Disease of Exploitation, Imperialism, and Terrorism* (New York: Seven Stories Press, 2008).

4. Nell Irvin Painter, *The History of White People* (New York: W.W. Norton, 2010).

5. Vanessa Machado de Oliveira, *Hospicing Modernity: Facing Humanity's Wrongs and the Implications for Social Activism* (Berkeley, CA: North Atlantic Books,

2021); Báyò Akómoláfé, "Homo Icarus: The Depreciating Value of Whiteness and the Place of Healing," August 19, 2017, https://www.bayoakomolafe.net/post/homo-icarus-the-depreciating-value-of-whiteness-and-the-place-of-healing.

6. Eckhart Tolle, *A New Earth: Awakening to Your Life's Purpose* (New York: Dutton/Penguin, 2005).

7. Graeber and Wengrow, *The Dawn of Everything*; John Mohawk, *Utopian Legacies: A History of Conquest and Oppression in the Western World* (Santa Fe, NM: Clear Light, 2000); Ned Blackhawk, *The Rediscovery of America: Native Peoples and the Unmaking of U.S. History* (New Haven, CT: Yale University Press, 2023).

8. "Prior to European colonization plains bison are estimated to have numbered between 30 million and 60 million animals . . . By 1889, only 512 plains bison remained after the ravages of westward expansion, market demand, and a deliberate effort by the US Government to eliminate the bison to subdue the Native people that relied so heavily upon them." World Wildlife Federation, "Plains Bison Facts," https://www.worldwildlife.org/species/plains-bison.

9. Asia Murphy, "Conservation's Biggest Challenge? The Legacy of Colonialism," *Live Science*, May 20, 2019, https://www.livescience.com/65507-conservation-colonialism-legacy.html; Emmanuel Kreike, *Scorched Earth: Environmental Warfare as a Crime Against Humanity and Nature* (Princeton, NJ: Princeton University Press, 2021).

10. Kreike, *Scorched Earth*; Ha-Joon Chang, *Bad Samaritans: The Myth of Free Trade and the Secret History of Capitalism* (New York: Bloomsbury Press, 2008); Ha-Joon Chang, *Kicking Away the Ladder: Development Strategy in Historical Perspective* (London: Anthem Press, 2002); Alnoor Ladha and Lynn Murphy, *Post Capitalist Philanthropy* (New York: Transition Resource Circle and Daraja Press, 2022).

11. Autodidact 17, "Dr. Martin Luther King Jr: 'I Fear I Am Integrating My People into a Burning House,'" *New York Amsterdam News*, January 12, 2017, https://amsterdamnews.com/news/2017/01/12/dr-martin-luther-king-jr-i-fear-i-am-integrating-m.

12. Greta Thunberg, "Greta Thunberg's Speech at the U.N. Climate Action Summit," NPR.org, September 23, 2019, https://www.npr.org/2019/09/23/763452863/transcript-greta-thunbergs-speech-at-the-u-n-climate-action-summit.

13. Milton Friedman, "A Friedman Doctrine—The Social Responsibility of Business Is to Increase Its Profits," *New York Times Magazine*, September 13, 1970, https://www.nytimes.com/1970/09/13/archives/a-friedman-doctrine-the-social-responsibility-of-business-is-to.html; *See also*, Rund Abdelfatah et al., "Capitalism: What Makes Us Free?" NPR.org, July 1, 2021, https://www.npr.org/2021/06/28/1011062075/capitalism-what-makes-us-free.

14. Ruby Sales with Krista Tippett, "Where Does It Hurt?" *On Being*, September 15, 2016, https://onbeing.org/programs/ruby-sales-where-does-it-hurt.

15. Ramachandra Guha, "Ramachandra Guha: Ten Reasons Why Gandhi Is Still Relevant," Scroll.in, January 29, 2023, https://scroll.in/article/1042767/ramachandra-guha-ten-reasons-why-gandhi-still-matters.

16. "Universal Declaration of Human Rights: History of the Declaration," United Nations, n.d., https://www.un.org/en/about-us/udhr/history-of-the-declaration.

17. Grace Lee Boggs with Angela Davis, "Grace Lee Boggs in Conversation with Angela Davis—Transcript, Web Extra Only," *Making Contact*, February 20, 2012, https://www.radioproject.org/2012/02/grace-lee-boggs-berkeley.

Chapter 3

1. Nick Hobson, "This 50-Year-Old Riddle That Continues to Stump Us Explains Why We Still Have a Strong Gender Bias," Inc.com, May 18, 2022, https:// www.inc.com/nick-hobson/the-100-year-old-riddle-that-continues-to-stump -us-explains-why-we-still-have-a-strong-gender-bias.html.

2. Laura Lambert, "Women Surgeons Defining Future of Surgery," *Good Notes*, University of Utah Health, July 30, 2021, https://uofuhealth.utah.edu/notes /2021/07/women-surgeons-defining-future-of-surgery.

3. I created "The Association Game (TAG)" from an exercise shared by Mahzarin R. Banaji and Anthony G. Greenwald in *Blindspot: Hidden Biases of Good People* (New York: Delacorte Press, 2013).

4. John T. Jost et al., "The Existence of Implicit Bias Is Beyond Reasonable Doubt: A Refutation of Ideological and Methodological Objections and Executive Summary of Ten Studies That No Manager Should Ignore," *Research in Organizational Behavior* 29 (2009): 39–69.

5. Banaji and Greenwald, *Blindspot*; Healthline, "Gender Bias in Healthcare," https://www.healthline.com/health/gender-bias-healthcare#examples; Jennifer L. Eberhardt, *Biased: Uncovering the Hidden Prejudice That Shapes What We See, Think, and Do* (New York: Penguin Books, 2020); B. D. Smedley, A. Y. Stith, and A. R. Nelson, *Unequal Treatment: Confronting Racial and Ethnic Disparities in Health Care* (Washington, DC: The National Academies Press, 2001), 764.

6. Amy J. C. Cuddy, Susan T. Fiske, and Peter Glick, "Warmth and Competence as Universal Dimensions of Social Perception: The Stereotype Content Model and the BIAS Map," *Advances in Experimental Social Psychology* 40 (2008): 61–149.

7. Banaji and Greenwald, *Blindspot*.

8. *See, e.g.,* Perception Institute, *The Science of Equality, Vol. 1: Addressing Implicit Bias, Racial Anxiety, and Stereotype Threat in Education and Health Care*, 2014, https://equity.ucla.edu/wp-content/uploads/2019/12/Science-of-Equality -Vol.-1-Perception-Institute-2014.pdf; Perception Institute, *The Science of Equality, Vol. 2: The Effects of Gender Roles, Implicit Bias, and Stereotype Threat on the Lives of Women and Girls*, 2016, https://equity.ucla.edu/wp-content/ uploads/2019/12/Science-of-Equality-Volume-2.pdf; D. Rooth, *Implicit Discrimination in Hiring: Real World Evidence*, IZA DP. No. 2764, 2007. There've been a few journalists and academics, most with dominant intersectional identities, who have thrown doubt on the IAT's validity and thereby efforts to address inequality and injustice in workplaces and societies. The fact that these few individuals, almost exclusively cis, straight, white, European-descent men who are college educated and dominant class, have held so much influence is an extension of their social power.

9. Shepard commented that "any knowledge or understanding of the illusion we may gain at the intellectual level remains virtually powerless to diminish the magnitude of the illusion" (p. 128). Roger N. Shepard, *Mind Sights: Original Visual Illusions, Ambiguities, and Other Anomalies, with a Commentary on the Play of Mind in Perception and Art* (New York: W.H. Freeman, 1990).

10. Amisha Ghadiali, "Alnoor Ladha on Post-Capitalism, Mystical Anarchism, and Solidarity—E123," February 2021, *All That We Are*

with Amisha Ghadiali, Spotify, 1:30:00, https://open.spotify.com/ episode/3wXj0Cwv3ddOjZtEHKdTEW (podcast).

11. Claude M. Steele, *Whistling Vivaldi: How Stereotypes Affect Us and What We Can Do*, rep. ed. (New York: W. W. Norton, 2011).

12. Gay Hendricks, *The Big Leap: Conquer Your Hidden Fear and Take Life to the Next Level* (New York: HarperOne, 2010).

13. Robin DiAngelo, *White Fragility: Why It's So Hard for White People to Talk About Racism* (Boston: Beacon Press, 2018).

14. Sanne Feenstra et al., "Contextualizing the Impostor 'Syndrome,'" *Frontiers in Psychology* 11 (2020): art. 575024, https://doi.org/10.3389/fpsyg.2020 .575024.

15. Brené Brown, *I Thought It Was Just Me (but It Isn't): Making the Journey from "What Will People Think?" to "I Am Enough"* (New York: Avery, 2007).

16. Jonathan Rothwell and Andre M. Perry, "How Racial Bias in Appraisals Affects the Devaluation of Homes in Majority-Black Neighborhoods," Brookings, December 5, 2022, https://www.brookings.edu/articles/how-racial-bias-in-appraisals-affects-the-devaluation-of-homes-in-majority-black-neighborhoods.

17. Cassi Pittman Claytor et al., *The Racial Bias in Retail Study*, December 2020, http://arks.princeton.edu/ark:/88435/dsp014b29b913g; Nick Thompson and Diana Magnay, "Oprah Winfrey Racism Row over Switzerland Shop Incident," CNN, August 11, 2013, https://www.cnn.com/2013/08/09/world/oprah -winfrey-racism-switzerland/index.html.

18. Erich Fromm, *The Heart of Man: Its Genius for Good and Evil* (Riverdale, NY: American Mental Health Foundation Books, 2010).

19. Philip Ball, "Strangers Are Just Relatives You Haven't Met Yet," *Nature* (1999), https://doi.org/10.1038/news990311-2.

Chapter 4

1.   Emily Tannenbaum, "Here's Every State That Has Passed the Crown Act," *Glamour*, July 27, 2022, https://www.glamour.com/story/the-crown-act -banning-hair-discrimination.

2.   Isabel Wilkerson, *Caste: The Origins of Our Discontents* (New York: Random House, 2020).

3.   About *Adivasis*, he wrote, "Thirteen million people living in the midst of civilization are still in a savage state, and are leading the life of hereditary criminals!" B. R. Ambedkar, *Annihilation of Caste: The Annotated Critical Edition* (London: Verso, 2016), 249–51.

4.   Brené Brown, *Braving the Wilderness: The Quest for True Belonging and the Courage to Stand Alone* (New York: Random House, 2017).

5.   Joan Howarth, *Shaping the Bar: The Future of Attorney Licensing* (Stanford, CA: Stanford University Press, 2022).

6.   *Inequality for All*, directed by Jacob Kornbluth, RADiUS-TWC, 2013.

7.   Alnoor Ladha and Lynn Murphy, *Post Capitalist Philanthropy* (New York: Transition Resource Circle and Daraja Press, 2022).

8.   David Loy, *Money, Sex, War, Karma: Notes for a Buddhist Revolution* (Boston: Wisdom Publications, 2008).

Chapter 5

1. Isabel Wilkerson, *Caste: The Origins of Our Discontents* (New York: Random House, 2020).

2. Alan H. Goodman, Yolanda T. Moses, and Joseph L. Jones, *Race: Are We So Different?* 2nd ed. (Hoboken, NJ: Wiley-Blackwell, 2020).

3. Jessica Dickerson, "Toni Morrison Breaks Down the Reality of Race on *The Colbert Report*," *HuffPost*, November 21, 2014, https://www.huffpost.com /entry/toni-morrison-colbert_n_6199402.

4. *Race: The Power of an Illusion*, three episodes produced by California Newsreel in association with the Independent Television Service, 2003.

5. Francisco Bethencourt, *Racisms: From the Crusades to the Twentieth Century* (Princeton, NJ: Princeton University Press, 2013).

6. George M. Fredrickson, "The Historical Origins and Development of Racism," *Race: The Power of an Illusion*, California Newsreel, 2003, https://www. racepowerofanillusion.org/articles/historical-origins-and-development -racism.

7. Steven T. Newcomb, *Pagans in the Promised Land: Decoding the Doctrine of Christian Discovery*, 3rd ed. (Golden, CO: Fulcrum, 2008).

8. Bethencourt, *Racisms*; Ibram X. Kendi, *Stamped from the Beginning: The Definitive History of Racist Ideas in America* (New York: Nation Books, 2016).

9. Blake A. Watson, *Buying America from the Indians: Johnson v. McIntosh and the History of Native Land Rights* (Norman: University of Oklahoma Press, 2012).

10. Isabelle Charmantier, "Linnaeus and Race," Linnean Society of London, September 3, 2020, https://www.linnean.org/learning/who-was-linnaeus /linnaeus-and-race.

11. Stuart Ewen and Elizabeth Ewen, *Typecasting* (New York: Seven Stories Press, 2011).

12. Nell Irvin Painter, *The History of White People* (Princeton, NJ: Princeton University Press, 2010).

13. Ewen and Ewen, *Typecasting*.

14. Goodman, Moses, and Jones, *Race: Are We So Different?*

15. Audrey Smedley, "What Role Does the Bible Play in Our Society of Racial Inequality Today?" PBS, https://www.pbs.org/race/000_About/002_04- experts-02-07.htm; *see also*, Audrey Smedley, *Race in North America: Origin and Evolution of a World View* (Boulder, CO: Westview Press, 1993).

16. "President's State of the Union Address Refers to Human Genome Project," National Institutes of Health National Human Genome Research Institute, January 27, 2000, https://www.genome.gov/10002102/2000-state-of -the-union-and-hgp.

17. The Japanese emulated the West in the late 19th and early 20th centuries by adapting the story of race to suit their colonial missions in Korea, China, Taiwan, and other parts of Asia; *see* Bethencourt, *Racisms*.

18. Eli Meixler, "Nobel Laureate James Watson Loses Honorary Titles Over 'Reprehensible' Race Comments," *Time*, January 14, 2019, https://time.com /5501811/james-watson-loses-honors-race-comments.

19. Jay L. Garfield and Bryan W. Van Norden, "If Philosophy Won't Diversify, Let's Call It What It Really Is," *New York Times*, May 11, 2016, https://www.nytimes.com/2016/05/11/opinion/if-philosophy-wont-diversify-lets-call-it-what-it-really-is.html.

20. Tom Heyden, "The 10 Greatest Controversies of Winston Churchill's Career," BBC.com, January 26, 2015, https://www.bbc.com/news/magazine-29701767.

21. Resmaa Menakem, *My Grandmother's Hands: Racialized Trauma and the Pathway to Mending Our Hearts and Bodies* (Las Vegas, NV: Central Recovery Press, 2017).

Chapter 6

1. bell hooks, *Feminist Theory: From Margin to Center* (Cambridge, MA: South End Press, 1984).

2. Sandra Slater and Fay A. Yarbrough, eds., *Gender and Sexuality in Indigenous North America, 1400–1850* (Columbia: University of South Carolina Press, 2011); Gregory D. Smithers, *Reclaiming Two-Spirits: Sexuality, Spiritual Renewal and Sovereignty in Native America* (Boston: Beacon Press, 2022); Indian Health Service, "Two-Spirit," n.d., https://www.ihs.gov/lgbt/health/twospirit.

3. Netflix series, *Live to Lead*, S1 E6: Gloria Steinem, December 31, 2022.

4. Nayyirah Waheed, *Salt* (self-published, 2013).

5. "LGBT+ Pride 2021 Global Survey: A 27-Country Ipsos Survey," Ipsos, June 2021, https://www.ipsos.com/sites/default/files/ct/news/documents/2021-06/LGBT%20Pride%202021%20Global%20Survey%20Report_3.pdf.

6. Nurith Aizenman, "Men Are Hunters, Women Are Gatherers. That Was the Assumption. A New Study Upends It," NPR, July 1, 2023, https://www.npr.org/sections/goatsandsoda/2023/07/01/1184749528/men-are-hunters-women-are-gatherers-that-was-the-assumption-a-new-study-upends-it.

7. David Graeber and David Wengrow, *The Dawn of Everything* (New York: Farrar, Straus and Giroux, 2021).

8. Adam S. Green, "Killing the Priest-King: Addressing Egalitarianism in the Indus Civilization," *Journal of Archaeological Research* 29 (2020): 153–202, https://doi.org/10.1007/s10814-020-09147-9.

9. Stephen Luntz, "Rise of Sexual Inequality in Ancient China Revealed in Bones," IFLScience, https://www.iflscience.com/rise-of-sexual-inequality-in-ancient-china-revealed-in-bones-39863.

10. Munya Andrews, *Journey into Dreamtime* (Sydney: Evolve Communities, 2018).

11. Stuart Ewen and Elizabeth Ewen, *Typecasting* (New York: Seven Stories Press, 2011).

12. Yuval Noah Harari, *Sapiens: A Brief History of Humankind* (New York: Harper, 2015).

13. Ewen and Ewen, *Typecasting*.

14. Ewen and Ewen, *Typecasting*.

15. Vivian Ho, "Did Christian Homophobia Come from a Mistranslation of the Bible?" *The Guardian*, December 1, 2023, https://www.theguardian.com/film/2023/dec/01/christian-homophobia-bible-mistranslation-1946-documentary.

16. Rama Tirtha, *Swami Ram Tirath: His Life and Teachings* (Ann Arbor: University of Michigan Library, 1908).

17. Ewen and Ewen, *Typecasting*.

18. Rebecca Ratcliffe, "Nobel Scientist Tim Hunt: Female Scientists Cause Trouble for Men in Labs," *The Guardian*, June 10, 2015, https://www.theguardian.com/uk-news/2015/jun/10/nobel-scientist-tim-hunt-female-scientists-cause-trouble-for-men-in-labs.

19. "Full Transcript: President Summers' Remarks at the National Bureau of Economic Research, Jan. 14 2005," *The Harvard Crimson*, February 18, 2005, https://www.thecrimson.com/article/2005/2/18/full-transcript-president-summers-remarks-at.

20. Mary Gibson, *Born to Crime: Cesare Lombroso and the Origins of Biological Criminology* (Westport, CT: Praeger, 2002).

21. Ewen and Ewen, *Typecasting*.

22. Ewen and Ewen, *Typecasting*.

23. Ewen and Ewen, *Typecasting*.

24. Samuel White Swan-Perkins, "Five Two-Spirit Heroes Who Paved the Way for Today's Native LGBTQ+ Community," KQED, November 20, 2018, https://www.kqed.org/arts/13845330/5-two-spirit-heroes-who-paved-the-way-for-todays-native-lgbtq-community.

25. Ruth Maclean, "No Shame. No Sorrow. Divorce Means It's Party Time in Mauritania," *New York Times*, June 4, 2023, https://www.nytimes.com/2023/06/04/world/africa/mauritania-divorce-parties.html.

26. The World Bank, "Nearly 2.4 Billion Women Globally Don't Have Same Economic Rights as Men," WorldBank.org, March 1, 2022, https://www.worldbank.org/en/news/press-release/2022/03/01/nearly-2-4-billion-women-globally-don-t-have-same-economic-rights-as-men.

27. "Climate Crisis, Fragmentation, and Collective Trauma," Science and Nonduality, YouTube, November 3, 2021, https://www.youtube.com/watch?v=6RWfad60fmM&ab_channel=ScienceandNonduality.

28. "Expanding the Spectrum of Love," Plum Village, June 27, 2023, https://plumvillage.org/articles/expanding-the-spectrum-of-love.

Chapter 7

1. *The Buddha: History of Buddhism*, directed by David Grubin, narrated by Richard Gere, PBS, 2010.

2. Gordon W. Allport, *The Nature of Prejudice* (Cambridge, MA: Addison-Wesley, 1954).

3. Vandana Shiva, "The Violence of Reductionist Scientists," *Alternatives* 12 (1987): 243–261, https://doi.org/10.1177/030437548701200205.

4. "Haiti's Forced Payments to Enslavers Cost Economy $21 Billion, The New York Times Found," Equal Justice Initiative, June 13, 2022, https://eji.org/news/haitis-forced-payments-to-enslavers-cost-economy-21-billion-the-new-york-times-found.

5. Alnoor Ladha and Lynn Murphy, *Post Capitalist Philanthropy* (New York: Transition Resource Circle and Daraja Press, 2022); David Harvey, *A Brief History of Neoliberalism* (Oxford: Oxford University Press, 2005).

6. Danielle Vilaplana, "Ethnobotany and Ethnocide: An Interview with Wade Davis," Voices for Biodiversity, May 7, 2012, https://voicesforbiodiversity.org/articles/ethnobotany-and-ethnocide-an-interview-with-wade-davis.

7. Vanessa Machado de Oliveira, *Hospicing Modernity: Facing Humanity's Wrongs and the Implications for Social Activism* (Berkeley, CA: North Atlantic Books, 2021).

8. Tiokasin Ghosthorse, "3/12/23—Vanessa Machado de Oliveira Andreotti," *First Voices Radio,* March 12, 2023, https://firstvoices.transistor.fm/episodes.

9. Mehrsa Baradaran, "The Spirit of the Law: Race and Legal Hypocrisy," 28th Annual Derrick Bell Lecture on Race in American Society, Center on Race, Inequality, and the Law, November 14, 2023.

10. Andrew Cooper, "The Likably Unlikely Monk," *Tricycle: The Buddhist Review*, Fall 2009, https://tricycle.org/magazine/likably-unlikely-monk.

Chapter 8

1. Douglas S. Massey and Stefanie Brodmann, *Spheres of Influence: The Social Ecology of Racial and Class Inequality* (New York: Russell Sage Foundation, 2014); Douglas S. Massey, "American Apartheid: Segregation and the Making of the Underclass," *American Journal of Sociology* 96 (1990): 1153–1188, https://doi.org/10.1086/229532.

2. Designing Justice + Designing Spaces, "Mission and Vision," n.d., https://designingjustice.org/about/#mission.

3. Daniel Cox, Juhem Navarro-Rivera, and Robert P. Jones, "Race, Religion, and Political Affiliation of Americans' Core Social Networks," Public Religion Research Institute, August 3, 2016, https://www.prri.org/research/poll-race-religion-politics-americans-social-networks.

4. Malcolm Gladwell, *The Tipping Point: How Little Things Can Make a Big Difference* (Boston: Back Bay Books, 2002).

Chapter 9

1. Matthew Rozsa, "The Psychological Reason That So Many Fall for the 'Big Lie,'" *Salon*, February 3, 2022, https://www.salon.com/2022/02/03/the-psychological-reason-that-so-many-fall-for-the-big-lie.

2. Sasha Alyson, "The Origin of Modern Schooling," Karma Colonialism, n.d., https://karmacolonialism.org/the-origin-of-modern-schooling.

3. Ellwood Patterson Cubberley, *The History of Education: Educational Practice and Progress Considered as a Phase of the Development and Spread of Western Civilization* (Boston: Houghton Mifflin, 1920).

4. Vanessa Machado de Oliveira, *Hospicing Modernity: Facing Humanity's Wrongs and the Implications for Social Activism* (Berkeley, CA: North Atlantic Books, 2021); Detlef Müller, Fritz Ringer, and Brian Simon, eds., *The Rise of the Modern Educational System: Structural Change and Social Reproduction 1870–1920* (Cambridge, UK: Cambridge University Press, 1989).

5. Bob Pepperman Taylor, *Horace Mann's Troubling Legacy: The Education of Democratic Citizens* (Lawrence: University of Kansas Press, 2010).

6. T. B. Macaulay, "Minute by the Hon'ble T. B. Macaulay, dated the 2nd February 1835," Bureau of Education, n.d., https://franpritchett.com/00generallinks/macaulay/txt_minute_education_1835.html.

7. Sathnam Sanghera, *Empireland: How Imperialism Has Shaped Modern Britain* (New York: Pantheon Books, 2023).

8. Senjuti Millik, "Colonial Biopolitics and the Great Bengal Famine of 1943," *Geojournal* 88 (2023): 3205–3221, https://www.ncbi.nlm.nih.gov/pmc/articles /PMC9735018; Sandhya Ramesh, "Proved by Science: Winston Churchill, Not Nature, Caused 1943 Bengal Famine," *The Print*, March 31, 2019, https:// theprint.in/science/proved-by-science-winston-churchill-not-nature-caused -1943-bengal-famine/214942.

9. Patricia Burch, ed., *System Failure: Policy and Practice in the School-to-Prison Pipeline* (New York: Routledge, 2022).

10. National Alliance on Mental Illness, "Mental Health in Schools," n.d., https:// www.nami.org/Advocacy/Policy-Priorities/Improving-Health/Mental -Health-in-Schools.

11. Robin Wall Kimmerer, "Speaking of Nature," *Orion*, June 12, 2017, https:// orionmagazine.org/article/speaking-of-nature.

12. Akilah S. Richards, *Raising Free People: Unschooling as Liberation and Healing Work* (Oakland, CA: PM Press, 2020); Kerry McDonald, *Unschooled: Raising Curious, Well-Educated Children Outside the Conventional Classroom* (Chicago: Chicago Review Press, 2019).

Chapter 10

1. "SRK—Fair and Handsome New Ad," YouTube, n.d., https://www.youtube .com/watch?v=xZTsuwYgl48&ab_channel=TheSrkBigFans.

2. A. Guttmann, "Media Usage in the U.S.—Statistics and Facts," *Statista*, December 18, 2023, https://www.statista.com/topics/1536/ media-use/#editorsPicks.

3. Brother Anandamoy, "A World in Transition," YouTube, October 21, 2022, https://youtu.be/Qhce8SDz6I8?si=mb1fy_ZCwtXoZspr (at 36:36).

4. Jonah Sachs, *Winning the Story Wars: Why Those Who Tell—and Live—the Best Stories Will Rule the Future* (Boston: Harvard Business Review Press, 2012).

5. Jennifer L. Eberhardt, *Biased: Uncovering the Hidden Prejudice That Shapes What We See, Think, and Do* (New York: Viking, 2019).

6. See Judson Brewer's *The Craving Mind* (New Haven, CT: Yale University Press, 2017) for an overview of our brain's reward-based system.

7. Maria Ressa, *How to Stand Up to a Dictator: The Fight for Our Future* (New York: Harper, 2022).

8. *"Ek Anek Ekta* (1974)." You can watch the full video here: https://www .youtube.com/watch?v=R-tTOJ1RvUY.

9. Pamposh Raina, "The Cartoon That Taught Indians the Meaning of 'Many,'" *New York Times*, May 18, 2012, https://archive.nytimes.com/india.blogs. nytimes.com/2012/05/18/the-cartoon-that-taught-indians-the-meaning -of-many.

10. Dartmouth College, "Revisiting Fred Rogers' 2002 Commencement Address," March 27, 2018, https://home.dartmouth.edu/news/2018/03/revisiting -fred-rogers-2002-commencement-address.

11. Living Mandala, "The Spring of Sustainability 2012," n.d., https://www
.livingmandala.com/Living_Mandala/Spring_of_Sustainability_2012.html.

12. Thích Nhât Hânh, "Please Call Me by My True Names," June 3, 2020, https://
plumvillage.org/articles/please-call-me-by-my-true-names-song-poem.

The Promise of Breaking Bias

1. *The Buddha: History of Buddhism*, directed by David Grubin, narrated by
Richard Gere, PBS, 2010.

2. Alnoor Ladha and Lynn Murphy, *Post Capitalist Philanthropy* (New York:
Transition Resource Circle and Daraja Press, 2022).

3. Paramahansa Yogananda, *Autobiography of a Yogi* (Los Angeles: Self-Realization
Fellowship, 2015).

ABRIDGED BIBLIOGRAPHY

For an in-depth bibliography, visit **anuguptany.com**.

Akómoláfé, Báyò. *These Wilds beyond Our Fences: Letters to My Daughter on Humanity's Search for Home*. Berkeley: North Atlantic Books, 2017.

Alexander, Michelle. *The New Jim Crow: Mass Incarceration in the Age of Colorblindness*. New York: New Press, 2010.

Ambedkar, B. R. *Annihilation of Caste: The Annotated Critical Edition*. London: Verso, 2016.

Blackhawk, Ned. *The Rediscovery of America: Native Peoples and the Unmaking of U.S. History*. New Haven, CT: Yale University Press, 2023.

Boggs, Grace Lee and Scott Kurashige. *The Next American Revolution: Sustainable Activism for the Twenty-First Century*. Berkeley: University Of California Press, 2012.

Brewer, Judson and Jon Kabat-Zinn. *The Craving Mind: From Cigarettes to Smartphones to Love—Why We Get Hooked and How We Can Break Bad Habits*. New Haven, CT: Yale University Press, 2017.

Crenshaw, Kimberlé. *On Intersectionality: Essential Writings*. New York: New Press, 2017.

Dirks, Nicholas B. *Castes of Mind: Colonialism and the Making of Modern India*. New Delhi: Permanent Black, 2003.

Ekman, Paul and Eve Ekman. *Atlas of Emotions*. https://atlasofemotions.org.

Elkins, Caroline. *Legacy of Violence*. New York: Vintage, 2023.

Ewen, Stuart and Elizabeth Ewen. *Typecasting*. New York: Seven Stories Press, 2011.

Guha, Ramachandra. *Savaging the Civilized: Verrier Elwin, His Tribals, and India*. Chicago: University Of Chicago Press, 2016.

Gunaratana, Bhante Henepola. *Mindfulness in Plain English*. Somerville, MA: Wisdom Publications, 2015.

Haney López, Ian. *Dog Whistle Politics: How Coded Racial Appeals Have Reinvented Racism and Wrecked the Middle Class*. New York: Oxford University Press, 2014.

——— *White by Law: The Legal Construction of Race*. New York: NYU Press, 1996.

Hânh, Nhât Thích. *Living Buddha, Living Christ*. New York: Riverhead Books, 2015.

——— *Understanding Our Mind: 50 Verses on Buddhist Psychology*, Berkeley: Parallax Press, 2002.

Hanson, Rick, and Richard Mendius. *Buddha's Brain: The Practical Neuroscience of Happiness, Love & Wisdom*. Oakland, CA: New Harbinger Publications, 2009.

Harvey, David. *A Brief History of Neoliberalism*. Oxford: Oxford University Press, 2005.

Lee, Ilchi. *Brain Wave Vibration: Getting Back into the Rhythm of a Happy, Healthy Life*. Sedona, AZ: Best Life, 2009.

Levine, Peter A. *Waking the Tiger: Healing Trauma: The Innate Capacity to Transform Overwhelming Experiences*. Berkeley, CA: North Atlantic Books, 1997.

Lugones, María. "Heterosexualism and the Colonial / Modern Gender System." *Hypatia* 22(1): 186–209. doi:10.1353/hyp.2006.0067.

——— "Toward a Decolonial Feminism." *Hypatia* 25(4): 742–759. doi:10.1111 /j.1527-2001.2010.01137.x.

Machado de Oliveira, Vanessa. *Hospicing Modernity: Facing Humanity's Wrongs and the Implications for Social Activism*. Berkeley, CA: North Atlantic Books, 2021.

Majied, Kamilah. *Joyfully Just: Black Wisdom and Buddhist Insights for Liberated Living*. Boulder, CO: Sounds True, 2024.

Marya, Rupa, and Raj Patel. *Inflamed: Deep Medicine & the Anatomy of Injustice*. New York: Farrar, Straus and Giroux, 2021.

Maté, Gabor. *In the Realm of Hungry Ghosts: Close Encounters with Addiction*. Toronto: Vintage Canada, 2008.

McGhee, Heather C. *The Sum of Us: What Racism Costs Everyone and How We Can Prosper Together*. London: Profile Books, 2022.

Menakem, Resmaa. *My Grandmother's Hands: Racialized Trauma and the Pathway to Mending Our Hearts and Bodies*. Las Vegas, NV: Central Recovery Press, 2017.

Narula, Smita. *Broken People: Caste Violence Against India's 'Untouchables.'* New York: Human Rights Watch, 1999. https://www.hrw.org/reports/1999/india/ India994.htm.

Perry, Bruce Duncan, and Oprah Winfrey. *What Happened to You?: Conversations on Trauma, Resilience, and Healing*. New York: Flatiron Books, 2021.

Shiva, Vandana, and Kartikey Shiva. *Oneness vs. the 1%: Shattering Illusions, Seeding Freedom*. White River Junction, VT: Chelsea Green Publishing, 2020.

Steinem, Gloria. *My Life on the Road*. Collingwood, Victoria: Nero, 2017.

Tejaniya, Sayadaw U., and Robert French. *When Awareness Becomes Natural: A Guide to Cultivating Mindfulness in Everyday Life*. Boulder, CO: Shambhala Publications Inc., 2016.

Teter, Magda. *Christian Supremacy: Reckoning with the Roots of Antisemitism and Racism*. Princeton, NJ: Princeton University Press, 2023.

Tharoor, Shashi. *Inglorious Empire: What the British Did to India*. London: Scribe Publication, 2019.

van der Kolk, Bessel. *The Body Keeps the Score: Brain, Mind and Body in the Healing of Trauma*. New York: Penguin Books, 2014.

Williams, Robert A. *Savage Anxieties: The Invention of Western Civilization*. New York: Palgrave Macmillan, 2012.

Wright, Robert. *Why Buddhism Is True: The Science and Philosophy of Meditation and Enlightenment*. New York: Simon & Schuster Paperbacks, 2017.

Yukteswar Giri, Swami S. *The Holy Science*. Los Angeles: Self-Realization Fellowship, 2020.

COMMUNITIES AND PRACTICES FOR SUPPORT

The list below contains communities and practices that supported my breaking bias journey and inspired me to develop the PRISM Toolkit. This is not an exhaustive list but a starting point for seeking practices and communities that embody *ubuntu* and inclusion consciousness.

If you'd like to add to this list, please visit **www.anuguptany.com**.

Learning and Practice Communities

* **Antiracist Development Institute (ADI)** is a research and practice institute that is building a coalition of lawyers, law professors, and other professionals who use systems design thinking to innovate and transform systems that create marginalization. Learn more: **dickinsonlaw.psu.edu/antiracist-development-institute**

* **BE MORE with Anu (BMA)** is my education technology benefit corporation that provides ongoing breaking bias trainings and data-driven audits for businesses, nonprofits, and governments. BMA also offers facilitator trainings, summits, and a *beloved community of practice* for professionals interested in advancing equity and belonging. Learn more: **bemorewithanu.com**

* **Echoing Green** is a curated global network of over 1,000 social enterprises and nonprofits that are working at the intersection of social justice and innovation, addressing the symptoms and root causes of bias. Learn more: **fellows.echoinggreen.org**

* **Education for Racial Equity** is a nonprofit that offers somatically informed antiracist educational events based on Resmaa Menakem's scholarship on somatic abolitionism. Learn more: **educationforracialequity.com**

* **Mirror Memoirs** is a storytelling and organizing community uplifting queer and gender-diverse people of color and allies who survived child sexual abuse as a strategy to end rape culture and other forms of marginalization. Learn more: **mirrormemoirs.com**

* **Move the Crowd** is a community of practice facilitated by Rha Goddess that is building a collective of conscious entrepreneurs who seek to transform the culture of capitalism and foster a new economy of True, Paid, Good. Learn more: **movethecrowd.me**

* **Resource Generation** is a network of people ages 18 to 35 with access to wealth who want to use their wealth and class privilege to enable equity, justice, and healing. Learn more: **resourcegeneration.com**

* **Yes!** supports social change movements worldwide by hosting transformational gatherings called "Jams" that provide co-creative brave healing spaces for advocates and practitioners working at the forefront of equity and justice. Learn more: **yesworld.org**

Spiritually Oriented Learning Communities and Practices for Healing

* **Body & Brain Yoga** is a diverse community of practitioners founded by Taoist master Ilchi Lee who are trained in holistic somatic and energy practices to integrate the mind with the body, heart, and soul. Learn more: **www.bodynbrain.com**

* **Insight Meditation Community** is a global network of meditation centers and Buddhist sanghas led primarily by Western Buddhists who teach and support Theravada Buddhist mindfulness practices. I've found sanghas and retreats for secondary identities like people of color, queer and gender-diverse people, and lawyers very enriching. Learn more: **www.dharma.org/resources/meditation-centers-and-communities**

* **Middle Collegiate Church** is North America's oldest continuous Christian Church and the world's most diverse, multicultural, and multireligious community. Led by the Rev. Dr. Jacqui Lewis, it embodies the Christian ethic of "love period." Learn more: **www.middlechurch.org**

* **The Plum Village Community** is a global community of mindfulness practice centers and monasteries founded by Zen master Thích Nhât Hânh. They offer retreats and teachings of engaged Buddhism and the art of mindful living. Learn more: **www.plumvillage.org**

* **Self-Realization Fellowship** is a worldwide organization founded in 1920 by Paramahansa Yogananda to spread the scientific techniques of Kriya Yoga and experience the oneness of all spiritual traditions. Learn more: **www.yogananda.org**

* **Spiritual Directors International (SDI)** is a nondenominational global membership community of spiritual companions and soul-care workers who support with ongoing spiritual intimacy and formation. Learn more: www.sdicompanions.org

Practices for Centering and Healing

* **Breathwork** encompasses intentional techniques, such as diaphragmatic breathing and forceful breath patterns, designed to optimize oxygen intake, reduce stress, and help calm you down, shifting your body and mind away from fight-or-flight mode while fostering a centered state of being.

* **Ecstatic dance** is a spontaneous and freeform movement practice accompanied by diverse music. It encourages individuals to express themselves authentically, fosters a sense of community, and often leads to a meditative and joyful state. It is a liberating way of practicing embodiment in a nonjudgmental group setting.

* **EMDR (eye movement desensitization and reprocessing)** is a therapeutic method that incorporates guided bilateral stimulation, typically through eye movements. It is designed to aid in the processing of traumatic memories, fostering a transformative shift in emotional responses and assisting individuals in stepping out of patterns of emotional reactivity or distress.

* **Group talk therapy occurs** with 5 to 10 other individuals and a certified clinician, generally around a particular subject such as divorce, addiction, codependence, or childhood sexual abuse. For me, it was incredibly liberating because it helped me feel less alone. In seeking this modality, it is important to ensure you feel safe and share authentically.

* **High-vibrational music** is music that has positive and uplifting healing effects on the heart, mind, body, and soul due to its positive energy and the enhanced consciousness it evokes. Such music can exist across genres but generally enables listeners to experience connection with life elements that transcend intellectual understanding.

* **HIIT (high-intensity interval training)** is a dynamic fitness approach featuring short bursts of intense exercise interspersed with rest, creating a shift in heart rate and effectively pulling us out of our heads, promoting physical exertion, and maximizing cardiovascular benefits in a time-efficient manner.

* **IFOT** is an indigenous approach to Focusing-Oriented Therapy (FOT), which works with complex trauma through the collective and intergenerational indigenous lens. IFOT is especially useful for indigenous and non-European people because of its approach to healing that acknowledges our connection to land and our ancestors.

* **Insight Dialogue** is a contemplative communication practice that weaves mindfulness and interpersonal inquiry, creating a transformative shift in dialogues by emphasizing deep listening, shared mindfulness, and mutual understanding. This fosters somatic insight and connection within interpersonal interactions.

* **Nonviolent Communication (NVC)** is a communication approach that emphasizes empathetic listening, honest expression, and the identification of needs, fostering a transformative shift in conversations by promoting understanding, resolving conflicts, and cultivating compassionate connections.

* **One-on-one talk therapy** with a certified clinician helped me understand why and how unwholesome habits interfered with my emotional and mental well-being. In seeking this modality, ensure you can build safety, trust, and empathy with your clinician.

* **Plant-medicine and psychedelic-assisted therapy** with certified clinicians has shown to be powerfully efficacious in mitigating the effects of chemical dependencies, addictions, PTSD, and complex traumas. These therapies work with sacred plants that have been and are stewarded by indigenous peoples for millennia.

* **Somatic Experiencing** is a therapeutic approach that focuses on the body's response to stress and trauma and offers healing by allowing you to renegotiate traumatic experiences through heightened awareness of bodily sensations.

* **Time in nature** has scientifically proven benefits like the reduction of stress hormones, lower blood pressure, and improved mood. Activities like forest bathing stimulate the

parasympathetic nervous system, providing experiences that contributes to overall mental and physical well-being.

* **Time with more-than-humans**, whether through pet interactions or nature observation, offers scientifically supported benefits, including reduced stress, improved mood, and even lowered blood pressure, fostering a transformative experience that enhances emotional well-being and strengthens our bond with the natural world.

* **Yoga** is a holistic practice with roots in South Asia that combines physical postures, breath regulation, meditation, and ethical principles to enhance physical and mental well-being, promoting flexibility, strength, stress reduction, and a sense of inner calm. It helped me get out of my head and work more skillfully with thoughts and ideas.

INDEX

NOTE: Page references in *italics* refer to PRISM Toolkit tools and figures.

C

D

F

G

H

Ham (biblical figure), 161–162

Ham's Redemption (Brocos), 162

Haney López, Ian, 102

Harari, Yuval Noah, xxxiii–xxxiv

Hardy, JoAnna, 305

The Heart of Man (Fromm), 97

Hebb's Rule, 12

hijras ("third gender"), 182

Hinduism, 181

Hirshfield, Jane, 216, 240

The History of White People (Painter), 46

hooks, bell, 175, 177, 259

Howarth, Joan, 127

Huineng (Zen master), 276–277

human diversity, defined, 3–4. *See also* diversity and identity

human relationships (HR), institutional bias and, 100–101

human trafficking as policy, 144–147

Hunt, Tim, 200, 202

"hurt people hurt people," 197

"hypersegregation," 248, 256

I

identity. *See also* diversity and identity

national vs. religious identity and social contact, 243–244

PRISM Toolkit, *17, 19–20, 21–22, 23, 25–26, 30–32*

Ilieva, Gabriela, 271

Implicit Association Test (IAT), 80

implicit bias, 80–81

inclusion consciousness. *See also* exclusion and inclusion

challenges to exclusion paradigms, 43–44

culture and, 239–240

defined, 34, 40–41

media and, 300

race in era of (1970s–present), 171–172

rise of, 62–67

ubuntu, 40

India

caste system of, xx–xxiii

Penal Code on homosexuality, 205

poverty in, 252–253

Indiana Jones and the Temple of Doom (film), 283, 299

indigenous peoples

casteism and, 116–118

theriocide and, 55, *55*

individuation, xxvi, 76

Inequality for All (documentary), 129

injustice, 232–233

Insight Meditation Society, 13

institutional bias, 86, *86,* 99–104

interbeing, 40–41

intergroup dialogue, 63

internalized bias, *86,* 86–92, *88*

intersectionality, 22–23, 201

invisibility, 285

Islam

Abrahamic faiths on gender, 191–194

Dhimmi system, 45, 48–52

Islamophobia, 122–124

"is-ness" of gender, 180–184

I-statements, xxx

J

jati systems, 115–118

Jefferson, Thomas, 166

Jesus, 43, 44, 62, 120, 192

Judaism

N

O

P

R

S

T

U

V

W

Y

Z

ACKNOWLEDGMENTS

All thanks first and foremost to our shared Creator, our God, Allah, or *bodhicitta*. Thank you to my beloved guru, Paramahansa Yogananda, paramgurus, the triple gem, saints of all religions, and all beings seen and unseen, known and unknown, who've guided my breaking bias journey and the writing of this book.

My deepest gratitude to His Holiness the Dalai Lama for blessing this book and our collective work of breaking bias. Your commitment to peace, nonviolence, kindness, joy, curiosity, and love—despite what you and our Tibetan siblings have experienced due to bias—humbles and inspires me every day. Thank you for being and for leading by example. Deep, deep bows.

Thank you, Mother Earth and your spirit in New York, Massachusetts, Sedona, Costa Rica, and Hawaii for providing the inspiration to write this book.

Much gratitude to generations of scientists, legal researchers, lawyers, judges, and scholars across disciplines who've kept the spirit of *ubuntu* alive through your truth-telling and truth-finding using modernity's approved methods of scientific inquiry. Thank you to the millions of racial justice, women's rights, queer rights, human rights, animal rights, and climate justice activists across the globe for your courageous efforts to realize equity, inclusion, and compassion in our political and economic institutions and systems. Thank you all for your patience and diligence to build a world where belonging replaces bias. This book stands on your shoulders.

Special thanks to Sunila Abeysekara, Derrick Bell, my biological and spiritual ancestors, *amma*, *badepapa*, and all ancestors around the globe—the enslaved, colonized, excluded, and subjugated—who were taken from us due to bias: may you continue to shine your wisdom and light on us.

Thank you, Katie Salisbury, for helping me conceptualize this project. Thank you to my agent, Jaidree Braddix, for taking a chance on this project, and many thanks to my incredibly patient editor, Anne Barthel, and Patty Gift, for supporting me in blowing up this project across space and time. Thank you, Dr. Kamilah Majied for your thoughtful comments to enable the words of this book reach even more humans across intersectionalities. Thank you to the Hay House team for your deep love for what you do to shift human consciousness.

Thank you to my dharma family at NYIMC, BCBS, IMS, and Spirit Rock. You remain one of my spiritual homes. Thank you for offering me the liberating teachings of the Buddha and for providing me with a refuge to break so many biases. Special shoutout to my "Exploring the Heart of Freedom" teachers and cohort, especially my fellow Loons and Herons, who were so patient with me as I was writing this book.

Thank you to my many dharma teachers for your love and guidance over the years, including, Larry Yang, Gina Sharpe, Bonnie Duran, Yifa Faxi, DaRa Williams, Sebene Selassie, Madeline Klyne, Sharon Salzberg, Joseph Goldstein, Kamala Masters, Mindah Lee Kumar, Tara Brach, Spring Washam, Roxanne Dault, Jill Shepard, Willian Edelglass, and Pascal Auclair. Deep bows.

Thank you to my SRF/YSS sangha and monastics for preserving the ancient teachings of Krishna and Jesus and the liberatory practice of Kriya Yoga. Thank you, Middle Church and Rev. Jacqui Lewis for embodying *love period*. Thank you for loving all of God's creation, while putting on a great show and reminding us of the gift of laughter, music, dance, and spirit. Ever since that Easter service in 2010, you've helped me to taste freedom in my heart, body, and soul. We are building a beloved community, together.

Thank you to my team at BE MORE, especially Caroline Horste, for always holding down the fort as we continue to support others to break bias and build a beloved community. Thank you, Josh Babcock, for translating my handwritten drawings into the beautiful figures and tables in this book. And thank you to everyone who's been a part of BE MORE. You've helped me grow tremendously.

Thank you to my social entrepreneurship family at Echoing Green, Antiracist Development Institute at PSDL, TED, B Corps, Move the Crowd, NYU Reynolds, NYU Law, and Goldman Sachs 10,000

Small Businesses for making work worthwhile and giving me pathways to negotiate work within the constraints of late-stage capitalism.

Thank you to all of my friends, students, partners, and collaborators who've helped me step up, grow up, and show up. Thank you to my Reworlding siblings. You've nurtured and nourished the ideas presented in this book. I love, love, looove you! Together, we are reworlding!

Thank you, Ian Fuller, Stan King, Daniel Aitken, and Manoj Dias for being my heartful brothers. Thank you, my dearest rainbow brothers for showing me the many healing ways to be in a queer male body. Thank you, Jen Angeli for adopting us in Sedona and introducing me to the wonders of energy and Body & Brain Yoga.

Thank you, Susan Davis. I don't know who I'd be without you—thank you for loving me unconditionally, you'll always be my queer guardian angel.

Thank you, Dhanu Miskin, Qinza Najm, Reka Prasad, Leslie Booker, Lola West, Terry Lafrazia, Rha Goddess, Helen Kramer, Amina AlTai, Priya Gupta, Ananta Ajmera, Nitika Raj, Julie Fahnestock, Yul-san Liem, Heather Box, Priya Iyer, Janet Bell, Danielle Conway, TaWanda Stallworth, Lisa Braff, and the many powerful women who've been my friends, coaches, mentors, advisors, therapists, and collaborators ever since that fateful night.

Thank you, mummy-jaan, for growing with me, for being my cheerleader, and for the priceless gift of faith. You make it all feel so easy. I am so grateful to be your son.

Thank you to my *janu*, Justin, for all of the silly ways you love me and for being my sunshine, day in and day out. I could not have completed this project without the levity and joy you bring to my life every day. You are my gift from the universe and I will continue to love you for lifetimes to come.

Thank you, Vasudha, Arusha, Daddy, Partha, Michael, my nibbles, Rhea and Sanvi, and our extended biological and chosen families across India, North America, and beyond for your presence and love.

Last, but not least, thank you to you my dear reader for undertaking this journey with me. Your companionship is what makes our breaking bias journey worthwhile. ♥

ABOUT THE AUTHOR

ANU GUPTA is an educator, lawyer, scientist, and the founder and CEO of BE MORE with Anu, an education technology benefit corporation that trains professionals across corporate, nonprofit, and government sectors to advance diversity, equity, inclusion, and belonging (DEIB) and wellness by breaking bias. His work has reached more than 300 organizations, training more than 80,000 professionals, impacting over 30 million lives.

As a gay immigrant of color, he came to the work of breaking bias after almost ending his life due to lifelong experiences with racism, homophobia, and Islamophobia. The realization that bias is learned—and can be *un*-learned—helped lead him out of that dark point and inspired a lifelong mission to build a global movement for social healing based on principles of mindfulness and compassion. A peer-reviewed author, he has written and spoken extensively, including on the TED stage, the Oprah Conversation, *Fast Company*, and *Newsweek*.

Anu is a trained meditation and yoga teacher with over 10,000 hours of meditation practice. He has a JD from NYU Law, an MPhil in development studies from Cambridge University, and a BA in international relations and Middle Eastern and Islamic studies from NYU. Rooted in his ancestral Buddhist and Kriya yoga lineages, he is also a student of Sufi, Taoist, Christian, and animist wisdom. He lives in New York City with his partner.

www.anuguptany.com

Hay House Titles of Related Interest

We hope you enjoyed this Hay House book. If you'd like to receive our online catalog featuring additional information on Hay House books and products, or if you'd like to find out more about the Hay Foundation, please contact:

Hay House LLC, P.O. Box 5100, Carlsbad, CA 92018-5100
(760) 431-7695 or (800) 654-5126
www.hayhouse.com® • www.hayfoundation.org

―――

Published in Australia by:
Hay House Australia Publishing Pty Ltd
18/36 Ralph St., Alexandria NSW 2015
Phone: +61 (02) 9669 4299
www.hayhouse.com.au

Published in the United Kingdom by:
Hay House UK Ltd
The Sixth Floor, Watson House,
54 Baker Street, London W1U 7BU
Phone: +44 (0) 203 927 7290
www.hayhouse.co.uk

Published in India by:
Hay House Publishers (India) Pvt Ltd
Muskaan Complex, Plot No. 3,
B-2, Vasant Kunj, New Delhi 110 070
Phone: +91 11 41761620
www.hayhouse.co.in

―――

Let Your Soul Grow

Experience life-changing transformation—one video at a time—with guidance from the world's leading experts.

www.healyourlifeplus.com

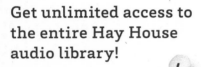

gratefulness   social cohesion   ~~homophob~~

fairness   ~~bigotry~~   gratitude   ~~hatred~~   kindne

~~xenophobia~~   equity   ~~nationalism~~   collaborati

mercy   ~~sexism~~   ~~transphobia~~   freedo

~~speciesism~~   inclusion   ~~fascism~~   forgivene

optimism   ~~wetiko~~   compassion   celebrati

~~greed~~   wisdom   ~~classism~~   ubuntu   ~~nazi~~

love   ~~ageism~~   bliss   ~~microaggressions~~

belonging   ~~patriarchy~~   ~~sizeism~~   heali

appreciation   empathy   ~~racism~~   ~~entitlem~~

~~ignorance~~   empowerment   ~~prejudice~~   happine

hope   ~~colonialism~~   courage   tendern

~~separation~~   awe   ~~supremacism~~   pea

safety   enchantment   ~~ableism~~   trust   ~~selfishn~~

~~poverty~~   contentment   ~~extremism~~   connect

curiosity   ~~egotism~~   passion   ~~fanatici~~

diversity   ~~insensitivity~~   ~~apathy~~   welln

~~exclusion~~   well-being   ~~ection~~   understand

generosity   ~~detachment~~   tranquility   equanin

~~antisemitism~~   serenity   liberty   ~~islamoph~~

cooperation   ~~hinduphobia~~   interbeing   jus

~~misogyny~~   collective identity   oneness   ~~caste~~

equality   ~~colorism~~   sympathy   thankfulr